INJUSTICE AND THE REPRODUCTION OF HISTORY

Demands for redress of historical injustice are a crucial component of contemporary struggles for social and transnational justice. However, understanding when and why an unjust history matters for considerations of justice in the present is not straightforward. Alasia Nuti develops a normative framework to identify which historical injustices we should be concerned about, to conceptualise the relation between persistence and change and, thus, conceive of history as newly reproduced. Focusing on the condition of women in formally egalitarian societies, the book shows that history is important to theorise the injustice of gender inequalities and devise transformative remedies. Engaging with the activist politics of the unjust past, Nuti also demonstrates that the reproduction of an unjust history is dynamic, complex and unsettling. It generates both historical and contemporary responsibilities for redress and questions precisely those features of our order that we take for granted.

Alasia Nuti is Lecturer in Political Theory at the University of York. Her work is situated at the intersection of analytical political theory, critical theory, gender studies and critical race theory. Her work has appeared in the *Journal of Political Philosophy, Ethics and International Affairs, Feminist Theory, Political Theory* and *Ethics and Global Politics.* Alasia was also awarded the prestigious Elizabeth Wiskemann Prize for the study of inequality and social justice from the Political Studies Association.

INJUSTICE AND THE REPRODUCTION OF HISTORY

Structural Inequalities, Gender and Redress

ALASIA NUTI

University of York

CAMBRIDGE
UNIVERSITY PRESS

CAMBRIDGE
UNIVERSITY PRESS

University Printing House, Cambridge CB2 8BS, United Kingdom

One Liberty Plaza, 20th Floor, New York, NY 10006, USA

477 Williamstown Road, Port Melbourne, VIC 3207, Australia

314-321, 3rd Floor, Plot 3, Splendor Forum, Jasola District Centre, New Delhi - 110025, India

103 Penang Road, #05-06/07, Visioncrest Commercial, Singapore 238467

Cambridge University Press is part of the University of Cambridge.

It furthers the University's mission by disseminating knowledge in the pursuit of education, learning and research at the highest international levels of excellence.

www.cambridge.org
Information on this title: www.cambridge.org/9781108412667
DOI: 10.1017/9781108325592

© Alasia Nuti 2019

First published 2019
First paperback edition 2022

A catalogue record for this publication is available from the British Library

ISBN 978-1-108-41994-9 Hardback
ISBN 978-1-108-41266-7 Paperback

For Gabriele

Contents

Acknowledgements   *page* viii

1   Introduction   1

2   De-temporalising (Historical) Injustice   13

3   The Structural Reproduction of Unjust History   30

4   History, Injustice and Groups   52

5   Defining Women as a Group   82

6   Women and the Reproduction of Unjust History in Egalitarian
    Contexts   105

7   The Policy of the Unjust Past   128

8   The Politics of the Unjust Past   153

9   Conclusion: Responsibility and the Process of Redress   178

References   195
Index   219

Acknowledgements

Some of the core ideas of this book were developed as part of my PhD thesis. I wish to thank my supervisors at the University of Cambridge, Duncan Kelly and Duncan Bell, for their guidance, encouragement and comments during my doctoral studies; their precious advice on the academic world; and their assistance in turning the thesis into a book project. I am also indebted to Jude Browne and Anne Phillips, who have been the best examiners one could hope for. It is fair to say that without their enthusiasm for the project and constructive criticisms, this book would have not been published. In particular, Anne has been a major source of inspiration and help for many years, and I cannot thank her enough for her unfailing support. I would also like to thank the University of Cambridge and Pembroke College for providing me with financial support during my PhD studies.

I wrote the book proposal during a year of post-doctoral fellowship at the Centre for Advanced Studies Justitia Amplificata ('Rethinking Justice – Applied and Global'), located at the University of Frankfurt and the Free University of Berlin. I wish to thank Rainer Forst and Stefan Gosepath for inviting me there. I am especially grateful to Rainer for many discussions (and sometimes heated exchanges) on the importance of the past, which have always propelled me to refine my thoughts. The year in Frankfurt and as a fellow at the Forschungskolleg Humanwissenschaften in Bad Homburg was incredibly productive but also tremendously fun. This was thanks to an incredibly talented and lively community of political theorists, including Nathan Adams, Daniel Callies, Julian Culp, Cristian Dmitriou, Dmitrios Efthymiou, Eszter Kollar, Malte Frøslee Ibsen, Brian Milstein, Darrel Moellendorf, Yasemin Sari, Antoinette Scherz, Johannes Schulz, Isaac Taylor, Luke Ulaş and Melissa Williams.

At the University of York, I have found a new home thanks to exceptionally welcoming colleagues. I am particularly grateful to the members of the Political Theory Cluster for our many inspiring exchanges and, especially, to Matthew Festenstein for having been a true mentor during my first years in York with his calm and wisdom.

During all these years, I have particularly benefitted from stimulating discussions with Daniel Butt, Lior Erez, Signy Gutnick-Allen, Laura LoCoco, Catherine Lu, Maeve MacKeown, Valeria Ottonelli, Jennifer Page and Jeff Spinner-Halev. Laura, Lior and Jennifer all deserve some extra credit. Jennifer and I had many written and Skype conversations on historical injustice that deeply influenced my way of thinking about it and exemplified academic collaboration at its best. Laura and Lior have become two of my best friends, with whom I shared all moments of anxiety and joy since the start of my PhD programme.

I presented material of the book at the following conferences and seminars: the London Graduate Conference in the History of Political Thought (Senate House London, 2014); the Association for Legal and Social Philosophy Annual Conference (University of Leeds, 2014); the Society for Women in Philosophy (SWIP) Ireland Annual Conference (Dublin, 2014); the Collegio Giasone del Maino (University of Pavia, 2015); the Multi-disciplinary Gender Research Seminar (University of Cambridge, 2015); the 8th Princeton University Graduate Conference in Political Theory (2015); the POLIS PhD Colloquium (University of Cambridge, 2015); the Frankfurt Colloquium in Political Theory (2015); and the Workshop in Political Theory at the University of York (2016). I thank all the participants in these events for their thought-provoking questions and especially Isabella Litke and Jeff Spinner-Halev for their written comments.

At Cambridge University Press, John Haslam, Tobias Ginsberg and Joshua Penney provided excellent support throughout the entire process, and I am extremely thankful to two anonymous referees for their insightful comments, which pushed me to strengthen and clarify some arguments of the book. For some very efficient linguistic assistance and help with the index, I am grateful to Harry David.

It seems ages since I moved from Italy, and I must confess that I have never regretted that choice. However, I have always missed some people whom I could not bring with me. I wish to thank Serena Badano, Luca Lagomarsino, Maurizia Pera and especially my parents, Antonella and Gianni, for being able to erase the geographical distance separating us and for their love and support.

There is one person for whom no acknowledgement will ever be enough: Gabriele Badano, my partner. Gabriele has always believed in me much more than I have ever done and has followed all the (very often painful) steps of this book. I have inflicted on him more crises, bad moods and insecurities than a normal person could understandably bear. He has always reacted by being at the same time an amazing, supporting and caring partner and an outstanding scholar with whom to discuss any argument and unpack any intuition. There are no words to express the unique daily experience that sharing my life with such a special person is. This book is dedicated to him.

CHAPTER I

Introduction

Rome, 1960: Enrica, a seventeen-year-old teenager coming from a low-income family, finds out she is pregnant by Cesare, a law student with whom she has had a long-term affair while he has been engaged with another woman. Reaching the conclusion that she cannot keep the baby, but abortion being illegal in Italy, Enrica resorts to dangerous means, as many other women did before her throughout history. After having unsuccessfully attempted to miscarry by drinking a glass full of magnesium sulphate and having a steaming bath, she pays a visit to a local backstreet abortionist. Describing her atrocious experience in that squalid apartment, Enrica says, 'I felt forged by the long needles . . . Suddenly, when they started to probe in depth, the pain became acute and went through me like an electric shock. All my body was torn apart. I screamed . . . I put my hand over my mouth and bit it. The crochet hook shrank and widened inside me, leaving me in pain and worn-out'.[1]

Rome, 2010: Valentina is a twenty-eight-year-old woman who wishes to become a mother but has a very rare and serious genetic disease and cannot access state-funded assisted reproduction. Five months into her pregnancy, she discovers that her foetus inherited her disease; she then decides to get an abortion. Since her gynaecologist is a conscientious objector, Valentina embarks on an exhausting search for another doctor; finally she is admitted to a hospital. The medical staff starts the procedure to induce labour through a pessary, and Valentina's ordeal begins. Because, after a change of shift, all the hospital staff are registered as conscientious objectors, she is left completely alone with her husband. Valentina recalls that 'it was a nightmare. After fifteen hours of agonising pain, during which I vomited and fainted several times and my husband screamed and searched for help in vain, I gave birth [to a dead foetus] abandoned in the bathroom'.[2]

---

[1] This story is drawn from Dacia Maraini's (1963) novel *L'età del malessere* (The age of discomfort), 114–15, my translation.
[2] Pasolini (2014; my translation).

Like Valentina, many women in Italy deciding to terminate their pregnancies have to travel inter-regionally or abroad, are left alone during the procedure and, if unsuccessful, try other means. Recently, this unjust situation has (rightly) sparked much outrage from the Italian and international presses. Many have framed such an injustice as a 'return to an unjust past' and specifically to a time of obscurantism in which Italian women such as Enrica had to risk their lives to get abortions – an era that seemed long gone.[3]

This framing gets us on the right track for thinking about the current unjust situation in Italy. However, it is not fully satisfactory. Certainly, there are important new elements that differ between Enrica's and Valentina's stories, such as the existence of a law (1978's Law 194) that should guarantee women the right to safe abortion in Italy and some constraints on that right that women face (e.g. the spread of 'conscientious objection' among doctors, nurses and anaesthetists), which urge us to go beyond a mere discourse on the return of a past era and also reflect on the *changes* in how the right to abortion has been threatened in Italy. Most importantly, the return-to-the-past narrative paradoxically still offers an overly progressive account of the development of reproductive justice in Italy. It seems to suggest that the passage of Law 194 in 1978 did bring about the revolutionary cultural and social transformation dreamed of by the Italian feminist movement struggling for women's emancipation but that now, suddenly, women in Italy face a 'regressive' turn back in time. What this framing fails to capture is the enduring challenging economic, social and cultural conditions in which women have been exercising their self-determination when deciding whether to have and raise a child in Italy, conditions which question the very idea that the past has ever gone away.[4] Such a narrative thus does not fully conceptualise the *continuity* (and changes) in the reproductive injustice suffered by women in Italy.

What is compelling in return-of-the-past narratives that are often constructed in public discourse is that they refer to the past (and sometimes

---

[3] See, e.g., Gallo (2016).
[4] Such conditions include, for instance, a family-centred and gendered model of care in which women are expected to undertake the bulk of caring and domestic labour within the household; the poor public support given to balance family responsibility and employment to parents and, in particular, single mothers; the limited assistance provided to those raising a disabled child; and the stigma attached to single motherhood and disability (e.g. Badassi and Gentile 2016; Falcinelli and Magaraggia 2013; Pacelli, Pasqua and Villosio 2013; Sabbadini 2018).

even a distant one) as being present and thus invite us not to dismiss history while analysing our present conditions. Although such narratives point to the political urgency of the presence of the past, they do not entirely capture the complexity of the relation between past and present in thinking about justice. Does an unjust history thus theoretically and normatively matter? And if so, why is that the case?

For someone interested in these questions, the burgeoning literature on historical injustice – injustices committed in the past – within normative political theory is an obvious starting point precisely because by arguing that we have obligations of justice to redress the unjust past, it refuses to dismiss that past. This literature is particularly interesting as it directs our attention not to more recent injustices but to wrongs committed in the distant past involving both original perpetrators and victims that are now dead,[5] such as the seizure of indigenous land by settlers in North America, South America and Australasia; the unjust history of colonialism; the transatlantic slave trade and the institution of slavery in the US. Accounts of historical justice do take history (and our responsibilities to repair its injustice) seriously, but they face serious conceptual challenges in showing why we should worry about wrongs committed in a distant past and what is the normatively salient relation between past and present generations.[6]

A first difficulty lies in identifying which injustices committed in history call for contemporary redress. Indeed, claiming that history is fraught with injustices would be an understatement of history itself. Should we repair all the wrongs that occurred in the past? Or should we focus only on some specific injustices? In this case, what criterion should be used to distinguish past injustices that should be redressed from those that should not?

A second problem is constituted by the passing of time, which, according to many sceptics of historical justice, seriously weakens claims of responsibility to repair or compensate for injustices of a distant past. For instance, too many counterfactuals seem necessary to establish how our present would look if historical injustice had not happened.[7] Moreover, the

---

[5] Ivison (2008, 509); Meyer (2014); Perez (2012, 153); Spinner-Halev (2012a, 320).

[6] In this respect, accounts of historical injustice encounter challenges that are distinct from those faced by other literatures that focus on a cruel and divisive past – most notably the field of transitional justice, which revolves around the aftermath of civil conflicts and large recent violations of human rights (e.g. the Rwandan genocide in 1994 during the Rwandan Civil War). Indeed, it is immediately more intuitive to see why Tutsi and Hutu cannot easily cast aside their past of violence and conflict than to establish why, in a world fraught with injustices, we should care about offering redress for the injustice of slavery to African Americans whose progenitors were enslaved. For an overview of the specific issues of transitional justice, see Eisikovits (2014).

[7] Waldron (1992, 9–11).

more time passes, the more difficult it becomes to, for example, determine whether entitlement to holdings that have been violated (e.g. indigenous rights to their land) survives in the present and whether current generations (e.g. present-day African Americans) are harmed because of past wrongs (e.g. slavery). In short, many critics of historical justice argue that 'claims about justice and injustice must be responsive to changes in circumstances',[8] and thus, with the passing of time, instead of thinking we should redress the unjust past, we should focus on the here and now as 'present circumstances are the ones that are real'.[9]

Like accounts of historical injustice, this book aims to vindicate the normative significance of unjust history in our considerations of what justice requires. However, it does so by developing an alternative framework to think about the theoretical and normative relation between past and present and what redressing an unjust history entails, which is more compelling yet more unsettling than mainstream cases for historical justice. Or so I hope to show. The chief argument of this book is that the unjust history that should normatively matter in justice-based considerations is present because it has been reproduced over time through different means, and it still is so. The reproduction of unjust history is pervasive as it shapes the background conditions in which some present wrongs occur and relations between agents are established. At the same time, it is dynamic because it is enabled also through agents' actions and interactions. In this respect, like return-of-the-past narratives, the book does conceptualise history as present; however, it does so in a more complex way.

A distinguishing feature of the conception of historical injustice developed throughout the book is that it does not deny that many changes have taken place over the time that has passed since past injustices, such as slavery in the US, were committed. Nor does it dismiss the importance such changes should have when we reflect upon what justice demands. On the contrary, it argues that if we want to understand how injustices are reproduced over time, we also need to consider the various and substantial changes undergone by our societies (and the transnational order). A further distinctive characteristic of such a conception is that it significantly

---

[8] Waldron (1992, 25).
[9] Waldron (2002, 159). Note that many critics of historical justice do not claim that memory and the acknowledgement of an unjust distant past are irrelevant to the present. For instance, Jeremy Waldron, in his famous argument for superseding historical injustice, recognises that we should condemn an unjust past to show our commitment to a just future and that memory is important for communities to construct a common identity (1992, 5). What critics of historical justice usually dispute, and its supporters instead argue for, is that redressing a distant past is a demand of justice.

broadens our understanding of historical injustice by advancing a case for thinking of the normative significance of the unjust past not only in relation to wrongs, such as slavery, colonialism and the destruction of indigenous communities – which usually dominate the literature on historical injustice – but also in relation to other groups that have suffered from systematic injustices in history.

To do so, the book concentrates on the condition of women in societies that have endorsed anti-discrimination legislation and formal equality of opportunity, thereby merging the literature on historical injustice with debates over gender injustices and inequalities. With very few exceptions, gender dynamics within groups that suffered from past injustices are neglected in accounts of historical justice.[10] Moreover, the very injustices women were subjected to over history within, for example, so-called liberal democratic societies, such as the denial or violation of their political, economic, sexual and reproductive rights, are rarely considered within theories of historical justice and redress, let alone being a central case of why history should matter for considerations of justice.[11] This neglect is puzzling if one thinks that women have arguably been one of the groups that have been most systematically oppressed and unjustly treated over history nationally and transnationally and that nowadays such a history is largely recognised as unjust within liberal democratic societies. It is important to point out that such a neglect cannot be easily corrected by simply adding the past injustices against women to the cases that mainstream accounts of historical injustice should focus on. This difficulty is at least partially due to the narrow understanding of groups that is endorsed within the literature. Let me anticipate some observations.[12]

The literature on historical injustice has started to look at members of groups (as opposed to mere individuals) as rightful claimants of reparations or compensation for past injustices in an attempt to reply to the so-called non-identity problem, which philosophically challenges the ground for intergenerational obligations. In short, according to proponents of the

[10] For instance, in her recent account of justice and reconciliation in world politics, Catherine Lu argues that gender dynamics are important to think about the responsibilities not only of the colonisers but also of governments in the colonies for wrongs occurring during colonial rule (2017, 132–38). Lu also mentions that women as a group are relevant to issues of past injustice (161), but she does not extensively focus on it.

[11] Note that my critical target here is the normative literature on redress for historical injustice. I do not want to suggest that within political theory, there is no 'historical argument' to advance the condition of women such as their political representation (e.g. Williams 1998, 8).

[12] A reconceptualisation of the relation between groups and historical injustice will be advanced in Chapter 4.

non-identity problem, an act harms someone only if that person is made worse off as a result of it. Since (1) many past wrongs led to the very existence of contemporary descendants of original victims and (2) existing (or, more precisely, living a life worth living) is always better than not having been born, descendants of victims of past wrongs cannot be harmed by these wrongs, as they would have not existed if such wrongs had not been committed and thus should not receive reparation or compensation for them.[13] To overcome or sidestep the non-identity problem and develop notions of harm and identity over time, some supporters of historical justice have tried to identify different types of harm from that captured by the non-identity problem – namely, harm that members of groups that suffered from past injustice experience because of their constitutive attachment to those groups[14] – whereas others have concentrated only on those groups, such as nations, that are allegedly regarded as displaying an enduring shared collective identity as claimants of rectification.[15] The assumption underpinning accounts of historical injustice thus is that for a group to endure over time, its members must share a common identity and strongly identify with their group. Even those diminishing the importance of the non-identity problem for matters of historical injustice, such as Jeff Spinner-Halev, endorse a similar understanding of groups.[16] In his account of 'enduring injustice', Spinner-Halev argues that only those groups that have developed a shared collective narrative centred on their past injustices, which ties the knot among group members, can suffer from enduring injustices.[17] In other words, groups suffering from enduring injustice must be characterised by a collective identity based (at least significantly) on past wrongs its members identify with that continue over time.

Anyone familiar with debates within feminist theory over what defines women as a group is aware that a conception of groups centred on a common identity and members' attachment to that identity cannot (and should not) be applied to women because it neglects the important differences among women and runs the risk of constructing a common identity that actually promotes particular interests and experiences.[18]

---

[13] For a seminal formulation of the non-identity problem, see Parfit (1984, 351–80), while for discussions of this problem in the context of historical injustices, see Boxill (2003); Cohen (2009); Kershnar (1999); and Sher (2005).
[14] E.g. Herstein (2009).   [15] E.g. Butt (2009, 23–24); Tan (2008, 451).
[16] Spinner-Halev (2012b, 83–84). See also Butt (2009, 106).   [17] Spinner-Halev (2012b, 59–61).
[18] E.g. Crenshaw (1991); hooks (1982, chapter 5); Mohanty (1991); Young (1997a). I will discuss the difficulties with defining women as a group and yet the importance of this task at length in Chapter 5.

Trying to fit women into the understanding of groups that underlies mainstream accounts of historical justice would amount to misinterpreting what makes women a group.

The impossibility of simply adding women to our understanding of groups should also lead us to ask whether the very conception of groups at play in the literature on historical injustice, which assumes common identity and attachment as necessary conditions for a group's continuance, is not actually flawed. Indeed, it seems that groups such as women do persist over time, for instance as groups suffering from injustices. The partiality of such an understanding of groups becomes immediately evident in a theory such as that of Spinner-Halev, which explicitly focuses on enduring injustices. Stipulating that only those groups that have developed a shared collective narrative on their history of injustice can be said to suffer from enduring injustices is misguided. Would we say that, for example, since the Romani people and Sinti have traditionally not constructed a composite collective narrative on the past injustices they experienced, they are not the target of persisting injustices in Europe?[19] Determining that a group suffers from a persisting injustice should depend on whether injustices against them endure over time and not on whether such a group has developed a collective narrative on their (unjust) past.

In other words, considering gender in discussions over the normative significance of the unjust past for considerations of justice is fruitful because, as the historian Joan Scott points out, analysing women as a group 'not only add[s] new subject matter but . . . also force[s] a critical re-examination of the premises and standards of existing scholarly work'.[20] It prompts one to put forward a different account of groups and of 'descendants'[21] that, as we will see, will also offer a more sophisticated understanding of the nature of the injustice suffered not only by women but also by those other groups that are usually at the centre of the literature on historical injustice and of contemporary responsibilities for reparation and redress.

---

[19] For Ian Hancock (one of the leading scholars in the field of Romani studies), in the case of the Romani people and Sinti, the lack of a collective narrative about the past injustice is (at least partly) due to the Romani attitude not to conceive of themselves as victims of an unjust past, which is in turn also a result of a never-ending history of injustices. The Romani people, Hancock argues, 'are traditionally not disposed to keeping alive the terrible memories from [their] history. Nostalgia is a luxury for others' (2008, 93).

[20] Scott (1986, 1054).

[21] To anticipate, I will conceptualise 'descent' beyond family and biological lines and show that this reformulation captures who should count as descendant in cases of past injustices and what is normatively salient in being a descendant (see § 4.2).

The book can be thought of in three parts. The first part aims to develop a framework to reflect on the normative significance of unjust history in considerations of justice – a framework that is able to theorise the presence of the past and overcome some shortcomings of existing accounts of historical injustice by reflecting on what history means, analysing injustice and theorising groups. Chapter 2 argues that if we want to understand the importance of historical justice, we need to endorse an apt conception of history. After having discussed the problems the two main approaches to historical injustice – backward-looking and forward-looking justifications – encounter as a result of their under-theorisation of history, I will make a case for 'de-temporalising injustice' by building on some insights into history provided by Reinhart Koselleck. 'De-temporalising injustice' entails avoiding the conceptual separation between past and present and endorsing a structural conception of history. In particular, it means thinking of history itself as made up of long-term structures that outlive unjust (past) events and reveal the continuum between past and present. How should 'long-term structures' be defined? And how do they persist over time?

Chapter 3 replies to these questions by merging a structural view of history with a structural conception of injustice. Arguably, the most influential notion of structural injustice in political theory is the one advanced by Iris Marion Young.[22] This notion captures important lessons social movements offer on the nature of injustice, such as the fact that injustices (1) are about not only the distribution of goods, resources and wealth but also the relations in which persons stand with one another and vis-à-vis national and transnational institutions;[23] (2) result from complex dynamics in which many actors participate; and (3) tend to become normalised and not to be perceived as injustices.[24] According to Young, structural injustices occur when 'social processes put large groups of persons' in a systematic position of vulnerability, 'threat of domination[,] or deprivation of the means to develop and exercise their capacities', while the same processes 'enable others to dominate or to have a wide range of opportunities for developing and exercising capacities available to them'.[25] By combining a structural account of history with Young's understanding of 'structures', I identify a specific type of injustice – 'historical-structural injustice' – constituted by the structural reproduction of an unjust history over time

---

[22] See, e.g., Young (2000, chapter 3; 2006; 2011).   [23] Young (1990, chapter 1).
[24] Young (1990, 95; 2011, 59–62).   [25] Young (2011, 52).

and through changes. By focusing on the example of stereotypes, I will show that the conception of historical-structural injustice offers a more complex understanding of persistence and change than, for instance, Spinner-Halev's theory of enduring injustice. By theorising unjust history as structurally reproduced, the account of historical-structural injustice will overcome the serious obstacles that mainstream theories of past justice encounter. Furthermore, this account significantly broadens the array of groups that can be said to suffer from the new reproduction of history and thus calls for a reconceptualisation of groups.

Chapter 4 is precisely devoted to this task and puts forward a dynamic taxonomy of structural groups. Specifically, I will argue that there are many types of structural groups and that they should be envisaged as components of a spectrum. The idea of the spectrum is particularly congenial to capture both the similarities and the differences that structural collectives display vis-à-vis one another. The spectrum will be constituted by three categories of structural groups: (1) 'historical-structural groups' (e.g. women and gay men); (2) 'non-historical-structural groups' (e.g. the homeless and veterans); and (3) 'historical groups with structural dynamics' (e.g. nations). I will contend that the idea of the spectrum not only offers a compelling alternative to mainstream accounts of groups endorsed by scholars of historical injustice, one which, for instance, reconceptualises the notion of 'descendants', but also significantly elaborates on the conception of structural groups delineated by Young. In particular, I will argue that thinking in terms of the spectrum is fruitful for mapping out the various structural groups that are present in our societies and thinking about (1) how to remedy the injustices they suffer from and (2) historical and contemporary responsibility for redress.

The account of historical-structural injustice developed in the first part at a general level contributes to both the literature on historical injustice and the growing scholarship on structural injustice. As for historical injustice, my account of historical-structural injustice challenges the theoretical and normative divide between past and present injustice through the idea of de-temporalisation, and it identifies and theorises a type of injustice that has been reproduced in such a pervasive way that we cannot fully understand (some) existing injustices without accounting for the dynamic presence of history. In so doing, my account shows why a 'present'-focused egalitarianism is misguided when it comes to certain current injustices. Moreover, by pointing out the interdependence between persistence and change, it shows that the passage of time is not such a challenge when it comes to certain injustices.

The account of historical-structural injustice also enriches our understanding of structural injustice. In particular, it advances the case for *a pluralistic account of structural injustices*, which highlights both the similarities and the differences between types of structural injustice by looking at the role unjust history plays in their formation and persistence. This is necessary because, especially through the influential and latest work of Young's, structural injustice has become a framework deployed to characterise many instances of oppression and marginalisation (e.g. women, sweatshop workers, the homeless, temporary migrants and the unemployed).[26] Although there is much to admire in this attempt to think about how mechanisms of injustice analogously operate, the risk of turning 'structural injustice' into an umbrella term is that we lose sight of (1) the heterogeneous nature of the injustices at stake, (2) the different means that are required to address them and (3) the different types of responsibilities they generate. Therefore, my account of historical-structural injustice maintains and defends the centrality of the paradigm of structural injustice by enhancing it and diversifying among (equally important) structural struggles.

The second part of the book zooms in on women as a group and specifically on the position of women in formally egalitarian societies, which is one paradigmatic example of historical-structural injustice. Defining women as a group is not as straightforward as it may seem. Chapter 5 faces the challenge that defining women traditionally poses according to feminist scholarship: the charge of essentialism and risk of neglecting intersectionality. Although there are many attempts to theorise women as a group within the feminist literature, I extensively engage with Young's account of 'seriality' as one of the most logical and compelling starting points. I contend that, although promising, the idea of seriality still contains problematic essentialist elements, fails to take intersectionality into full consideration and misses some crucial ways in which being a member of the group of women operates in persons' lives. Such shortcomings, however, should lead to an improvement of the idea of 'seriality' rather than its outright rejection; an account of women as a historical-structural group can provide such an improvement.

Chapters 6 and 7 aim to show how the conception of historical-structural injustice is particularly suitable to capture the condition of injustice suffered by women in formally egalitarian contexts. Chapter 6

---

[26] On women, sweatshop workers and the homeless, see Young (1997a, 2004, 2011, chapter 2). On temporary migrants and the unemployed, see Nuti (2018) and Woodly (2015), respectively.

points out that some of the enduring inequalities characterising women in liberal democratic societies (viz. the dramatic presence of violence against women and the gendered division of both paid and unpaid labour) cannot be explained without considering the history of discrimination and oppression that women suffered as a group as well as the reproduction of that history. Chapter 7 demonstrates that the conception of historical-structural injustice offers a normative framework through which it is possible to assess and design policy proposals that can contribute to tackling persistent issues of gender inequality. In particular, by critically examining solutions implemented to overcome intimate-partner violence, horizontal occupational segregation and the gendered division of domestic labour, I identify the necessary features that must generally be displayed by measures devised to address injustices that are both historical and structural (i.e. 'transformative measures').

In addition to refining the account of historical-structural injustice developed in the first part, Chapters 5, 6 and 7 engage with some of the most lively and long-standing debates in feminist theory, such as how to define women as a group without neglecting differences among women. Moreover, unravelling the structural reproduction of unjust history is particularly fruitful in understanding why certain dimensions of gender inequality and difference are unjust and how they persist in egalitarian settings. Obviously, much more work needs to be done to explore the role unjust history plays in contemporary gender injustice and within specific contexts than I can aspire to do in this book, but I hope I will at least show that this is a valuable project to be further pursued.

A particularly valuable general lesson that should be learned from the presence of the unjust past in the condition of women in egalitarian contexts is that a necessary (yet not sufficient) tool to redress historical-structural injustices is promoting historically sensitive policy making.

The third part of the book shows that de-temporalising injustice also has far-reaching implications for thinking about the 'politics of the past' – that is, the ways redress for past injustices is demanded in political struggles and the responsibilities arising from the reproduction of historical injustice and structural injustice. Chapter 8 directly engages with the channels whereby the unjust past is reclaimed in contemporary politics by focusing on the history of racial injustice in the US. I criticise theorists of structural injustice, such as Catherine Lu and Young, who reject reparations claims for racial injustices of a distant past (e.g. slavery), and I argue for the existence of backward-looking obligations of repair that fall on certain agents from within a structural approach by examining the history of

reproductive injustice against African American women and putting forward the novel notion of 'structural debt'. In addition to reparations
claims, the unjust past is at the centre of another form of activist politics
and specifically of a type of activist discourse that is largely under-theorised
yet becomes crucial for redress once we recognise the unjust past as
structurally reproduced in new ways. To identify and conceptualise such
a discourse, which I call 'counter-historical institutional justifications',
I draw on how the narrative developed by the prison-abolitionist movement in the US connects the injustice of slavery to the contemporary
workings of US society so as to criticise its present institutional and
structural setting (and, in particular, the penitentiary system). Such narratives show how important and unsettling redressing an unjust history
can be.

Chapter 9 concludes by reflecting upon how we should think about
contemporary responsibility for structural injustice (of a historical nature
or not). I argue against accounts of a shared responsibility based on
contribution and contend that responsibility within unjust structures
must be more sensitive to the different types of agents participating in
them than structural-injustice theorists have recognised so far. Before
doing so, I pull together my arguments and advance the idea of redress
as a process. Overcoming injustices that are both historical and structural
entails an intersectional process of redress, which is constituted by many
measures, including reparations, historically sensitive policy making and
counter-historical institutional justifications.

Redressing historical-structural injustices generates both historical
accountability and contemporary responsibilities, and it entails a radical
transformation of our societies and transnational order and many of our
familiar ways of organising our social, political, economic and cultural life.
On the other hand, as women in Italy and many others probably know too
well, the neat division between the past and the present is just a dangerous
illusion preserved to the advantage of a few. Redress is thus a fundamental
demand of justice that should not be postponed any longer.

CHAPTER 2

De-temporalising (Historical) Injustice

What does 'history' mean? Or, better, which way of conceptualising history can guide our normative reflections on historical injustices? Normative accounts of historical justice do not usually ask these questions. Nor do they interrogate the particular conception of history upon which they hinge. To be sure, as Pier Pierson argues, this is a common mistake of political science in general, which tends to neglect the different temporal features of social, political and economic events, thereby limiting its illumination of our social world.[1] However, when it comes to accounts of historical injustice, such a neglect seems particularly puzzling and worrisome. Since these accounts are precisely driven by the intuition that history does matter when thinking about justice, their normative analysis should be underpinned by an understanding of history that is suited (rather than inapt) for supporting that intuition.

This chapter discusses how history and historical events should be approached if we want to understand and vindicate the normative signifi-cance of history in considerations of justice. It puts forward an approach to history that, borrowing from Reinhart Koselleck's terminology, I call 'de-temporalising injustice'. De-temporalising injustice means showing that unjust history should be envisaged as present in a deep and dynamic way. In particular, it entails reconceptualising history (and unjust historical events) as long-term structures. Not only does this approach argue that the unjust past cannot be separated from the present when justice and injustice are considered but also it reveals the logical consistency of the 'present-past'. De-temporalising injustice is necessary to capture (1) the relation between past and present injustice, and consequently (2) the complex interplay between persistence and change. One far-reaching implication of de-temporalising injustice is that, unlike many accounts of historical injustice, it clarifies why a strong commitment to egalitarian

---

[1] Pierson (2004).

justice in the present would not downplay the importance many attach to an unjust history. Moreover, conceiving of history as being inherently constituted by long-term structures represents a privileged starting point to understand *when* and *why* historical injustices normatively matter and to theorise *how* historical injustices as long-term structures are not past but newly reproduced into the present. Or so I argue.

Before doing so, however, let me examine the theoretical difficulties that many mainstream accounts of historical justice encounter as a result of their under-theorisation of history.

2.1 Historical Injustice and the Problems of History

The debate over historical injustice can be analytically systematised into two main approaches based on the temporal direction of obligations of historical justice: (1) backward looking and (2) forward looking. The backward-looking approach suggests we have current obligations to redress historical injustice per se; the significance of historical injustice lies in the fact that an injustice was committed and has not yet been rectified. To wit, obligations of historical injustice are triggered by the *past*; the connection between past and present injustices is neither a necessary nor a sufficient condition for duties of historical justice to arise. Conversely, forward-looking approaches point out that past injustices are important to repair existing broken relationships and address present inequalities. It is the *present* and the idea of a better *future* that asks us to look back to the past. The two approaches run into serious yet different difficulties.

There are some influential accounts of historical injustice that can be labelled backward looking in the sense defined above. Famously, Robert Nozick includes a principle of rectification for past injustices in his entitlement theory; the principle aims to return or compensate for holdings (e.g. property, resources, belongings) that have been originally acquired or received from others in an unjust way (e.g. by coercing, defrauding, stealing from them). Although Nozick is aware that rectification, as he describes it, is highly encumbered by the need to overcome uncertainty about important details of all past violations that took place and to determine counterfactually what would have happened without their occurrence, he still forcefully argues that to give back or compensate for 'tainted' holdings remains a matter of justice.[2]

---

[2] Nozick (1974, 150–53). Daniel Butt argues that a 'libertarian' outlook extends beyond self-confessed libertarians and it is implicitly endorsed by many accounts of international (although not domestic)

Another example of an influential backward-looking approach is David Miller's liberal nationalist account of nations' responsibility, which includes an obligation to set the national record straight – that is, to repair the wrongs committed by co-national ancestors. For Miller, what triggers such an obligation is only the intergenerational bound between co-nationals; thus, that obligation stands independently of the present conditions of the descendants of those who originally suffered the wrong.[3]

Finally, accounts focusing on the status and rights of the dead are clearly backward looking. For instance, W. James Booth contends that a dead victim of injustice remains a 'persisting member of a community of justice, demanding recognition and receiving at last what was owed him'.[4] In a similar vein, Michael Ridge points to the existence of 'posthumous harm and benefit' to argue that providing reparations to the descendants of deceased victims of past injustice represents the best way to give those who were wronged in the past (and not compensated for it) what they are owed as a matter of justice.[5]

Although very different, all backward-looking approaches consider past injustices as significant per se, thereby avoiding difficult speculations about the possible connections between past and present injustices. This avoidance may be tempting; however, it comes at a high price. Indeed, backward-looking approaches immediately raise a serious objection, which I call the *impracticability objection*: if all the injustices that occurred in the past are important, redressing historical injustice is an impractical task. If the unjust past per se is worth being rectified, as backward-looking approaches suggest, it seems there is no principled reason why we should be more concerned with French colonialism in the Caribbean than with, say, the atrocities committed by Louis IX, king of France during the European crusades against Arabs in Tunis (North Africa) in 1270, or why we should try to benefit dead American slaves by improving the welfare of their descendants but not do the same with, say, descendants of victims of the Tribunal del Santo Oficio de la Inquisición (i.e. the Spanish Inquisition), which from the second half of the fifteenth century to almost the middle of the seventeenth century tortured and hanged, beheaded or burned at the stake 'heretics' and false or relapsed converts. In other words, there is no criterion for distinguishing between the types of past injustices that call for redress and those that do not.

---

justice, which should thus also include principles of rectification for past violations of norms of just international relations (2009, chapter 3).
[3] Miller (2007, 146, 251; 2008, 561).   [4] Booth (2011, 757).   [5] Ridge (2003, 44).

This impracticability turns the search for historical justice into a quixotic enterprise as the number of injustices committed over history is obviously incredibly vast.[6] More importantly, it strengthens a long-standing worry that many critics of the very idea of historical justice have voiced: redressing past injustices would divert our attention, energy and resources from present injustices. Since there are arguably plenty of pressing injustices in our present world, trying to repair past injustices would entail neglecting 'the suffering and the deprivation over which we still have some control' in the present.[7] One may reply that present injustices should be prioritised over repairing the past; the fact that we have obligations of historical justice independently of present conditions does not imply that the former should outweigh the latter. However, since bringing about a just world is arguably quite a demanding goal, it is likely that the attempt to redress historical injustices would never start if we adopted that view. In other words, why should we be concerned with past injustices if present injustices should always take precedence?

Unlike backward-looking approaches, forward-looking ones start with the claim that reparations for what happened in the past are instrumental to tackle an unjust or problematic present condition. Such an instrumentality can be framed in pragmatic terms: since many are sympathetic to repairing past wrongs but are sceptical about contemporary duties of egalitarian distribution at an international (or domestic) level, reparations for past injustices may be the most (argumentatively) effective way to bring about a more equal distribution of resources.[8]

However, the majority of forward-looking approaches conceive of the instrumental role of the unjust past not just pragmatically. Some focus on how relations of trust between different groups within societies or between different nations (or states), which are deemed necessary to guarantee domestic and international stability and cooperation, are damaged because of past injustices. As Leif Wenar puts it, 'The past wrong is relevant because it poisons the groups' future life together'.[9] Because in these cases, contemporary mistrust is the legacy of an 'unresolved' past, acknowledging

---

[6] Ridge tries to offer a temporal threshold to circumscribe those past injustices calling for redress – i.e. focus on those past injustices whose victims still have immediate descendants. This is only because persons 'generally care less about descendants three and four generations down the line' (2003, 52). Note, however, that (1) this claim may not be true as some may be concerned with the future of their lineage; (2) even if it were true, since meeting the dead's desires is what matters, we can benefit the more distant dead by promoting some of their other reasonable interests; and (3) Ridge's criterion would also dismiss the very cases for reparations for historical injustices he aims to defend, e.g. reparations for slavery in the US (formally abolished in 1865).

[7] Waldron (1992, 26).   [8] Butt (2009, 13–17); Tan (2007, 281).   [9] Wenar (2006, 403).

and repairing that past is an important way of restoring (or building) relations of trust and mutual recognition.[10] In the case of indigenous peoples in the US, Canada and Australia, some observe that their mistrust towards settler societies is compounded by the indigenous peoples' particular interpretation of their present condition. For them, present claims of land and self-government are intrinsically linked with their unjust history in the wider society. As Duncan Ivison argues, such claims 'rest . . . on the recognition of the historical injustices carried out against them by various colonial powers'.[11]

Other forward-looking approaches emphasise how inter-group inequalities (regarding income, health and education) are the legacy of historical injustices. Supporters of reparations for slavery and Jim Crow argue that there is no other plausible explanation for substantial contemporary gaps in all measures of well-being between African Americans and white Americans apart from their being the outcomes of 'a history of slavery, segregation, and discrimination'.[12] In other words, we need to be concerned about the past (and repair it) because that past is causally connected to present injustices and inequalities.[13]

Unlike backward-looking approaches, forward-looking ones avoid prioritising the past over the present, and they offer general criteria to select which past injustices we should focus on: only those past injustices that can be used to argue for present distributive justice or build mutual trust or that are causally connected to present inequality should be repaired. Thus, forward-looking approaches are less open to the impracticability objection. Moreover, they can ease the worry that historical injustice would move present justice to the background; indeed, it is precisely because we aim to solve a normatively problematic condition that we need to repair the past.

There is much to admire about forward-looking approaches; nevertheless, as they stand, they raise another powerful objection, which I call the *redundancy objection*. This objection states that a strong commitment to principles of present distributive justice would make claims of historical justice not compelling. In other words, once a world in which opportunities and resources are more equally distributed has been created, the unjust past would lose its significance.[14] To be sure, historical arguments

---

[10] Freeman (2008); Hendrix (2005, 774–75); Ivison (2002, 371); Lu (2017, 180); Thompson (2002, 83–85); Wenar (2006, 403–4).
[11] Ivison (2000, 100). See also Thompson (2002, 66).   [12] Hall (2004, 9).
[13] E.g. Hall (2004, 9); McCarthy (2004, 753); Valls (2007); Valls and Kaplan (2005); Williams and Collins (2004).
[14] Vernon (2003).

may be useful to bring about more distributively just outcomes when the arguments are deployed against libertarians who reject state redistribution.[15] Nevertheless, the redundancy objection continues, this sort of argument cannot convince those who already endorse principles of distributive justice at the domestic (or global) level of the normative importance of past injustices.

Regarding the issue of trust, the egalitarian sceptic may think the actual sources of mistrust lie elsewhere – namely, in the present mistreatment and disadvantage of certain groups – or that, rather than repairing the past, there may be other ways to build the mutual recognition and assurance that are necessary to sustain a system of social (and international) cooperation. For instance, eradicating poverty and creating equal access to opportunities and resources for members of disadvantaged groups may well reduce inter-group hostility and build relations of trust between historically disadvantaged groups. Obviously, the fact that groups, such as indigenous peoples, interpret their present disadvantage as intrinsically connected to the unjust past is noteworthy. However, for the egalitarian sceptic, this does not imply that such an interpretation should be accepted at face value. The fact that we should respect those who suffer from an injustice by listening to their specific understanding of their condition does not necessarily entail taking it as an indisputable truth.[16] Nor should we regard this interpretation as something immutable which cannot be modified by those who now hold it if present unjust circumstances change.[17] Therefore, according to the redundancy objection, focusing on the past when considering present injustices is superfluous, as the past is not necessary for creating a present and future just world, and it may even neglect other possible ways to address present disadvantages or mistrust issues.

Likewise, it may be true, the egalitarian sceptic would argue, that intergroup inequalities are a legacy of the past, but this does not normatively

---

[15] Goodin (2013, 490).

[16] One may agree with Judith Shklar that accounts of injustice are incomplete without including the particular understandings of it that those who suffer from these injustice have (1990, 35–36), without thinking that such understandings are the sole (and the only valid) face of the injustices under consideration.

[17] Note that indigenous and formerly colonised peoples endorse anti-modern conceptions of history centred on the logical consistency of the present-past which resonate with the one advanced in this chapter (e.g. Chakrabarty 2007; Nandy 1995; Seth 2004). However, the reason we should endorse these conceptions of history is not exclusively that they are proposed by victims of injustice, although suffering from injustice may give a privileged standpoint on the workings of that injustice. Such conceptions are also compelling because they are apt to conceptualise the presence of the unjust past and its normative implications.

matter as they are 'objectionable on grounds of distributive justice'.[18] Thus there is no need to look to the past to challenge present injustices; as Tommie Shelby, among others, contends, 'If poor Blacks need greater resources to achieve full citizenship, then they are owed this investment regardless of whether their ancestors were enslaved'.[19] I do not intend to endorse this egalitarian scepticism; I only claim that, as they stand, accounts focusing on the necessity of repairing the unjust past because of its effects on present inequalities do not offer an interpretation of the relation between past and present injustices that is sufficiently compelling to rebut the egalitarian (present-focused) critique. What is needed (and will be provided in the next sections and following chapter) is a more complex and dynamic understanding of history and of its presence.

In sum, critics of historical justice resist both backward-looking and forward-looking arguments that historical injustice is not superseded by present injustice,[20] either because they deem the latter more important than the former or because if enough changes in the distribution of resources and opportunities were brought about, considerations of historical justice would eventually vanish.

The debate over historical injustice seems to have reached an impasse, which amounts to a theoretical difficulty in explaining the normative importance the unjust past has for present-based considerations of justice. It appears particularly challenging to conceptualise (1) how (and whether) the (unjust) past remains significantly present, notwithstanding the possible changes over time and the ones we may reasonably expect (or hope) to occur in the future and (2) how such a presence cannot be dismissed if one is concerned with present injustices. In other words, the current debate over historical injustice suffers from an *under-theorisation of history*, specifically of how persistence and change are interrelated.

In the next section, I explore this under-theorisation of history by suggesting that we need to 'de-temporalise' justice by moving beyond a 'modern' conception of history, a conception that is still implicitly at play in the debate over historical injustice.

2.2 The Temporalisation of Injustice

To analyse in what sense both critics and the majority of supporters of historical justice undertheorise history, I briefly draw on some observations about modernity and history developed by Koselleck. Since my reference

---

[18] Shelby (2011, 396).   [19] Shelby (2011, 396).   [20] Waldron (1992, 25).

to Koselleck may seem puzzling and unjustified, and somehow sketchy, let me specify its role in my overarching argument. In analysing modernity, Koselleck is engaged in a very different project from mine – namely, he aims at unpacking the practice of history and the construction of historical time within historiography as a discipline. By drawing on Koselleck, I do not want to reduce the complexity of his reflections on the practice of history. Nor do I aim to suggest that Koselleck is the only possible source to reconceptualise history in our normative assessment of historical injustices. I selectively draw on some of Koselleck's observations as an arguably imaginative way to argue for the importance of reflecting upon what history should mean in theories of historical justice. As Koselleck challenges the reductive way historical time is constructed within historiography, so do I question the neglect of history in accounts of historical injustice. Koselleck's view is instructive as it immediately conceives of historical time as a political and social issue. For Koselleck, historical time is always experienced and embedded in social and political institutions; thus such an experience affects how political and social issues are conceptualised and normatively assessed.[21]

Koselleck offers a powerful analysis of modernity centred on the peculiarity of modern historical time. For our purposes, it is not necessary to discuss all the nuances and aspects of Koselleck's understanding of modernity but just its main points.[22] For Koselleck, since the eighteenth century, the relation between the past, present and future has radically changed. Before the advent of modernity, it was widely believed that the past would have offered invaluable lessons for the future, as the time to come would not have substantially varied from what had previously happened. Individuals have since then started to perceive themselves as the members of a new time (*Neuzeit*) depicted as entirely different from the past and completely projected towards a better future, a future which 'broke with the conditions of all previous history'.[23] Recalling Kant's well-known words, modern individuals conceived of themselves as not yet living in an age of enlightenment.[24] Modernity is marked by the phenomenon of *acceleration*; since the eighteenth century, especially during the French Revolution and industrialisation, the expectations of a time to come, now deprived of its religious meaning and secularised through the ideal

---

[21] Koselleck (2005, xxii).

[22] For instance, I omit Koselleck's controversial interpretation of the genesis of modernity – famously developed in his *Kritik und Krise* – because the tenability of his discussion of the conception of historical time that he sees as typical of the Enlightenment does not rely on it.

[23] Koselleck (2005, 198).   [24] Kant ([1784] 2004, 58).

of progress, became the dominating temporal experience. Consequently, the perception of incessantly speeding towards a different and better future led to a progressively long distance from what happened in the past.[25] Not only does time accelerate towards the future but the latter is also conceived as constantly bringing about newly unexpected events; that is, it is 'an open future'.[26]

According to Koselleck, during modernity the phenomenon of temporalisation (*Verzeitlichung*) of history has occurred; the past and future are relocated with respect to each other in such a radical way that the space of past experience ceases to be the basis for the expectancy of the future. To wit, the past starts being conceived as separated from the present and the future.[27] This does not mean history as a discipline becomes insignificant. Conversely, since modernity, history – or rather, the study thereof – has performed an important and legitimising function. Due to the differentiation between past and present, it became possible to consider history as the study of a distant past whose otherness confirmed the exceptionality of the new time. It is only when the past is experienced and conceptualised as not inhabiting the present that it can be regarded as a detached object of investigation and history can turn into a distinctive discipline.[28]

The temporalisation of history inaugurated by modernity can cast some light on the conceptual difficulty in grasping the 'present-past' that accounts of historical injustice seem to encounter. One may suggest that both critics and (at least the majority of) supporters of historical justice have inherited from modernity an understanding of history which regards the past either as disjointed from the present (and the future) or, at the very best, as having some effects on the present.

Critics of historical justice and backward-looking approaches *temporalise injustice* by neatly separating the unjust past from present conditions of inequalities and injustices. Critics temporalise justice not only by restating that it is present and future justice, as distinct from past justice, that we should worry about but especially by insisting that we have in the present all the normative resources to assess and address contemporary injustices. In doing so, the possibility that the unjust past can remain present to such an extent that many contemporary injustices cannot be fully conceptualised, let alone overcome, without addressing its presence is simply ruled

---

[25] Koselleck (2005, 40–41).   [26] Koselleck (2002, 165).   [27] Koselleck (2005, 4, 11).

[28] Koselleck's point interestingly resonates with postcolonial analyses of the emergence of the discipline of history as the exclusive mode in which a society should relate to the past and of how this led to the marginalisation and even eradication of all those other non-modern forms of experiencing the past (Chakrabarty 2007, 237–55; Nandy 1995, 44; Seth 2004, 88–90; Skaria 1999).

out. Backward-looking approaches share with sceptics the temporalisation of justice; by identifying the sources of obligation for historical justice in the past, they accept the separation of past and present injustice but think the former should be redressed per se. Thus backward-looking approaches argue that the past still has claims on the present; however, they also reiterate that the past (and the considerations of justice stemming from it) should not be theoretically and normatively confused with what present injustices are. The past and the present cannot be regarded as the same.

It is also now possible to spot some differences between two forward-looking approaches which contend that past wrongs should be considered in relation to present injustices on different grounds. Pragmatic accounts can be said to somehow temporalise justice in principle, even though not in practice, because they do not theoretically and normatively engage with the possibility that the past remains present; the link between past and present, when it is made, is argumentatively purely strategic.

Conversely, forward-looking approaches contending that unrepaired past injustices wreck the prospect of building trust relations between citizens and among states or that present inequalities can be seen as the legacy of historical injustices do not temporalise injustice in the same way that critics of historical justice and backward-looking approaches do. Nevertheless, when it comes to spelling out how the past remains present and why more egalitarian changes in the distribution of resources and opportunities cannot offset the effects of the past, these approaches encounter serious difficulties. In other words, by being unable to explain the relation between persistence (of the past) and changes (in the present and the future), they cannot successfully rebut the proposal of simply temporalising injustice. Moreover, conceiving of history as present only in terms of its effects is still theoretically compatible with thinking of it as separate – that is, as placed in a different dimension. To wit, the past can be still regarded as not the same as the present, even if the impact of the former on the latter is recognised.

Having reconstructed the account of historical time inaugurated during modernity, the theoretical obstacles forward-looking approaches face no longer appear so puzzling. Indeed, they can be seen as resulting from a failure to outright reject a modern understanding of historical time. To be sure, forward-looking approaches pointing in particular to a causal link between existing inter-group inequalities and the historical injustices committed to such disadvantaged groups recognise how the past takes its toll on the present in a significant way. However, to de-temporalise injustice and thus fully theorise the 'present-past', we should move beyond a modern understanding of historical time and reconceptualise history itself, and not just its effects, as present. In this way, it will become clearer why (1) persistence and change are not contradictory but actually interdependent and (2) the realisation of present and future justice cannot be achieved without tackling an unjust history.

2.3 A Structural Conception of History

A modern conception of historical time is inherently inapt to fully conceptualise the present-past. We need instead to be able to immediately direct our normative analysis to the logical consistency of an unjust history that is not really past. To do so entails unpacking the very meaning of history.

Koselleck instructively argues that there are two different yet interdependent levels of temporal extension: 'events' and 'long-term structures'. Events occur in a determinate moment and are perceived as unique. Although events can display different durations – that is, they can last for longer or shorter times – their internal coherence 'is rooted in temporal sequence'.[29] No matter exactly how long an event lasted, what confers unity to its existence is the possibility to narrate its beginning and end. With an event, there is always a 'before' and an 'after', which are regarded as distinct from the 'now' wherein the event happens.[30] Unlike events, long-term structures endure over time and cannot be reduced to a series of events. As Koselleck states, long-term structures 'include those temporal aspects of relations not covered by the strict sequence of experienced events',[31] and they elucidate phenomena, such as stability and change, that otherwise would remain inexplicable. Therefore, long-term structures outlive the mere individual experience of a chronological sequence of events; far from being enclosed in the lifetime of single individuals, their influence extends over *intergenerational* groups of persons and resists the passing of time. For Koselleck, long-term structures, unlike events, cannot be narrated in terms of what happened before and after them.[32] Nevertheless, just because they endure, it does not mean that long-term structures do not display a temporal dimension or that they are somehow outside time. Conversely, by persisting over time, they acquire a processual and systemic dimension. Importantly, Koselleck observes that when long-term structures become particularly persisting, they tend to be taken for

---

[29] Koselleck (2005, 104).   [30] Koselleck (2005, 104).   [31] Koselleck (2005, 107).
[32] Koselleck (2005, 109).

granted and are internalised by the groups experiencing them, thereby making their transformation even more difficult to achieve.[33]

For Koselleck, although distinct, events and long-term structures are linked to one another through a complex relation of interdependence. Events rely on long-term structures that were already present and resist their end. Long-term structures do not merely correspond to what existed before the event and what remains after it terminates; they are the conditions under which an event can occur.[34] More precisely, for Koselleck, long-term structures lie at the root of the *repetition* of events; the mere possibility for two analogous events to repeat depends upon the continuing presence of such structures. Without resorting to long-term structures, it would be nearly impossible to make sense of the repetition of similar events, and history would appear to be constituted by incongruous events.

That said, Koselleck warns against interpreting the interconnection between events and long-term structures as one of mere causality. Although long-term structures provide the background conditions for the occurrence of an event (and of a series of similar events), they do not directly cause events. Moreover, the comprehension of an event cannot be completely reduced to the structures that contribute to its occurrence. Although they are the conditions under which events happen, long-term structures cannot be captured by observing the sequence of similar events. Trying to identify the common denominator between two analogous events or to abstract the more general features from the particularities of specific events overlooks the complexity of long-term structures and their workings. On the other hand, the fact that an event actually takes place is determined by further factors. The relation between events and long-term structures can be clarified by resorting to the difference between possibility and reality. While for an event to be possible some long-term structures have to be in place, a possible event becoming a reality results from a unique combination of structural and non-structural elements. In other words, an understanding of the occurrence of an event that merely refers to long-term structures is not exhaustive, but without considering long-term structures, how a particular event could happen in the first place remains unexplained.[35]

Koselleck elucidates his point by providing an example that draws on one of the most famous chapters of German history: the victory of Frederick the Great, king of Prussia, in the Battle of Leuthen over the Austrian army under the command of Charles of Lorraine (5 December 1757). This battle is not

---

[33] Koselleck (2005, 108).   [34] Koselleck (2002, 124).   [35] Koselleck (2002, 58).

only well known because it secured Frederick the Great's control of Silesia during the Seven Years' War. It is especially renowned because the Prussians were able to defeat a much larger army through a strategic manoeuvre. Koselleck mentions this example to show how, while the surrounding and pre-existing structures (e.g. the organisation of the Prussian army, and the social and economic conditions of the kingdom) made this unexpected victory possible, they did not fully determine the defeat of the Austrian enemy.[36] Other, non-structural factors, such as the foggy weather, the Prussian army's knowledge of the terrain (once their training ground), arguably a bit of chance and not least Frederick the Great's exceptional military skills, need to be considered if one wants to explicate why such a victory happened. In this regard, 'December 5, 1757 remains a unique event in its chronologically immanent sequence'.[37]

The irreducibility of events to those long-term structures that are their conditions of possibility is of paramount importance; however, the alternative conception of historical time introduced by Koselleck still emphasises the crucial role long-term structures play as constitutive components of history. Given the presence of long-term structures, history cannot be conceived as entirely new, because when something apparently new occurs, there are always long-term enduring structures that made it possible. In particular, Koselleck observes that if we are interested in how certain issues persist over time, and to what extent we are 'dealing with problems that, although unique, are persistent and respond to permanent challenges',[38] the structural dimension of history cannot be disregarded.

By immediately endorsing a *structural understanding of history*, it is possible to de-temporalise injustice – that is, theorise the present-past. History can be seen as embedded (and, as we will see, reproduced) in the present through long-term structures. The explicit adoption of a structural understanding of history offers a privileged starting point to theorise *historical* injustices. In particular, focusing on the structural dimension of history immediately prompts us to think about past injustices not only in terms of singular events with a clear beginning and a putative end but also (and especially) as long-term structures. In other words, when we consider an injustice that occurred in the past such as slavery in the US, we cannot simply approach it as an event that spanned across a roughly precise amount of time (e.g. from the arrival of enslaved Africans to the British

---

[36] Koselleck (2002, 125).   [37] Koselleck (2002, 125).   [38] Koselleck (2006, 103).

colony of Jamestown, Virginia, in 1619 to ratification of the Thirteen Amendment on 18 December 1865).[39] By approaching it that way, we neglect the structural dimension of history. That is, slavery in the US as a historical phenomenon was also characterised by long-term structures that constituted its possibility of existence and that may have outlived the end of the 'event' of slavery, and thus it should also be normatively analysed as such.

The structural dimension of the institution of slavery in the US is given by (1) the long-term structures (e.g. economic, political and ideological) that were in place before the beginning of slavery and under which the establishment of the institution of slavery was possible; (2) those long-term structures, such as the creation of racial hierarchies, that sustained the institution of slavery over time during its different phases; and (3) those long-term structures (e.g. of economic dependency, political disenfranchisement, institutional violence, cultural disempowerment and psychological oppression) established in the US by slavery that not only may have outlasted the abolishment of the 'peculiar institution' but may also keep being reproduced nowadays and be the structural conditions under which other events can occur.[40] To be sure, in this section, I do not intend to make any historiographic claim about the origins, development and impact of such a complex phenomenon as the institution of slavery in the US, which is the object of an extensive body of literature.[41] My argument is merely conceptual and normative; here, the example of the institution of slavery is given to show how the endorsement of a structural understanding of history results in majorly transforming how we theorise historical injustices and their normative relevance. It immediately compels us to embrace 'the uncertainty whether the past really is past, over and concluded, or whether it continues, albeit [perhaps]

---

[39] Note that not all those who conceptualise slavery in the US in terms of an event would agree with this specific demarcation of the extension of that institution. For example, some may date the beginning of slavery earlier by pointing out that Spanish and Portuguese settlers had already brought slaves from Africa to the 'New World' in 1501 by turning Santo Domingo into the first international slave port. I do not dispute that the specific demarcation of an historical event can be the object of (lively) controversies among historians. Nor do I want to suggest that the demarcation we draw has no implications for how we may understand a historical event and its importance. What I intend to suggest is that there is something conceptually (and normatively) problematic about considering slavery in the US (as a historical injustice) only in terms of an event with a specific demarcation, whatever such a demarcation may be.

[40] See, e.g., Berlin (2000); Eltis (2000); Harris (2004); Johnson (1999).

[41] Indeed, one of the arguments developed in Chapter 8 (§ 8.3) is that activists, rather than the political theorists, play a crucial role in signalling the ways a historical injustice is newly reproduced in the present.

in different forms'[42] and to conceive of historical injustices as potentially being present through long-term structures.

In the next chapter, I will provide a more fully fledged account of historical injustices and the de-temporalisation approach, which relies on this structural interpretation of history and shows that, once considered in terms of long-term structures, the (unjust) past cannot be dismissed if we want to address (some) present injustices and inequalities. Before doing so, however, let me dispel some doubts that a structural understanding of history may generate, especially when it is adopted to think about injustice. Although some of these doubts will hopefully be removed in the following chapters, it is best to anticipate some observations.

First, one may worry that although a structural understanding of history is better equipped to capture persistence over time than a modern conception of historical time, it encounters more difficulties in grasping and theorising *change*. By mainly focusing on what remains over time, this understanding of history is bound to underappreciate the significance of what instead changes; even worse, it may not have the theoretical resources to do otherwise. Although this is a legitimate concern, it is misplaced when it addresses the specific structural conception of history elaborated in this chapter, which provides the basis for the account of historical injustice defended in the book. Indeed, the fact that we especially need to approach past injustices as long-term structures does not entail arguing that these injustices persist over time in the same form as they originally appeared. Conversely, change becomes fundamental in understanding the endurance and, specifically, the reproduction of an unjust history. It is only when the modifications undergone by societies (and the international sphere) since the past injustices under consideration occurred are fully taken into account that one can comprehend how the present-past can still operate and be reproduced. Change is necessary for persistence, or, as famously said in *The Leopard*: 'If we want things to stay as they are, things will have to change'.[43] Therefore, the structural conception of history elaborated here gives change a crucial role.

What, however, such a conception does imply is a different account of persistence. Persistence cannot simply be regarded as a legacy (of the past); it should be seen in terms of *structural reproduction*. Historical injustices do not merely remain present as something passively handed down from a distant era which blocks the progress that otherwise would have been achieved. As I will show in the next chapter, they significantly structure the

---

[42] Said (1994, 1).   [43] Tomasi di Lampedusa ([1958] 2007, 19).

present by establishing (at least partially) the background conditions in which individuals and collective agents interact. In this sense, historical injustices keep being reproduced and reactivated in the present. Importantly, this semantic shift – from legacy to long-term structures – also provides the basis for an understanding of the relation between historical unjust long-term structures that remain present and contemporary (and future) unjust events that is more complex than the one underlying 'causalistic' forward-looking approaches, as the latter are based on a too direct link between past injustice and present inequalities.[44] In particular, dropping the language of legacy to endorse that of structural reproduction helps theorise the dynamic interplay between persistence (of an injustice) and change, an interplay that is crucial precisely to understand how historical injustices persist over time. In other words, it enables one to appreciate how historical injustices are *newly* reproduced and, as I will argue in Chapter 8 (§ 8.1), to attribute historical accountability to powerful agents for the significant role they have played in that reproduction over time.

Second, one may object that my structural conception of history offers too reductionist an account of the relation between events and long-term structures, thereby neglecting Koselleck's warning to not conflate one with the other. Specifically, we seem to be caught in a dilemma. On one hand, to show why the past is normatively significant even if (or especially when) one holds egalitarian commitments in the present, we need to resort to a structural conception of history and offer a substantive account of unjust long-term structures. On the other hand, the more specific such an account is, the more likely the temptation to trace the occurrence of a present event back to the pre-existence of long-term structures becomes. Tracing it in this way seems particularly troubling when we focus on questions of injustice as it risks undermining the agency of those who committed a wrong and thus their liability for it. This is a serious worry which I will come back to in the next chapter. For now, let me observe that a structural conception of history is not necessarily a determinist one. As already emphasised, recognising the structural dimensions of history does not mean regarding the actual occurrence of an event (e.g. a wrong, crime or injustice) as fully determined by the long-term structures that ground its condition of possibility. It merely attributes 'explanatory autonomy' to

---

[44] To anticipate, fully de-temporalising injustice by embracing a structural conception of history will have important normative implications. It will mean that waiting for the present achievements or deploying present resources to overcome the present-past would not be a viable option, thereby offering a reply to the redundancy objection (§ 3.3).

long-term structures[45] by arguing that how a particular event (and repetitions of analogous events) could happen in the first place remains unexplained without considering such structures. Moreover, long-term structures do not reproduce a historical injustice on their own; they are reactivated precisely by human agency.

In sum, in this chapter I showed how the impasse reached in the debate over historical injustice amounts to an under-theorisation of the modern conception of historical time on which both critics and supporters of historical justice rely (or fail to fully reject). I also argued that we need to de-temporalise injustice – that is, fully conceptualise the present-past – and that this can be done by endorsing a structural account of history. Approaching history in terms of long-term structures immediately directs our normative enquiry to its presence and offers a conceptually advantageous starting point to understand how history can persist under new circumstances and when and why an unjust history should matter in our considerations of justice. However, to convincingly show how, unlike backward-looking and the majority of forward-looking approaches, de-temporalising injustice does not turn historical justice into an impractical task or make it redundant, a more detailed account of historical long-term structures and their reproduction needs to be provided. This is precisely the aim of the next chapter.

---

[45] For a definition of the notion of 'explanatory autonomy', see MacDonald and Pettit (1980, 122–25).

CHAPTER 3

The Structural Reproduction of Unjust History

The 2010 movie *Even the Rain* (*También la Lluvia*), directed by Icíar Bollaín, compellingly recounts the Cochabamba Water War, a series of violent demonstrations that erupted in the city of Cochabamba in Bolivia between December 1999 and April 2000. The protests were sparked by the privatisation of the city's municipal water company (Semapa), which was sold to a transnational consortium (Aguas del Tunari) involving the US Bechtel Corporation. The privatisation of water was part of a larger privatisation programme of national resources adopted by the Bolivian government to reduce the debt incurred after its long military dictatorships and bloody civil wars, and also to implement the directives given by the World Bank and thus be eligible for further loans.[1] The movie tells the story of a film crew, headed by director Sebastián and his executive producer Costa, who go to Bolivia to make a revisionist movie about Christopher Columbus's conquest of Latin America but arrive in the country during the intensifications of water protests. The reality of the riots enters the fiction when Daniel, the local actor cast for the role of the indigenous chief who led a rebellion against Spanish conquistadores, becomes one of the leaders of the community protests in Cochabamba and refuses to stop his involvement with the rioters – a decision that results in continuous clashes with the police.

The peculiarity of *Even the Rain* consists not only in drawing continuous parallels between the expropriation of indigenous lands and resources by Columbus and the Spanish conquistadores and the contemporary dispossession of water by the Bolivian government and transnational organisations. The movie is especially distinctive in constructing a powerful narrative that de-temporalises history; that is, it conceives of history itself as present. In particular, such a narrative tries to show how the injustice

---

[1] On the Cochabamba Water War and the national and international context in which the protests took place, see Assies (2003) and Perreault (2006).

against indigenous peoples initially committed by European settlers is reproduced in the fabric of the Bolivian society and the transnational order in complex and intertwined ways and through different means: from the interplay between transnational capitalistic interests and domestic politics, to individuals' behaviours (e.g. Costa's decision of setting the movie on Columbus's exploitation of indigenous resources in Bolivia, one of the poorest countries of the 'New World', to save on the budget, and Sebastián's obsession with his movie and indifference towards the ongoing plight of 'the dispossessed') and to the everyday interactions among the crew and the local population and actors.

Like *Even the Rain*, this chapter argues for the complexity and normative unavoidability of the reproduction of unjust history.[2] Although it cannot even aspire to make that case as powerfully as done by the multiple narrative layers of the movie, it contends that historical injustices, as long-term structures, have established the background conditions in which persons interact and that these conditions are crucial to grasp how injustices can endure over time. The chapter offers an account of historical injustice – which I call *historical-structural injustice* – that is sensitive to how historical long-term structures can operate under new circumstances and explains why egalitarians who strive for justice in the present cannot dismiss the structurally reproduced past. Specifically, by developing such an account, this chapter has three goals. First, it aims to point out that the structural presence of an unjust history has both 'radical' (e.g. violence) and more 'banal' (e.g. stereotypes) dimensions and that the latter should not be neglected as they significantly interplay with the former. Second, it tries to show the interdependence of persistence and change by suggesting that change is actually an important element of the very reproduction of history. Third, it aims to overcome the difficulties that, as seen in Chapter 2, the majority of approaches to historical justice encounter by identifying a criterion that allows distinguishing which historical injustices need to be considered and, more importantly, by showing that the unjust past cannot be superseded by present-based considerations of injustice because the former structures the latter.

---

[2] Note that even such a movie seems to remain entangled in the complexity of the reproduction of the unjust history it intends to denounce. As a review in the *New York Times* lucidly observes, the audience is left wondering whether 'its makers exploited the extras recruited' to play sixteenth-century indigenous people (Holden 2011).

3.1   Structural Processes and Unjust History

In Chapter 2, I argued that (unjust) history should be conceived as long-term structures. How should historical structures be defined? And what is their normative significance? Before answering these questions, a caveat is in order. In this chapter, I cannot offer a full-fledged account of historical structures; nor can I develop a blueprint for how historical long-term structures should be identified. Not only is it true that such a task is inevitably contextual and thus any detailed description of historical structures is bound to neglect crucial historical specificities but also it is a task that should be pursued by other agents and in the praxis of activist politics (rather than from the armchair of the political theorist). Indeed, as I will suggest in Chapter 8 (§ 8.3), this crucial task is undertaken in a more fruitful way by activist groups fighting for justice who have been constructing narratives that identify and specify unjust historical structures and thus suggest how a particular unjust history is reproduced in the fabric of a society (or the transnational order). That said, let me offer some thoughts on how historical structures should be approached by starting with the notion of structure.

As already mentioned in the Introduction, Iris Marion Young has developed an influential and arguably compelling account of the relation between structures and injustices. In particular, Young usefully suggests that reflecting 'structurally' on injustice means endorsing a specific outlook on society which does not zoom in on a 'small set of institutions' but looks at the whole society in a specific way, namely by seeing 'patterns in relations' between persons.[3] Observing society through a wide-angle lens means going beyond the Rawlsian idea that there is a 'basic' structure – a limited set of institutions that can be said to have a profound impact on persons' lives from the start – and that justice applies only to it. It does not mean neglecting the important role of institutions but simply means revealing and questioning processes that significantly contribute to creating conditions of vulnerability and threats of domination but are usually largely unchallenged and left unscrutinised by an exclusive focus on institutions. For instance, as suggested by Young, a structural account of injustice brings about processes of 'normalisation' – that is, the elevation of

---

[3] Young (2011, 70). It is important to note that a structural-injustice approach is not confined to the nation-state. On the contrary, as Young's case of sweatshop labour shows, it does not only apply even to the workings of our global order but also prompts us to reflect upon the interconnections between 'domestic' and 'global' injustices by revealing transnational structural processes (e.g. those characterising financialised capitalism) that affect persons both at a domestic and a global level (Young 2011, chapter 5).

'the experience and capacities of some social segments into standards used to judge everyone' – as a crucial mechanism whereby injustices are produced.[4] As Young (drawing on the social model of disability) argues, the injustice to which physically disabled persons are subjected cannot be grasped without considering the ableist normalisation of how bodies should function, say in the urban infrastructure.[5]

Structures can be analytically divided into two types: (1) environmental and (2) rules based. 'Environmental' structures include all those physical imprints on our surrounding world that result from many persons' deeds and decisions over time.[6] For instance, Young notices how the highways and suburban-tract housing that characterise many cities represent the material effects that the status and economic value of the automobile, which was endorsed by many persons (especially in the 1960s and 1970s), had on city planning.[7] These material effects outlive and continue to shape the urban landscape even if today many dwellers do not own a car, either because of the high cost of petrol or because they opt for more environmentally friendly means of transport. 'Rules-based' structures consist of both formal and informal rules that mould the ways persons interact. Admittedly, many different structural processes fall into this category: from legal rules, formal institutions and occupational hierarchies to norms, expectations, conventions, symbols and even dress codes.[8]

In describing the workings of structures and, in particular, how they operate in persons' lives, Young observes how persons passively experience environmental structures, which are, however, as mentioned, 'the products of previous actions'.[9] Although highways do not mark our urban surroundings by chance, we do not encounter them as the outcome of 'past praxis' but as mere features of our environment that we have to deal with; in this sense, they are 'practico-inert'.[10] However, such structures profoundly affect persons' lives by *constraining* and *enabling* their present and future possibilities. Consider, for example, the case of public toilets, which usually separate female from male restrooms. Public toilets are a physical feature of our environment that we tend to passively experience, yet they represent a material effect of the decision to divide humankind into two genders. For

---

[4] Young (2006, 95).   [5] Young (2006, 94–95).   [6] Young (2011, 53).   [7] Young (2011, 54).

[8] Young (2011, 54). 'Environmental' and 'rules-based' structures are often interdependent, as the example of the automobile shows. The status symbol of the automobile has created the social expectation of owning a car, which has in turn incentivised the building of highways. Similarly, the existence of highways to connect the inner city with the outskirts and close cities has strengthened, for example, the expectation that persons should own a car to get a job.

[9] Young (2000, 96).   [10] Sartre (1976, 318) quoted in Young (2011, 53).

a woman who has a masculine appearance or a transgender woman, public toilets are deeply constraining not only because they limit her possibilities to express and live her non-conforming gender identity but also in that they channel her choices into what may be dangerous directions (e.g. risking to be mistaken as a man in a female bathroom).[11] At the same time, more feminine and cisgender women do not experience 'gendered' public toilets as constraining but instead may even regard these restrooms as enabling them to feel safer in a public yet intimate space.

Moreover, structures can be seen as creating a 'multi-dimensional space of different social positions among which a population is distributed'.[12] Structures *position* individuals in relation to one another, and every specific position is defined interdependently with other positions within the structures. For example, we cannot understand the privileges that the Brahmins ('the priests'), the highest caste in India, have without considering their systematic relation of hierarchy with lower castes, such as the Shudras ('the servants').[13] This feature of structures is crucial. Although structures are the result of sedimented interactions, they are also productive – that is, they sustain and create positions of asymmetries within societies (and the transnational order).[14]

Structures also have a third characteristic: they 'exist only in the action and interaction of persons; they exist not as states but as processes'.[15] That is, by acting within structures, collective and individual agents contribute to *reproducing* them. In greater detail, structures should be regarded as providing 'rules and resources' for agents to orientate their actions in the world.[16] However, by relying on the knowledge of structures pre-existing their actions, agents reproduce them. Now, the process of reproduction of structures can be unreflective: for instance, persons do not necessarily act in accordance with structures intentionally or consciously; they may unconsciously or habitually rely on them in the exercise of their agency. Structures are also embodied and enacted through an internalisation of what is expected (e.g. in terms of behaviour, preferences, dress code) of persons within determinate structural positions – that is, the 'habitus'.[17] Habitus contributes to maintaining the endurance of practices and their

---

[11] On the so-called bathroom problem, see Halberstam (1998, 366).
[12] Blau (1977, 4) quoted in Young (2011, 56).   [13] Young (2000, 94).
[14] I will return to the idea of structural positions in Chapter 4.   [15] Young (2000, 95).
[16] Giddens (1979, 64) quoted in Young (2000, 95).
[17] Bourdieu (1984) quoted in Young (2011, 61). For Young, because structures are reproduced by many (collective and individual) agents also through routinised actions, structures can produce outcomes that run counter to agents' aims; they have 'counter-finalities' (Young 2011, 63).

perception as correct because it places 'the active presence of past experiences [in each individual] in the form of schemes of perception, thought and action'.[18] It constitutes the embodiment of cultural capital.

Having indicated what structures refer to and their complex mechanisms, it is important to point out how many (although not all) environmental and rules-based structural processes do not simply stem from the sedimentation of past deeds and decisions but are also significantly connected with past *unjust* actions – that is, with historical injustices. Consider, for example, how the *banlieues*, which designate the urbanised zones around French cities and are usually inhabited by the poorest and most marginalised dwellers, can be seen as an environmental structural incarnation of France's colonial history. Indeed, such suburbs not only are populated by many migrants from France's North African ex-colonies (e.g. Algeria, Tunisia and Morocco) or French citizens of North African origins but also have been the centre of violent riots expressing the failure of the French model of integration. The *banlieues* can be regarded as an example of how France has not effectively come to terms with her unjust colonial past or, better, of how that unjust history remains structurally present in the material urban environment and continues to produce second-status citizens.[19] To wit, French colonial history is 'objectified' in the material environment of the French cities.[20]

Similarly, societies are structured by many formal and informal rules related to historical injustice; some of them may appear harmless at first sight, although they clearly have a far-reaching symbolic significance. Consider rules deciding national festivities and, in particular, the case of the annual celebration of Christopher Columbus's discovery of the Americas, which has marked a federal festivity in the US since 1937 (i.e. Columbus Day). Some, such as the American Indian movement, strenuously argue that the decision to commemorate the European settlement of the Americas and its ongoing practice is not so meaningless in that it (intentionally or not) contributes to neglecting the responsibility for the genocides committed against indigenous peoples (and for their enduring condition of oppression). To further prove how several structural processes shaping persons' interactions are intrinsically connected with historical injustice, let me focus on stereotypes.

---

[18] Bourdieu (1984, 54).
[19] Hussey (2014). A further example of how the urban landscape can incorporate an unjust history is obviously the 'black ghetto' in contemporary American cities (Hayward 2013; Young 2000, 96–97).
[20] For a compelling analysis of how material objectification reproduces identities, see Hayward (2013).

Stereotypes, which refer to 'qualities perceived to be associated with particular groups or categories of people',[21] constitute a particularly interesting case to show the close relation between unjust history and structures for a twofold reason. First, this is because of the growing empirical and normative attention to stereotypes. The pervasive and damaging effects stereotypes have in persons' lives have been extensively analysed by social psychologists in the last decades, and it is only quite recently that some political theorists have started to examine closely the role stereotypes play in sustaining inequalities.[22] Second, stereotypes are a component of those processes of 'normalisation' which, as seen, a conception of structural injustice (historical or not) must bring to the forefront. Stereotypes, even if they are activated by individuals, are not simply in our heads but are a component of structures because they constitute 'cultural schemas' that orient our actions in relation to others and 'make the structure of our social milieu seem right and natural'.[23]

Obviously, not all stereotypes are negative, and not all negative stereotypes can be said to be related to unjust history. However, it is worth pointing out how for many historically oppressed and marginalised groups, unjust history does provide much of the content of those stereotypes associated with them. Stereotypes can be said to stem from unjust history in at least two interconnected ways. First, many stereotypes were originally and systematically deployed *to justify historical injustices*, such as the segregation of and violence against certain groups. Consider the stereotypical association of African Americans with criminality. As Angela Davis, among others, argues, such an association stems from the slavery system and the defence of racial discrimination.[24] In the aftermath of the Civil War and the abolition of slavery, former slave states in the South passed new legislation which revisited the slave codes that previously gave slave owners absolute power over the enslaved, in order to regulate the behaviour of free blacks in ways similar to those that had existed during slavery. This legislation, called the black codes, aimed at seriously restricting African Americans' freedom and also compelled them to work for low wages or for free in order to pay debts. Most importantly, such codes proscribed a range of actions (e.g. vagrancy, drunkenness and absence from work) that were criminalised only if the person was black.[25] This discriminating criminal legislation 'tended to racialize penality and link it closely to previous

---

[21] Schneider (2003, 24).   [22] Most notably, see Anderson (2010, chapter 3).
[23] Haslanger (2012, 174).   [24] Davis (2003, 28–39). See also Loury (2002, 69).
[25] Davis (2003, 28–39); see also Manos (2015, 50). For a historical account of black codes, see Wallenstein (2004).

regimes of slavery'.[26] In this sense, the stereotype that links blackness with criminality was constructed precisely to justify the reproduction of legal segregation and differential treatment of African Americans.

In the case of unjust histories of inter-group relations, stereotypes have provided a powerful tool to rationalise the establishment and sustainment of a system of subjugation and the use of violence when the subordinated group is perceived as a threat to the interests of the dominant one. This can be seen when examining, for example, the stereotype of indigenous peoples as uncivilised and its crucial legitimising role in the infamous Trail of Tears – that is, the forced expulsion of indigenous nations such as the Cherokee from their lands after the Indian Removal Act signed by the US president Andrew Jackson on 28 May 1830. Although the 'threat' presented by the Cherokee 'was not so much the savage, drunken Indian as the civilized one who ... would beat the white man at his own game – raising cotton',[27] it was precisely the available stereotype of indigenous peoples as uncivilised, unclean and primitive that was activated to persuade the public of the rightness of the brutal removal. Similarly, in the case of European colonialism in Africa and Asia, as Albert Memmi suggests, the stereotyping of the colonised as 'lazy' served the purpose of exploiting their economic resources and especially their labour force by paying them otherwise indefensible inadequate wages.[28]

The second interconnected way stereotypes of groups that suffered from historical injustice are significantly connected to that unjust history is by *offering an alternative narrative* of what actually happened. This is the case of those stereotypes that romanticise a historical injustice. Consider the popular stereotype of the 'Indian' princess, which has nourished literature, cinema and even cartoon works in the US (and worldwide).[29] This stereotype has become particularly influential through the mythicised story of Pocahontas, a noble woman (daughter of the chief of many tribal nations in Tsenacommacah, Virginia) who saves a white man while falling in love with him, and, once held captive by the English, happily embraces their allegedly superior culture by converting to Christianity, rebelling against her people and marrying another English settler.[30] The stereotype of the 'Indian' princess helped construct a romantic and idyllic narrative of the relations between indigenous women and white men, which were instead

---

[26] Davis (2003, 31). For another account of the historical connection between the stereotypical and statistical association of blackness with danger, see Muhammad (2011).

[27] Wallace (1993, 62).   [28] Memmi ([1965] 2003, 123).   [29] Bird (1999).

[30] For some critical analyses of the stereotype of the 'Indian princess' embodied by Pocahontas, see, e.g., Jackson (1996) and Sardar (1996), who focus on Walt Disney's popular depiction.

characterised by sexual violence and forced assimilation.[31] More precisely, these kinds of stereotypes worked alongside other (even more) negative ones (i.e. the stereotype of indigenous women as sexually available and immoral 'squaws') to originally justify the injustice. While the stereotype of the 'Indian' princess enabled the justification of the forced assimilation as something that 'good' indigenous women desired, the dissolute squaw legitimatised the extreme violence against 'bad' indigenous women.[32] However, 'romanticised' stereotypes also retrospectively perform an important ideological function precisely by developing a false and poetic interpretation of a 'past' injustice. By being retold and reproduced over time, even or especially after the injustices were committed, the stereotypical story of the 'Indian' princess facilitates the neglect of the dark chapters of the history of the 'New World' and thus makes governments and their citizens feel less responsible for them.

Why is the connection between historical injustices and the origins and content of negative stereotypes significant? Such a connection, for example, can explain how persons are subjected to dissimilar forms of stereotyping depending on the context. For instance, many African Americans who have emigrated to Europe argue that, although European countries are prejudiced against racial minorities, the type of stereotyping they are subjected to in places such as France is radically different from that which they suffered in the US. Moreover, once their American accent makes them less likely to be mistaken for someone with North African origins, they are less vulnerable to stereotypical associations than when they were in the US.[33] This disparity can be easily traced back to the different history the African American identity has in the US (vis-à-vis France). That said, the connection between historical injustices and stereotypes is of paramount importance also for a normative reason. By confirming how structural processes such as stereotypes not only are a mere sedimentation of past actions but also are linked to historical injustices, such a connection helps show how even these normalised structural processes of interaction should be regarded as mechanisms whereby historical injustices are reproduced – that is, as crucial aspects of the 'structural presence of the unjust history'. It is to this presence and its workings that now I will turn.

---

[31] Smith (2005).

[32] On the binary 'princess/squaw' as fundamental to understanding the historical stereotyping of indigenous women, see Green (1975).

[33] Steele (2010, 79–84).

3.2   Historical-Structural Injustice and Its Banal Radicality

The stereotypical association of members of a group with a determinate feature can be intentionally and deliberatively invoked to justify the oppression of a group, as seen in the previous section. However, as social psychologists argue, today in many egalitarian contexts stereotypes *also* operate at a more unintended level as implicit biases – that is, as 'unconscious and relatively automatic features of prejudiced judgment and social behaviour'.[34] To see how stereotypes function, consider their workings in employment decisions. The link between the stereotyping of a group and a determinate occupation can be made *directly*. An occupation may be believed to require qualities that only or mostly members of a specific group are putatively thought to have or, for example, that members of a group that suffered from historical injustice such as African Americans do not stereotypically possess. When intelligence, determination, trustworthiness and capacity for compromise are considered as essential attributes to be, say, a successful manager, and African Americans have historically been stereotypically depicted as unclever, idle, unreliable and impulsive (especially vis-à-vis white men), an African American applicant for a managerial position may immediately appear as unsuited for the job. Thus, in a country such as the US, in which African American men are stereotypically seen as criminal, it is not surprising that, compared to white men with an identical résumé, African American men without criminal convictions tend to have the same chances of being called for an interview as white men with a criminal record – chances that are obviously much lower than for white men without a criminal history.[35] The (historical) stereotypical association of blackness with criminality makes every African American man a potential offender and thus less employable than a white man.[36]

Stereotypes operate in an even more subtle way: by creating an *indirect* association between group membership and access to a specific occupation or position. In greater detail, criteria of merit are often constructed in a way that privileges the qualifications and characteristics of applicants from the group seen as stereotypically best suited to the job. For instance, an experiment discovered that when asked to evaluate and rank the credentials for admission into university, assessors tended to redefine the criteria to

---

[34] Brownstein (2015).   [35] Pager (2007, 91–93). See also Bushway (2004).
[36] This stereotypical association can also be seen at work during interviews when African American candidates are, for example, more likely to be asked about their criminal history or even to take drug tests than, ceteris paribus, white men (Gooden 1999; Holzer, Raphael and Stoll 2006).

match the qualifications and skills white applicants had. Thus, if an African American applicant happened to have stronger scores on the standardised tests used for college admission in the US (SAT) and lower school grades than a white applicant, school grades were regarded as more important than test scores in admission to university; however, if test scores were the weaker credential of the African American applicant vis-à-vis a white counterpart, evaluators reconceived the entry criteria to highlight the importance of SAT scores.[37] This more indirect working of stereotypes is particularly congenial to self-professed egalitarian contexts as it subconsciously allows persons to preserve their self-image as impartial assessors (and even supporters of equality and non-discrimination) while producing the outcome stereotypically expected.[38] The indirect use of stereotypes is ubiquitous and pervades all the interactions between persons in which there is space for subjective judgements – that is, potentially the entire 'everyday realm of social relations'.[39]

It is important to stress that stereotypes are activated not only because they help persons to organise their social surroundings and conserve cognitive energy but especially because persons 'are motivated to perceive their world as fair and legitimate',[40] and stereotyping reassures that injustices are just misfortunes and existing inequalities depend on individuals' faults.[41] In other words, through indirect stereotypes persons are able to regard their social world as just and, even when they recognise certain outcomes and patterns – for example, racial inequality – as problematic, they can rationalise their behaviour within the social world as unbiased and unrelated to such problems. To be sure, the pervasive and often unconscious working of stereotypes does not mean that, in societies with a history of racial injustice such as the US, racial stigmatisation only stems from unconscious and indirect mechanisms. Such an assessment would be not only erroneous but also dangerous as it might lead one to misconceive recent overt racist terroristic attacks (e.g. the Charleston church massacre in South Carolina in June 2015) and rallies (e.g. the white-supremacist

---

[37] Hodson, Dovidio and Gaertner (2002).   [38] Norton, Vandello and Darley (2004).
[39] Kang (2005, 1494). See also Reskin (2000)   [40] Fiske and Lee (2008, 18).
[41] It is also worth observing that the phenomenon of negative stereotyping is broader than the direct and indirect forms of 'external' stereotyping mentioned above. It also encompasses 'internal' stereotyping processes activated by members of the stereotyped group, from internalisation of the negative stereotype to 'stereotype threats', which refers to how the members of a stereotyped group can underperform in a context in which they tend to be stigmatised because of their fear of reinforcing the negative stereotype of their group (e.g. Steele 2010). The latter are particularly difficult to control as they are easily triggered by simple cues, e.g. ticking one's racial background on an exam paper (e.g. Murphy and Taylor 2011).

march in Charlottesville, Virginia, in August 2017) as mere episodes rather than manifestations of systematic forms of racism within such societies. However, neglecting the fact that racism has also become a matter of 'aversion'[42] – that is, of internalised stereotypes or biases that can be easily misread by those who hold them – is problematic as well. It underplays how, in societies with a history of racial injustice, racism also operates through subtler and less detectable mechanisms to which persons who do not regard themselves as racist contribute.[43]

Structural processes such as stereotypes become crucial in the context of historical injustices. While such processes cannot explain how past injustices began, they help us understand how historical injustices can be reproduced through change. In particular, they are fundamental to grasp the complexity of reproduction, which is constituted by both banal and radical forms and their interplay. This can be seen by briefly examining Jeff Spinner-Halev's recent compelling and comprehensive account of historical injustices as 'enduring injustices'. While that account focuses on the endurance of an injustice as what normatively matters in cases of past injustices, it fails to properly theorise how an injustice can endure over time. Spinner-Halev contends that enduring injustices result from *radical* injustices that occurred in the past that have been left to fester without being addressed with an effective solution. For Spinner-Halev, radical injustices involved hideous wrongdoings (e.g. exile, dispossession of resources and land, cultural extirpation, blatant and institutionalised discrimination and extreme and large-scale violence) such as the ones committed against indigenous peoples in the US, Canada and Australia as well as the Crimean Tartars, Indian Muslims and Palestinian Israelis.[44] Spinner-Halev argues that when injustices of this kind are neglected or not properly corrected, they become increasingly 'enduring' over time and affect their victims so dramatically that they are not able to 'feel at home in the world'.[45]

This conceptualisation of historical injustices as enduring neglects that when historical injustices endure, they also change the ways they operate.

---

[42] On the concept of 'aversive racism', see Hodson, Dovidio and Gaertner (2002, 460).

[43] Obviously, this does not mean that nowadays *systems* of racism and sexism are just *caused* by implicit biases that individuals hold and thus have no material basis. Nor am I suggesting that eradicating racism simply amounts to making individuals responsible for individual biases. However, I think that, as Robin Zheng has recently argued (2018, 19–25) in reply to Sally Haslanger (2015), implicit biases, such as unconscious stereotyping, have a structural basis, as they are part of our habitus and thus can be traced back to cultural schemas. Therefore, they should be considered in a broader and multifaceted account of (historical) structural injustice.

[44] Spinner-Halev (2012b, 7–9).   [45] Spinner-Halev (2012b, 7–9).

In particular, by insisting on the radicality of enduring injustice – that is, on persisting dimensions of an injustice that immediately are seen (or should be seen) as shocking and wrong – Spinner-Halev overlooks the important *banal* mechanisms whereby unjust history is reproduced. As said, these mechanisms, such as stereotypes, are banal not because they are insignificant but because we tend to perceive them as 'natural' components of our social world. More precisely, these mechanisms can be defined as banal in at least two respects. First, they are banal in that they are *routinised*. Persons tend to take them for granted and not reflect on them, thereby relying on them in an automatic way. Second, such mechanisms are banal because they appear somehow as *trivial*, petty (and excusable) weaknesses of the human condition. Especially when compared to other forms of wrongs (e.g. exile and confinement in protected yet deprived areas), persons' reliance on negative stereotypes does not seem to amount to such a grave misdeed. However, when they are systematically performed over time, these mechanisms actually contribute to serious problems of injustice.

To be sure, the ongoing sufferance of peoples that continue to be confined in reservations or in exile immediately stands out as normatively problematic and in need of redress. Nevertheless, this does not suggest that history endures only through continuous hideous wrongdoings or blatant discriminations. Conversely, the past also remains within a series of conventions, habits, stereotypes and expectations that profoundly affect persons' lives. These aspects of the endurance of unjust history are likely to be underestimated when the stress is only on radical dimensions. Moreover, the banal ways the unjust past remains present are not simply a further component of the endurance of history – one that needs merely to be added to more hideous discriminations. They also constitute a fundamental element in explaining how radical forms of an injustice are maintained over time, especially within societies that have undergone substantial *changes* and are nowadays at least formally committed to equality of opportunity and anti-discrimination legislation.

To see the relation between banal and radical forms of endurance, consider one of the arguably most radical dimensions of the injustice against African Americans: the 'criminalisation of race', which refers to the central role race plays in constructing the presumption of criminality and has been recently denounced by the Black Lives Matter movement. The criminalisation of race has implications even more far-reaching than those informal discriminations in employment decisions mentioned above. For instance, police officers extensively use racial profiling to decide whether to stop and search someone who is walking or driving, or to engage in enforcement, or even whether to shoot armed or unarmed persons who are perceived as undertaking a criminal activity, as in the notorious cases of the shooting of Amadou Diallo in 1999 by four New York City Police Department plain-clothes officers and the Ferguson unrest sparked by the fatal shooting of Michael Brown in August 2014, to name a few. It is not an exaggeration to claim that persons cannot feel at home in a society in which race is criminalised. However, this radical injustice cannot be explained without considering the banal dimensions of the presence of the unjust past. As recent social-psychological studies have shown, racial profiling is closely related to the historical stereotype linking blackness with danger. For example, by simulating a situation with possible hostile targets, several experimental researches demonstrate how participants – police officers (and laypersons) – are more inclined and quicker to shoot when the targets are identified as black.[46] What these studies significantly point out is that these race-based differentials in shooting decisions not only stem from explicit prejudiced opinions and attitudes towards African Americans but also result from largely unconscious expectations, stereotypes and biases that persons commonly hold.

As seen, the association of blackness with danger and criminality is closely connected to the historical injustice of slavery and racial segregation in the US as, for example, it was used to justify unequal criminal legislation. However, since the conditions for upholding the original form of the historical injustice have ceased to exist, that injustice, of which the linking of blackness with criminality was a crucial component, changed its mechanisms by being perpetuated – for instance, (although not exclusively) through unconscious and routinised processes. To wit, an exclusive focus on radicality is misleading as it neglects how changes in circumstances have also profoundly transformed the injustice under consideration. Societies such as contemporary liberal democracies have evolved and have undergone significant changes over time. Under these circumstances, to endure, injustices must adapt and transform the ways they operate – that is, through mechanisms that can work notwithstanding (and through) institutional changes. In this sense, radicality per se overlooks how endurance 'needs' changes. Instead, a more nuanced understanding of endurance, which regards changes as indispensable for persistence over time, reveals what may be called the *banal radicality of the reproduction of the*

---

[46] E.g. Correll et al. (2007a, 2007b). See also Payne (2001).

unjust past.[47] By that, I refer to the subtle and often difficult-to-tackle ways an unjust history can be reproduced in the present (e.g. the unconscious stereotype of African Americans as criminals), which provide the conditions of possibility for radical injustices to occur (e.g. the systematic shooting of unarmed African American men by the police).[48]

In sum, the idea of enduring injustice may be misleading when we aim to grasp how the unjust past remains present; what we need is a more dynamic conception of injustice, which recognises and theorises the relation of interdependence between persistence and change. Such a conception can be put forward by merging the structural understanding of history developed in Chapter 2 (§ 2.3) with a structural approach to injustice. The former points out how historical injustices cannot be regarded only in terms of events (with a clear beginning and end) but should be also (and especially) analysed in terms of long-term structures which endure over time and through generations. The latter not only provides an account of structural processes by defending their importance for considerations about justice but also problematises those more 'normalised' and habitual mechanisms of structural reproduction, such as stereotypes, that are crucial to comprehend how (past) injustices can endure through changes.[49] Rather than being conceived as merely enduring, historical injustices should be regarded as *historical-structural injustices* (hereafter HSI) that are newly reproduced over time. These injustices can be defined as

> unjust social-structural processes enabling asymmetries between differently positioned persons, which started in the past and are reproduced in a different fashion, even if the original form of injustice may appear to have ended.

[47] The expression 'the banal radicality' is inspired by Peg Birmingham's discussion of the compatibility between Hannah Arendt's notions of banal and radical 'evil' (2003). As for 'evil', the fact that an unjust history is reproduced in 'banal' ways does not downplay the radicality of both its normative significance and its seriousness.

[48] To reiterate, my stress on the link between unconscious stereotypes, norms and expectations and institutional racial violence in the US does not deny that deliberative and intentional attacks, which have historically characterised police engagement with African American communities and activism (e.g. during the Birmingham campaign of 1963–64 and the Black Panther Party's era) do not significantly occur anymore. My point is that not only does the criminalisation of race endure through overt police brutality but also it is reproduced through other more routinised and complex ways.

[49] Indeed, the main problem with Spinner-Halev's conception of enduring injustice is that it is not a *structural* account; that is, Spinner-Halev theorises neither historical endurance nor injustice in structural terms. This is why his stress on radicality, which per se would not necessarily exclude banal aspects of injustices and of their endurance, actually turns out to be theoretically and normatively problematic.

These injustices are *historical* injustices that have become part of the *structures* whereby societies (or the international sphere) are organised and regulated. Historical injustices (as long-term structures) are thus reproduced into the present. Let me unpack the relation between persistence and change. On one hand, in the case of HSI, historical and present injustices should be regarded as the *same* injustice. To use Walter Benjamin's allegorical and famous image of the angel of history, one has to look at historical and present injustices as a 'single catastrophe' rather than as a 'chain of events'.[50] On the other hand, the same injustice can be reproduced over time in different ways. These include not only subtler mechanisms, such as, as seen, unreflexively stereotyping, but also different institutional channels. For instance, as Clarissa Rile Hayward persuasively shows, after the abolition of an overt racial legislation and the imposition of sanctions for explicit racial housing discrimination, the reproduction of racialised spaces in the US has occurred through a series of interventions to safeguard 'local autonomy over taxation, public service provision, and land use' which have institutionalised the allegedly colour-blind narrative of Americans as home owning people.[51]

The conceptualisation of historical injustices as HSIs incorporates the interdependency of persistence and change. Historical injustices are conceived in terms of unjust long-term structures that endure over time and through institutional transformations by means of changes in how they operate. Changes over time in the workings of an injustice are necessary for that injustice to be reproduced, especially in contexts where a past has been repudiated as unjust formally and by many societal members.

At this point, a clarification is in order. Stressing the significance of both history and structure may seem somehow superfluous as structures are historical by definition. Indeed, the very concept of structure relies on the reproduction over time of social processes (however we spell them out). Although this is true, the need for maintaining the terminological distinction between history and structure, in the context of historical and structural injustices, is motivated by a twofold reason.

First, such a distinction is significant when we consider *historical injustices*. This is because, in theory, it is possible for someone to recognise that historical injustices were also constituted *in the past* by structural injustices without properly appreciating what it means for such historical injustices themselves to be long-term structures that are reproduced over time. Embracing a structural conception of history instead entails immediately

[50] Benjamin ([1942] 2003, 392).   [51] Hayward (2013, 185).

conceiving of historical injustices themselves as long-term structures. As already pointed out (§ 2.3), this has far-reaching implications for how the presence of the unjust past is conceptualised. A structural conception of history rejects an interpretation of such a presence in terms of its legacy, and it advances the more disturbing idea that the unjust past is present (when and) because it is newly reproduced by structuring the formally and informally institutional set-up of our societies (and international order). As I will argue in Chapter 8, thinking about historical injustices in terms of their new reproduction becomes crucial to (1) conceptualise the historical accountability and obligations of reparation that certain powerful agents have towards (some) injustices of a distant past and (2) investigate whether our very societies and transnational order are organised in such a way that it makes the reproduction of unjust history possible.

Second, it is important not to conflate history and structure when it comes to *structural injustices*. Indeed, as I will contend in Chapter 4 (§ 4.3), there are some injustices displaying a structural character which are, however, not historical in at least a relevant respect as they cannot be conceived as historical injustices that are newly reproduced. To be sure, all structural injustices derive from the reproduction of structural processes over time and thus are historical to a certain extent; nevertheless, to anticipate, not all present injustices that result from the accumulation of social-structural processes and are thus structural are the reproduction of systematically unjust history. Therefore, they cannot be regarded as historical *and* structural in the sense defined above.

3.3   When Historical Justice Is Neither Impractical nor Redundant

Conceiving of historical injustices as historical-structural injustices provides the theoretical resources to reply to the two distinct yet equally powerful objections to which, as seen (§ 2.1), backward-looking and forward-looking approaches to historical injustice are respectively vulnerable. Backward-looking approaches, which contend that the unjust past should be redressed per se, cannot provide a criterion for singling out which kind of historical injustices should be of present concern, thereby turning historical redress into an impracticable venture. Forward-looking approaches, instead, argue that repairing the past is instrumental to tackling a problematic present condition, such as inequality between groups, but they struggle to explain why the past is normatively important and not redundant for those who are committed to substantive equality in the present.

Unlike backward-looking approaches, the account of HSI does not claim that the unjust past grounds obligations of justice in the present per se. Quite the contrary, it claims that we should pay normative attention to the unjust past because *it is present* in terms of unjust long-term structures. From the perspective of HSI, we should focus not on all injustices that occurred in the past but only on those that are reproduced into the present. To be sure, the normative criterion for distinguishing between historical injustices that need to be addressed and those we can neglect (at least as far as justice is concerned), which is introduced by the account of HSI, may ultimately select more past injustices than the ones generally at the centre of the debate over historical injustices. This holds true in particular when we compare HSI with forward-looking approaches because, as seen (§ 2.1), backward-looking outlooks should be overly inclusive in that the whole past seems to call for redress. Precisely by showing how unjust history is reproduced even through normalised structural processes, HSI may bring to the forefront injustices we do not usually regard or theorise as being significantly connected with an unjust past. For instance, I will argue in the following chapters that the group of women, which is not usually included in the cases analysed by mainstream conceptions of historical injustice, is a paradigmatic example of HSI (Chapters 5–7). That said, the fact that the account of HSI is likely to be more encompassing than mainstream (forward-looking) conceptions of historical injustices is not necessarily a weakness. Conversely, HSI highlights the pervasiveness of the reproduction of unjust history and, as I will further explore (§ 8.3), aims to challenge what we have come to accept as natural features of our social world.

One may ask whether the criterion introduced by HSI can address the question of how to identify those historical injustices that are reproduced into the present. This is a legitimate query to which it is possible to provide only an indicative reply.[52] One way to start identifying such historical injustices would be to look for those structural positions in which persons are positioned within societies (and at a transnational level) that are rooted in a past of systematic discrimination and oppression. In the next chapter, I will provide a more fully fledged and nuanced account of the characteristics of those groups that can be said to suffer from HSI and of those historical collectives displaying structural dynamics. For now, it is worth clarifying that, because (unjust) history varies across societies, theoretically,

---

[52] This reply can be only indicative for reasons already given in § 3.1.

there may be a case in which groups of persons suffer from HSI within one society but not in another or in which they can experience different types of HSI depending on the context – as seen in the example of African Americans in France. Thus the particular unjust history of a determinate context plays a fundamental role in selecting those injustices that can be conceived as historical and structural.

Although potentially more encompassing than existing forward-looking approaches, the account of HSI has the advantage of providing a more nuanced explanation of why we cannot overlook an unjust history when we endorse equality in the present. This is not because the unjust past has left a legacy in the present or present inequalities and injustices can be regarded as the effect of historical injustices that happened long ago. The conception of HSI establishes a more nuanced yet more compelling relation between unjust past and present than the one envisaged by simplistic causalistic accounts. An unjust history cannot be neglected when and because it is not 'past' but reproduced into the present and shapes (yet does not determine) the contours of our social reality. It provides the background conditions in which persons interact with and relate to each other. In other words, it constructs (at least a central part of) the *script* in which persons daily act and reproduce with their actions (or inactions).[53]

To conceptualise the presence of the past as a sort of script that informs persons' interactions does not downplay individual agency. Nor does it entail disclaiming the accountability that persons should bear for having undertaken a determinate (unjust) course of action. Thus, in the case of the shootings of unarmed African American men by the police, insisting that the historical-structural processes behind daily racial interactions and relations in the US, and, in particular, the historical association between blackness and criminality, structure that wrong does not suggest that police officers have no choice but to follow a pre-existing script. And it does not imply that such officers should not be held accountable or even liable to be punished for their misdeeds.[54] Instead, the idea of the script highlights those historical-structural conditions without which the systematic shooting of African American men mistaken for criminals would not be possible in the first place. In this respect, HSI thus interprets that situation (or other cases of violence against members of certain groups) not merely as a wrong event committed by an individual perpetrator but also as an injustice

---

[53] I borrow the use of the script metaphor for the structural conditions of persons' interactions from Tilly (1998).

[54] For the compatibility of making individuals accountable for the wrongs that they committed, while also being sensitive to structural processes, see Young (2004, 2011, chapter 4).

which is made possible by the banal radicality of the structural reproduction of unjust history. Without a historical-structural outlook on societies, we can neither understand how certain wrongs are also injustices nor capture the full injury such injustices inflict.

In addition to pointing out how persons still choose to act or not to act under conditions that pre-exist their choices, the agency of individuals within historical-structural processes is crucial in another respect. As seen, (historical) structural processes are reactivated and reproduced precisely through persons' action (or inaction) – that is, through persons' reliance on them. Therefore, persons' individual actions and inactions do contribute to injustice. This is not to say structural injustices (historical or not) are the direct result of individuals' actions and that it is thus possible to establish to what extent one's actions contribute to the sustainment and reproduction of unjust structural processes.[55] However, the recognition of the interplay between individuals' actions (and their accumulation) and unjust structures is a distinctive component of a structural approach to injustice. The implication that should be drawn from such an interplay is not that all those individuals' actions that somehow help support and recreate unjust structural injustices should be monitored and penalised. What follows from the interrelation between individuals' deeds and structures is that we need to consider *the structural conditions of individuals' interactions*, including more informal and unreflective mechanisms such as stereotypes, as *sites* or subjects of justice – that is, features of societies that need to be regulated (and transformed) from the perspective of justice.[56]

Therefore, turning back to the redundancy objection, those who are committed to equality in the present cannot light-heartedly dismiss the normative significance of historical injustices. The unjust past (or, better, that remaining structurally present) cannot be superseded by present-based considerations of justice, because its presence (or, better, its new reproduction) deeply undermines the workings of contemporary institutions.[57] If we aim to overcome contemporary grave injustices (e.g. the police's abuse of force in their engagement with African American men), we must tackle the present-past (e.g. by dissolving the stereotypical association of

---

[55] Young (2011, 96). I will come back to issues of (individual and collective) agents' responsibility within unjust structures in § 9.2.

[56] On the debate over the site of justice, see Cohen (2000); Rawls (1999, 3; 2005, 282–83); Young (2011, 64–74).

[57] Moreover, as we will see, the unjust past may even more radically challenge the very normative desirability of our institutional set-up (§ 8.3).

blackness with criminality) because, as seen, such an unjust past creates the structural conditions that make systematic radical injustices possible.

Additionally, (certain) historical injustices structure society in *all* its daily dimensions, from street encounters to employment decisions. Even when principles of equality and non-discrimination are endorsed, implicit structural mechanisms are activated that jeopardise the realisation of such principles in a way that is prima facie compatible with a commitment to egalitarian values, such as by ad hoc reconstructing criteria of merit. Therefore, although a society may appear just from a present-based perspective of justice, it may turn out to be unjust when a historical-structural outlook is endorsed. If we really want to achieve egalitarian justice in the present, the unjust structural history should be faced. In sum, the unjust past is not thus a mere legacy that can be tackled by enforcing formal egalitarian legislation that is already in place, because it is that unjust history that produces the very background structural conditions in which formal egalitarian institutions operate.

It is worth stressing how difficult it is for persons to be 'going off scripts'[58] – that is, not to rely on, trigger and thus reproduce unjust historical-structural processes. As already contended, well-intended egalitarians are not spared from acting upon such processes, and even those who are aware of their existence and effects struggle not to reactivate them because such processes pre-structure any interaction.[59] Nor can we simply hope that, with the passing of time, historical-structural processes will progressively be weakened and that, for example, the stereotypical association of blackness with dangerousness in the US will become less frequent through encounters with non-aggressive African American men. Indeed, historical stereotypes (and stereotypes in general) are particularly resistant to the evidence from individuals of the stereotyped group that do not fit the negative stereotype.[60] This provides a further reason not to dismiss the structural reproduction of an unjust history and its banal radicality and to instead seriously devise remedies and strategies to unravel and directly tackle it.[61]

---

[58] Benson (2014).   [59] Benson (2014).

[60] This explains why methods of resistance employed by individuals to escape stereotyping are unsuccessful at eradicating such stereotypes. For example, an African American man's attempt to present himself as well educated and thus potentially less menacing by, say, whistling Vivaldi when walking past white couples (Steele 2010, 6–7) may ease those couples' anxiety towards *him*, but it is unlikely to deactivate that stereotype in the future interactions such persons will have with *other* African American men. This is because those who do not conform to stereotypes are (even unconsciously) perceived as the exception rather than the rule.

[61] I will discuss some possible courses of actions for gender injustices and inequalities in Chapter 7.

By explaining when historical injustices matter and why this is the case, the account of HSI de-temporalises injustice and brings to light the full injury of certain historical (and present) injustices, which precisely consists in *the ongoing reproduction over time of the same injustice* – an injustice whose injury cannot be captured if we regard the past per se as in need of repair or if we conceptualise the past as simply having some effects on the present (however significant such effects may be claimed to be). At this point, one may object that de-temporalising injustice means denying the very existence of 'historical' injustices. Now, de-temporalising injustice does not imply that there are not past injustices that are actually past.[62] It simply suggests that there are *some* historical injustices that are erroneously regarded as past but that are instead reproduced into the fabric of our societies (and international order), both at a macro- and a micro-level. To wit, when it comes to an injustice of this sort (i.e. an HSI), thinking in terms of 'past' and 'present' is theoretically and normatively problematic; we should conceive of it as an unjust history that keeps being newly reproduced.

In the next chapters, I will try to deepen our understanding of HSI by providing an account of those groups that suffer from the reproduction of the unjust past and then by concentrating on one particular case: that of women.

---

[62] Does this mean that repairing or apologising for injustices that are really 'past' is actually wrong? It is important to distinguish between (1) cases in which the original victims or perpetrators are still alive and (2) cases in which they are dead. Cases falling into (1) are actually uncontroversial, as few would argue that if someone who is still alive was wronged in the past by living perpetrators, the former should receive no reparation from the latter; in such cases, indeed, we usually hold the perpetrators not only morally but also legally responsible for the wrong and its repair. As for (2), should, for instance, in 1997, Tony Blair, in his capacity as UK prime minister, not have issued an apology for the Irish potato famine, which occurred between 1845 and 1852 and had such a disastrous impact on Ireland (assuming that that injustice – i.e. as long-term structures – had not been reproduced up to then)? My account neither criticises nor discourages similar actions. Sometimes, say, apologising for an injustice, even if it is actually past, may be a way (although not necessarily the only one) to improve relations between countries. Often, publicly talking or teaching about past injustices that do not persist (e.g. discrimination against Italian and Irish migrants in the US) has important educational purposes. My point is simply that, only when it comes to HSI, addressing them is an obligation of justice and that fulfilling that obligation should have priority over, say, any apology or reparation for injustices that are really 'past' *and* fall into (2).

CHAPTER 4

History, Injustice and Groups

One distinctive characteristic of a structural approach to (in)justice is to immediately focus on groups or, more precisely, on the positions created by social (and transnational) structures and on the relations in which persons stand in virtue of their structural position. As seen, structural injustice cannot be understood without considering how persons are positioned within structures (§ 3.1). Likewise, historical-structural injustice (HSI) can be fully theorised only when groups or positions are considered. This is because HSI affects individuals only insofar as they are members of certain historically based groups. HSI is thus *a group-affecting* type of injustice. That said, what groups can be claimed to suffer from HSI? And do all groups for which unjust history keeps being structurally reproduced display similar features?

This chapter aims to provide a classification of structural groups based on the role history plays in their formation and reproduction. It shows that it is possible to conceive of structural groups as parts of a *spectrum* and that analysing the commonalities such groups have, while maintaining their differences, is normatively fundamental to (1) grasp the kind of injustice they suffer from and (2) think about how to overcome it. Specifically, I argue that, in addition to offering an alternative conception of historical injustice, the account of HSI also enriches existing understandings of structural injustice by pointing out the theoretical and normative importance of recognising that only certain structural injustices are connected to unjust history when we reflect on the nature of such injustices and their remedies.

4.1 Classifying Groups

To provide a classification of groups which can serve as a tool to identify collectives that suffer from a historical injustice that is newly reproduced in the present, we need to focus on how (and to what extent) groups, in light

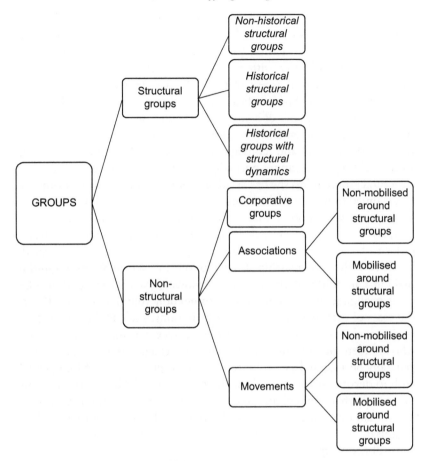

Figure 4.1 Taxonomy of structural and non-structural groups.

of their inner characteristics and mechanisms of membership, can be seen as affected by injustices that are structurally connected with an unjust history.

A useful start in drawing a taxonomy of groups in the context of historical and structural injustices is distinguishing between 'structural' and 'non-structural' groups (for a comprehensive summary, see Figure 4.1). One main difference between these two types of collectives lies in how membership is determined: while membership in structural groups (e.g. women, gay men, Italians) is non-voluntary as persons are included in such groups independently of their wills, members of non-structural groups (e.g. corporations, associations, social movements) have consented to their membership.[1] This stress on *voluntariness* calls for a clarification. To say that participation in structural groups is non-voluntary does not mean that persons do not identify with such a membership or that they do not consider it as a central aspect of their identity. However, as we will see below and in § 4.4, self-identification is neither necessary nor sufficient to be considered a member of a structural group (especially of those groups that are both historical and structural). What matters is to be externally recognised as such and consequently positioned within that group. Conversely, a person cannot normally be considered as a member of a non-structural group unless she has decided to enter that collective; I cannot be, say, claimed to belong to the World Wildlife Fund unless I have somehow joined the association. I may be externally regarded as someone who sympathises with the animal-rights activism of the association, but in order to be its member and subsequently reap the rewards and bear the burdens of that membership, I have to join the World Wildlife Fund by making a monthly donation to it. Obviously, external recognition plays a not-negligible role even for (at least some) non-voluntary groups. Besides the cases of exclusive clubs, some organisations, such as the ones helping victims and survivors of domestic violence, accept as volunteers only those who are identified as women. Thus, if I am recognised as a man, I cannot generally be accepted as a volunteer (or an employee) even if I desperately wish to devote my time to help such organisations.[2] The important point, however, is that although in this case voluntariness is not enough – because no woman can evidently be considered a member of a domestic violence organisation unless she has successfully applied for one of their positions – it is still necessary.

Structural groups are formed by the different formal and informal structures present within a determinate society and at a transnational level.[3] Structures of nationality, sexuality and class are only a few of the various ways in which our world is organised and that create some of the non-voluntary social groups generally existing within societies. Structural groups display many peculiar characteristics. First, they are *relational* in that, as Young argues, structural groups exist only through the continuous interaction between those who are positioned within such groups and those who are not; thus, they would not emerge and endure if persons

---

[1] Cudd (2006, 34–40).

[2] For example, in the UK, some women's organisations, such as Solace Women's Aid and Women and Girl Network, selectively hire only women following the Equality Act 2010 Schedule 9, Part 1.

[3] For a general account of structures, see § 3.1.

did not relate to each other.[4] In other words, rather than material entities, structural groups are better regarded as 'individuals *in* relations'.[5] Structural groups are relational in at least two respects. They are relational to the various and interconnected structures whereby societies are organised. Societies formally and informally distribute privileges, burdens, power and different statuses to their members according to precise categorisations.[6] To function properly and effectively, the different structures constituting societies (e.g. those regulating labour and the reproduction of the society itself) position persons into categories and assign each category particular roles and expectations. Consider, for example, how societies usually rely on gender categorisation in order to cover the majority of unpaid care work. Because of the cost and the fundamental importance of this work, which includes taking care of the elderly, the ill and children, societies would have to shoulder a particularly heavy burden if they could not count on the expectation that some persons, in virtue of their gender categorisation, would perform it.[7] Likewise, the division between menial and professional occupations on the basis of which many contemporary societies are regulated would be less easily maintained without relying on, for example, racial and ethnical categorisations. In turn, this reliance strengthens such categories by reinforcing the belief that they correspond to something natural and unchallengeable.

Furthermore, many structural groups are relational to other groups which are positioned in a comparatively better-off position.[8] This is because structural processes distribute disadvantages and burdens while allocating advantages and privileges. That is, structures tend to constitute a group with a disadvantaged structural position and at least one structural group that is in a position of advantage within such structures vis-à-vis the related underprivileged group. This dimension of the relational character of many structural groups crucially entails that often we cannot understand a particular structural position without simultaneously considering its mutually constituted structural counterpart(s). To exemplify, an analysis of those structural processes creating and reproducing the position of African Americans in the US would be significantly incomplete if it did not take into account how such a position is intrinsically related to that of white Americans – as seen in the previous chapter when examining stereotypes and employment decisions (§ 3.2).

---

[4] Young (2000, 89).   [5] May (1987, 5).
[6] Brubaker (2002, 184); Young (2000, 94). For a seminal work on categories, inequality and societal organisation, see Tilly (1998).
[7] I will return to the gendered division of unpaid labour in § 6.3.   [8] Young (1990, 42).

The second feature of structural groups is that membership is largely 'ascriptive',[9] not only because it is non-voluntary but also in that it is externally granted. It is by being positioned within certain structures that someone becomes a member of a structural group. Often that external positioning occurs when someone is recognised by society at large as displaying certain characteristics associated with a determinate structural group. It is important to examine in detail the mechanisms whereby membership in structural groups is given because they are more complex than they may initially seem. To do so, let me describe the scene of a movie directed by Spike Lee – *Bamboozled* (2000) – which masterfully and tragically represents how membership in structural groups is granted. In this scene, the police burst into the refuge of an underground militant rap group (the Mau Maus) that have committed criminal actions in defence of the 'black community' in the US. The collision with the police is fatal for all Mau Mau members, with the exception of one member (MC Serch), who is recognised as white and simply arrested. It does not matter that MC Serch, whose nom de guerre is emblematically One-Sixteenth Black, desperately declares that, by having one sub-Saharan African ancestor, he is African American – at least according to the infamous racist (no longer valid) 'one-drop rule' – and thus he has to die with the rest of his group. Following different categorisation rules, the police categorise him as non–African American by according to him the privilege (or, for MC Serch, the curse) of survival.

This scene is particularly instructive because it helps us introduce a necessary and sufficient condition for being granted membership in a structural group, which can be called *the authority condition*.[10] In short, to become a member of a structural group, one has to be recognised as such by someone who has the (e.g. social, legal, cultural) authority to do so in a determinate context. MC Serch's self-understanding as an African American is not authoritative in that situation; the fact that he conceives of himself as black is insufficient for him to be recognised as such by the police. Nor is it enough that other persons who are categorised as African

---

[9] On the idea of ascriptive groups, see Williams (1998, 16).

[10] Here, I draw inspiration from John L. Austin's theory of speech acts. For Austin, a speech act – i.e. an utterance that has a performative function (e.g. an apology) – is successful ('felicitous') only when some conditions are met. Particularly, it has to be pronounced by someone who has the authority to do so. For example, in the context of a Catholic wedding, the speech 'I declare you husband and wife' must be uttered by a priest to be effectively performed. If I stand up from the pew, approach the bride and groom to be and say that sentence, I have not married anyone, and thus in Austinian terms, the speech 'misfires' simply because I lack the authority to perform it (Austin [1962] 1975, lecture II).

Americans by the police considered MC Serch as an African American or that MC Serch himself has been an active member of an association whose goals focus on the protection of the African American community and he is willing to resort to violent means to achieve these purposes. In that context, the only agent that has the authority to recognise MC Serch as being positioned as an African American and thus grant him membership in that structural group is the police. And the police, as mentioned, perceive MC Serch as being differently positioned within societal structures from the other Mau Maus members. What is worth pointing out is that, while the authority condition is historical and contextual in that those who have the authority to position someone as a member of a structural group may change in different situations and over time, self-identification is never sufficient for such a condition to be met. In other words, I cannot ever have the exclusive authority to position myself into a structural group. As for MC Serch, when he wants to become a member of the Mau Maus, he needs already existing members to recognise him as an African American, whereas in the context of the police's bursting in, it is only the police's recognition that can satisfy the authority condition.

The scene from Lee's movie brings to light an important distinction, namely that between 'personal identity', which refers to how someone constructs her own sense of herself, and 'external categorisation', which is instead about others' perception of someone (societal institutions included).[11] I will address this distinction in the following sections (especially § 4.4) and chapter as it is fundamental in the general account of structural groups and in the specific conception of one such group, namely women, that I will put forward. However, here a clarification is in order. Obviously, there are significant overlaps between one's personal identity and external categorisation to such an extent that it is possible that the two completely match – as in the case of someone who thinks of herself as mainly an African American and is identified as such by society at large. Moreover, how one sees herself is often influenced by how others perceive her and vice versa. However, personal identity and external categorisation should remain analytically distinguished. This is because, as seen, although one person can take any particular aspect of her life as a characteristic of her personal identity,[12] it is not necessarily the case that she would be externally categorised according to that aspect. Indeed, as in the tragic example of MC Serch, the gap between one's personal identity and external categorisation can be so wide that the latter corresponds exactly to what one would never self-identify with. How

---

[11]   For a similar distinction, see, e.g., Appiah (1994, 152).   [12]   Copp (2002, 370).

persons are externally categorised becomes of paramount normative importance when theorising about structural injustices because of the very ways in
which such injustices are reproduced – for example, through daily interactions. For instance, it is when they are recognised as African American men
that such persons are perceived as potential criminals or as less suitable
candidates for certain jobs (§ 3.2). In this sense, for members of structural
groups, 'nomination is domination'.[13]

Before continuing to examine structural groups, let me provide a brief
description of non-structural groups because they will not be further
considered in this chapter (or in the rest of the book). Although wrongs
can be committed against these collectives, their non-structural nature
means they cannot suffer from an injustice that results from how persons
are positioned within societal and transnational structures and a fortiori
from HSI. Non-structural groups are collectives in which persons voluntarily decide to become members, usually share common goals, and consciously consider themselves as part of a unity. Because of this shared
identity and unity of intentions among members, a non-structural group
is usually considered as a 'collective agent' – that is, a 'we' that can perform
'joint-actions' and possess 'a moral [and legal] status different from that of
the discrete individual persons who compose [it]'.[14]

Non-structural groups can be classified according to their degree of
internal organisation. While, for example, corporative agents such as corporations and political parties have quite hierarchical and complex levels of
internal organisation, associations and especially social movements display
a less hierarchical internal layout. It is worth pointing out that although
structural groups do not display the conscious unity of agency, commitments and intents necessary to collectively advance claims and demands,
many non-structural groups mobilise precisely around the unjust condition
of structural groups and act to improve their condition. This is the case with
non-structural groups such as the anti-sweatshop movement, London
Friend and the Aboriginal Support Group, which strive to address the unjust
position that, respectively, sweatshop workers, LGBTQ+ persons and
Aboriginal Australians occupy within transnational and societal structures.
That said, members of these kinds of non-structural groups can be persons
who are *not* recognised as members of the structural groups for which they
advocate. In other words, membership in a structural group (e.g. gay men)

---

[13] Frye (1996b, 38).
[14] May (1987, 3). For a seminal account of non-structural groups, see Gilbert (1989, 222–23). Note that,
for Margaret Gilbert, only non-structural groups should be considered as proper groups.

and membership in a non-structural group that fight for overcoming the injustice that such a structural collective suffers from (e.g. London Friend) do not necessarily tally because the former is not necessarily a condition for the latter. Conversely, as I will suggest in Chapter 9 (§ 9.2), it may be argued that the collective mobilisation of persons who are not positioned in a structural group suffering injustice (e.g. straight and cisgender persons supporting and standing up for LGBTQ+ rights) as allies in the struggles fought by collectives organising around structural groups (e.g., London Friend) is important not least because such persons have a specific responsibility to address that (structural) injustice.

It is clear that these kinds of non-structural groups play a fundamental role in revealing, speaking out against and trying to tackle structural injustices. However, especially in the context of structural injustices that are also historical, it is also important to bear in mind that these collectives are not ahistorical. Indeed, they are embedded in those historical and structural processes in which they act. On one hand, this fact gives them a privileged knowledge of how societies have developed – a fact that, as we will see in Chapters 7 and 8, is vital to address HSI. On the other hand, this means they are likely to have inherited at least some of the biases and prejudices of the history they are part of. Such non-structural collectives may still remain caught in the dynamics and discourses they intend to challenge, and they may overlook how the structural groups they aim to support are internally heterogeneous. For example, associations for the rights of LGBTQ+ persons may ignore the specific issues of (or even discriminate against) those who are positioned as LGBTQ+ and are also recognised as members of a racial minority.[15] In this way, they not only neglect that structures of sexualities have been historically developed in tandem with racial structures but also they are bound to contribute to reproducing the HSI against such minorities.[16]

After these brief remarks about non-structural collectives, we can now turn back to structural groups and distinguish three categories on the basis of the role that history plays in the formation and reproduction of these groups: (1) historical-structural groups; (2) non-historical structural groups; and (3) historical groups with structural dynamics. As I will argue in § 4.5, these three categories should not be normally considered

---

[15] For instance, American LGBTQ+ organisations have been accused of anti-Latino racism; various demonstrations – e.g. the 21 April 2006 protest in San Francisco – have been held to denounce this discrimination. For an empirical study of racist exclusion experienced by Latinos within American LGBTQ+ communities, see Ibañez et al. (2009).

[16] We will turn back to the problem of the intersection of structures in Chapter 5.

as separate or completely different entities but instead as components of a spectrum. However, it remains important to analytically distinguish them to identify which kinds of (structural) groups suffer from HSI. In this sense, (1)–(3) represent ideal-types that can deepen our theoretical and normative understanding of HSI and, in general, of the multiple forms of structural injustices that can be present within societies and transnationally. With this caveat, let me start offering an account of historical-structural groups.

4.2 Historical-Structural Groups

Historical-structural groups (HSGs) can be defined as

> structural groups characterised by (1) a *systematically* unjust history of formal discrimination and exclusion that, although (2) decried by societies and now recognised as having been unjust, (3) is reproduced through other means.

The most distinctive characteristic of HSGs is the way their unjust history and present condition are connected in a relation of both persistence and change. HSGs have suffered from grave systematic forms of injustices in the past which were legally sanctioned and enforced. Slavery and discrimination laws, reclusion in mental hospitals or eugenic programmes, imprisonment for behaviours against nature, and formal denial of rights and entitlements have been just a few of the injustices that have been lawfully authorised against groups along, for example, race, ability, sexuality, ethnicity and gender lines. Today, at least within so-called liberal and democratic societies, such violations are rightly outlawed and considered as dark chapters of a past that should not be repeated. However, for HSGs this history is still structurally reproduced in that, as seen in Chapter 3, it not only endures through mechanisms that cannot be deactivated by the endorsement of anti-discrimination laws and a formal commitment to the value of equality of opportunity but also still structures societies (and the international order).

Therefore, to identify HSGs, the interconnection between history and structure should be unravelled. Three types of systematic past injustices, now rejected by liberal and democratic societies, can be hinted at as providing an indicative (and yet not exhaustive) list of the kinds of systematic wrongs that potentially have brought HSGs into existence. First, these groups may have been denied the right to vote and to participate in the body politic. As Judith Shklar argues regarding American citizenship, exclusion from political life has a powerful symbolic dimension: it does not simply entail preventing some persons from indicating their political preferences and advancing their claims, but, most importantly, this exclusion has also an *expressive* function in that it gives the status of second-class citizenship to those who are subjected to it. A group's disenfranchisement and 'exclusion from public life is a denial of [the] civic personality and social dignity'[17] of those recognised as members of that group.

Second, systematic legal exclusion from paid work or relegation to menial occupations is bound to have constructed HSGs. This is because of the social and public status attached to those who earn their own living through 'meaningful work'. Statutory denial of access to the labour force or assignment to servile or unskilled occupations confers to those who are affected by it an inferior public standing as being dependent or subordinate.[18]

Third, certain categories of persons have been systematically regarded as abnormal, morally deviant or physically and mentally repugnant.[19] In particular, HSGs may have been produced by the discourses of abnormality promulgated by 'scientific', philosophical and religious authorities and ratified by the state through legal measures (e.g. blacklisting, forced registration as sexual offenders, detention, sterilisation, forced hospitalisation, torture and even murder) precisely for the role such authorities played in regulating societies and defining what 'normality' was.[20] Obviously, this type of wrong was often committed against categories of persons who were disenfranchised or excluded from meaningful work and it precisely provided the rationale for their marginalisation. Nevertheless, it is important to consider this wrong as a distinct type of past injustice because there may have been categories of persons who were not always denied the right to vote or access to meaningful work (e.g. the case of gay and lesbian persons in certain countries such as the US) but were still systematically considered

---

[17] Shklar (1991, 39).
[18] Shklar (1991, chapter 2). Shklar's analysis about meaningful work, which is meant to capture the significance the institution of slavery has played in shaping US citizenship, can be generalised (at least in liberal democracies). This is not to deny that meaningful work (and thus exclusion from it) may have been particularly salient in the US because of its very history and particularly as a way to differentiate (and emancipate) the newly born country from the aristocratic European former coloniser (i.e. Great Britain). Nevertheless, even within societies with a strong aristocratic tradition, *forced* denial of work or legal relegation to menial occupations has been a sign of inferiority. On the general expressive significance of meaningful earning, see Phillips (1999, 67).
[19] For a seminal study on the historical and social construction of abnormality, see Foucault (2003a).
[20] On the case of gay and lesbian persons in the US, see Bronski (2011); Mogul, Ritchie and Whitlock (2011).

as abnormal according to religious, moral and scientific criteria,[21] and for these reasons were subjected to lawful punishment or degrading treatment.

Contemporary members of HSGs stand in a peculiar relationship with (dead) members of those groups that suffered from these kinds of past injustices. They can be defined as their *structural descendants* in that they have inherited their structural position – a social, transnational and international position constituted by injustices over history that are reproduced through different means. This changes the way 'descendants' should be normatively understood in the context of historical injustice in at least two interconnected respects: *who* descendants are and *what* they inherited.

As for the first respect, they should not be conceptualised in terms of family lines but from a structural perspective. Structural descendants are significantly connected to (dead) victims of past injustices. Had they been alive back *then*, they would have suffered from the original form of the injustice (which is now newly reproduced) because of their structural membership; they would have occupied the same position as their (structural) ancestors. Descendants may not share any biological tie with the original victims of past injustices that are now reproduced structurally; therefore, they may owe their *individual* existence neither to such ancestors nor to the past injustice under consideration. To put it in terms of the 'non-identity problem', had the injustice not been committed, *an unjust historical-structural position* connected with that injustice – in contrast with single individuals that presently occupy that position – would probably not exist today. Importantly, even if structural descendants happen to be biologically related to dead victims of the past form of injustice (or, more generally, it can be counterfactually proved that a determinate individual occupying that position would have not been born if that injustice had not been committed), this would not constitute a problem. What matters is that an unjust structural position would have still been nevertheless created and eventually occupied by someone else – that is, another (structural) descendant.[22] As we will see, this conceptualisation of the identity of descendants will be crucial in countering some

---

[21] For instance, Richard Freiherr von Krafft-Ebing's foundational and highly influential work *Psychopathia Sexualis* classifies homosexuality as a deviant pathology similar to paedophilia – i.e. paraesthesia ([1886] 2011, 230–40). It is only since 1 January 1993 that the World Health Organisation has removed homosexuality from its list of diseases.

[22] The notion of 'structural descendants', generally, challenges the way we should think about lineage, and particularly the narrow conceptions of identity and harm that the 'non-identity problem' relies on, thereby scaling down its force. I further explore the relation between 'structural descent' and the 'non-identity problem' in Nuti (n.d.).

objections against affirmative action and reparations for injustices of a distant past (§ 7.3 and § 8.1).

Second and relatedly, once descendants are considered in structural terms, it becomes clear that, unlike what is sometimes assumed in the debate over historical injustice,[23] the primary inheritance from victims of past injustices (that remain structurally present) is not misappropriated land, property or other divisible goods but a categorisation grounded on and bounded up with past systematic injustices. For such descendants, looking at the past does not mean determining the assets to which they are entitled, but it is indispensable to understand (1) their present condition (i.e. a condition in which history is structurally reproduced); (2) the full injury of that condition; (3) how to redress it; and (4), as I will argue in Chapter 8 (§ 8.1), the specific claims for reparations they rightly have against certain agents.

In this sense, HSGs are paradigmatic cases of HSI because somehow their very existence is intrinsically linked to the HSI they suffer from. Some theorists of oppression argue that oppression as an injustice can be committed only against a group 'who exists apart from the oppressive harm'[24] that it is subjected to. However, in the case of oppression that can be described as historical and structural, the existence of those oppressed groups cannot be easily separated from the injustice, because it is precisely through that injustice that such groups were created and are reproduced over time. Therefore, as we will see (§ 4.4), while other structural groups also suffer from historical and structural dynamics, HSGs are peculiar in that overcoming their HSI *may* result in such groups' disappearing within societies and transnationally, at least as categories whereby societies and the international order are structurally organised and regulated.

A clarification is in order. My discussion of HSGs focuses on groups that suffer from a historical injustice that is newly reproduced into the present. However, this does not mean there are no groups that are historical and structural while being *privileged* vis-à-vis the injustice in question. Indeed, as seen in Chapter 3 and § 4.1, structural injustices (historical or not) create and reproduce relations of asymmetrical power between different positioned persons. Precisely because privilege is rarely recognised (especially by those who hold it) as the result of an injustice, let alone a historical injustice that keeps being newly reproduced, the historical and structural

---

[23] This is particularly the case of accounts that take a Lockean framework of justice in holdings as their starting point to support their case in favour of or against historical justice (e.g. Boxill 2003; Butt 2009; Nozick 1974, chapter 7; Waldron 1992).

[24] Cudd (2006, 25).

character of groups that are privileged vis-à-vis a HSI needs to be unveiled. Indeed, all the types of policies tackling the HSI suffered by women that I will prescribe in Chapter 7 involve revealing the unjust historical-structural nature of the group 'men', of their relations to 'women' and of male privileges to men and societies at large. As I will point out in Chapter 9 (§ 9.2), members of privileged structural groups have specific responsibilities.

To further conceptualise the significance that (unjust) history has to HSGs, let me turn to another kind of structural group, namely non-historical structural groups. By analysing the difference between HSGs and non-historical structural groups, it will be possible to gain a more sophisticated understanding of structural injustice than the one advanced by already existing accounts, which tend not to (theoretically and norma-tively) appreciate the different forms structural injustices can take.

4.3   Non-historical Structural Groups

Non-historical structural groups (NHSGs) can be defined as

> structural groups formed by the accumulation of many lawful actions, decisions and rules which are not unjust when considered singularly but whose outcome creates an unjust condition. However, NHSGs do not have a systematically unjust history of *formal* exclusion and discrimination.

In defining NHSGs, I rely on Young's most recent formulation of struc-tural groups, which she describes through the case of the imaginary (yet sadly realistic) example of a single mother, Sandy, who is about to become homeless.[25] However, to show how NHSGs do indeed characterise liberal and democratic societies, I will focus on another case, namely that of veterans, which has lately received, especially in the US, public attention. After active military service, for veterans readjustment to civilian life is particularly difficult; besides likely physical disabilities, many experience serious psychological problems, such as depression and post-traumatic stress disorder.[26] Moreover, to escape from their harsh reality, many veterans become drug and alcohol addicts. A great number are homeless, unemployed and live in poverty.[27] As a result of these harsh conditions, the suicide rate among veterans in the US is 300 per cent of the national average.[28]

---

[25] Young (2011, 43–52).   [26] E.g. Brenner et al. (2011).
[27] For some data in the US, see USICH (2010); US Census Bureau (2016).
[28] Kemp and Bossarte (2012).

The group of veterans seems to be created by the combination of lawful actions and decisions whose consequences are largely unintended. For example, the termination of military conflicts, which increases the number of veterans, is clearly not arranged for the purpose of harming former soldiers. The surrounding peaceful setting to which veterans return is profoundly different from warfare, and it obviously cannot be converted to that. Many legal measures and institutional rules (e.g. the exhausting, long bureaucratic procedures to apply for postservice benefits, and governmental cuts in the provision of welfare services) play a role in putting veterans in a precarious position.[29] Moreover, the general shortage of health resources and also attitudes such as the understandable preference of many civilians not to be daily informed about the brutal reality of war contribute to isolating veterans.

As for the homeless, the group of veterans (as a vulnerable position within societies), too, largely stems not from individual misdeeds or large systematic violations but from decisions and structural processes that, although not unjust per se, lead to an unjust condition when they accumulate over time. As Young points out, this is not to deny that some individuals (e.g. a landlord deciding to evict a needy veteran) may have committed wrong actions against veterans that contribute to their vulnerable condition (e.g. a veteran having to sleep rough on the streets). The focus is simply on how a *group* such as veterans is not mainly caused by individual failure but is instead the outcome of structural mechanisms.[30] Emphasising the structural nature of the conditions of such groups is crucial to showing that they are unjust. To wit, such conditions are *structural* because they are the product of the aggregation of structural processes which are *unjust* in the sense used by Shklar – that is, because 'when nothing is done to end [the existence of a vulnerable position within society] when it begins [to be produced], there is an injustice'.[31] To the extent that the vulnerable conditions of veterans (and the homeless) are avoidable outcomes of societal processes, they should not be regarded as misfortunes but as injustices that must be addressed.

That said, groups such as veterans (and the homeless in Young's reconstruction) cannot be treated as HSGs.[32] There is a significant difference between the former and the latter that is neglected by many structural theorists such as Young: the role that *history* plays in forming (and

---

[29] Batkins (2013); Judd and Foot (2013).   [30] Young (2011, 62–65).   [31] Shklar (1990, 70).

[32] I specify that the homeless are not an HSG in Young's formulation because it may well be that, in certain contexts, the dynamics forming and reproducing the homeless are different from those identified by Young and thus more similar to HSGs.

reproducing) these two types of structural groups. While for groups such as the homeless and veterans the past is not per se systematically unjust, for HSGs the past is fraught with injustices. To clarify, I am not arguing that Young does not concede that the past is significant for structural injustices. Indeed, as a structural theorist, she recognises that looking at past decisions and actions is important to understand how certain conditions are structural;[33] for example, without considering decisions about housing rules and urban topography, one may think that the condition of the homeless is simply an individual failure, rather than the outcome of the aggregation of structural processes. However, Young does not acknowledge that structural groups such as the homeless and veterans suffer from a kind of structural injustice that is different from that characterising the condition of HSGs – one in which the past is not unjust.[34] To be sure, groups such as the homeless and veterans are not ahistorical; indeed, as structural groups, they are created and maintained by structures that are reproduced over time. However, in the case of HSGs, such structural processes are intrinsically bound up with a history of systematic injustices and these groups were created by and were the target of regular exclusion and discrimination over history. In other words, there are (at least) *two different kinds of structural injustices*: one that stems from an unjust history (injustices against HSGs) and one that does not (injustices against NHSGs). While the latter is created by the accumulation of structural processes over time, the former, as seen in the previous chapter, should be conceptualised in terms of historical injustices that keep being newly reproduced into the present as long-term structures (§ 3.2).

Highlighting the different types of past that are at the roots of the two kinds of structural groups and thus avoiding conflating HSI with structural injustices such as those of veterans and the homeless is crucial in at least two respects. First, from a *diagnostic* perspective, it is by examining *histories* of systematic injustices that we can identify which groups may today suffer from HSI and can be seen as the 'structural descendants' of those categories

---

[33] Young (2011, 182–83).

[34] More precisely, Young has progressively downplayed the significance of unjust history for a structural conception of injustice. While in her first works (and especially in *Justice and the Politics of Difference*), the unjust past was an important element of her analysis of the oppression of groups along, e.g. gender, race and sexuality lines (Young 1990, 122–55), the emphasis on history has become less considerable in her subsequent works, to the extent that in her *Responsibility for Justice* (2011), Young's focus is only on the accumulation of structures over time. Exegetically, this may be traced back to her attempt to formulate a conception of responsibility that is not backward looking and centred on blame (Young 2011, 108–9). However, what matters here is that Young fails to distinguish between different types of structural groups and of structural injustices.

of persons that were systematically subjected to injustices in the past. Conversely, to establish whether a collective suffers from a type of structural injustice similar to that of the homeless and veterans, what is needed is simply '*a plausible structural story*'[35] explaining how the conditions of such a collective result from the repetition, accumulation and combination over time of a chain of social processes which place members of that collective in a vulnerable position. Diagnostically, unlike what happens for NHSGs, the unjust systematic history also plays a pivotal role in understanding those mechanisms that reproduce the unjust condition of HSGs. The conditions of both HSGs and NHSGs are today maintained by informal and lawful means, rather than by formal discrimination and exclusion; however, as showed through the example of stereotypes, in the case of HSGs the unjust history provides much of the content of these means (§ 3.1). In other words, without considering that unjust history, we could neither identify HSGs nor fully grasp the ways their injustice is structurally reproduced in the present and the full injury of that injustice.

Second, recognising the difference in terms of history between HSGs and NHSGs goes beyond having merely a diagnostic value. Since the importance of a correct diagnosis lies also in the opportunity to provide appropriate and effective remedies, the distinct role the unjust past has in the formation of the two kinds of structural groups should also inform the actions taken to address their different types of structural injustices. For NHSGs, the point is to find solutions able to tackle those processes leading to a structural injustice that 'has existed recently, is ongoing'[36] and is likely to persist without any action. Regarding HSGs instead, the structural link between history and the present is what should be tackled to overcome the injustice. Because the unjust history informs the ways the injustice against HSGs is reproduced, it cannot be seen only as a diagnostic device, but should also be carefully considered when thinking about possible remedies. Indeed, as I will argue in Chapters 7 and 8, remedies to injustices that are both historical and structural should (1) be sensitive to the unjust history, (2) reveal its new structural reproduction and (3) avoid contributing to its reproduction when trying to overcome these injustices.[37]

HSGs, however, are not the only kind of group that displays structural features and is historical in a relevant sense, even though the affinities

---

[35] Young (2001, 16).   [36] Young (2011, 109).

[37] Moreover, in the case of groups that are both historical and structural, there are agents that should be historically accountable for their role in a history of injustice that has been reproduced over time (see § 8.1).

between these other groups and HSGs are usually overlooked. It is to these collectives that now we turn.

4.4 Historical Groups with Structural Dynamics

Historical groups with structural dynamics (HGSDs) can be broadly defined as

> groups that present a *multifaceted historical character* and, at the same time, are characterised by *structural dynamics*.

To analyse the features of HGSDs, I will focus on nations because the majority of the literature on historical injustice concentrates on collectives that are national communities, such as indigenous nations in settler societies such as the US, Canada and Australia. While in the previous section I showed that NHSGs and HSGs are different in a significant respect, here my aim is to point out the *similarities* between HGSDs and HSGs. This is because it is precisely the common features that HGSDs (e.g. nations) and HSGs (e.g. gay men) share that are largely overlooked by scholars of historical injustice and should instead be unravelled to gain a more comprehensive account of HGSDs such as nations and of why their history is important when we consider their unjust present.

To do so, let me start by examining how *membership* in nations is commonly thought to be granted and by looking at its actual mechanisms. It is quite undisputed that nations are ascriptive categories: persons are attributed a nationality at birth and, for at least a certain period, belong involuntarily to that nation.[38] However, liberal nationalists, who have arguably provided the most influential account of nations in analytical political theory and who usually support historical justice (see § 2.1), highlight that membership in a nation is also 'elective'.[39] According to liberal nationalists, from a certain moment onwards, co-nationals self-identify with their nationality and actively embrace it by mutually recognising each other as members of the same nation, taking material and psychological benefits from such a membership and valuing the very existence and endurance of the nation they belong to.[40] In this sense, from this moment – call it *the moment of conversion* – for a person to be part

---

[38] E.g. Canovan (1996, 55); Gans (2003, 43, 151); Margalit and Raz (1990, 446–47); Miller (1995, 42; 2007, 124).
[39] Tamir (1993, 87).   [40] E.g. Miller (1995, 22–24).

of a nation is a 'daily plebiscite'.[41] That is, what may have been initially an external imposition becomes a wilful endorsement.

The importance of the moment of conversion in liberal nationalists' normative defence of the value of nations and of the justifiability of national attachments should not be underestimated. Indeed, it may be argued that it is precisely the emphasis on that moment that makes it possible for liberal nationalists to conciliate nationalism with liberal tenets and thus distinguish a liberal endorsement of nations from communitarian strands of nationalism. The fact that co-nationals can be seen as having, at a certain point, freely decided to be members of their nations gives a typically liberal flavour to an ascriptive categorisation that would otherwise be suspiciously regarded as arbitrarily inflicted. From a liberal (and nationalist) perspective, in virtue of that alleged moment, nationality should not be treated as an arbitrary category like class; conversely, nations should be regarded as 'historical and ethical communities' whose members share an identity, perspectives and aims.[42] In this sense, for liberal nationalists, nations display a sort of unity of agency – that is, they are collective agents whose members perform 'joint-actions' or, at least, 'take decisions together'.[43] For instance, because nations display unity of agency, which is guaranteed by what I have called the moment of conversion, and historical continuity, they are conceived as collectively responsible to redress their past actions and to remedy current unjust states of affairs. In other words, if nations can act, then they can (and should) also bear responsibility for their unjust deeds and help address morally unacceptable situations.[44]

Regarding the issue of membership, the moment of conversion has, in theory, two correlated implications: persons can choose to (1) renounce their national identity and (2) embrace another one through, for instance, naturalisation processes.[45] This obviously entails being willing to relinquish the benefits granted by the former membership while also accepting the obligations stemming from the new one. However, what is worth stressing is that the moment of conversion 'turns the adherence to a culture and the assumption of national obligations into voluntary acts

---

[41] Renan ([1882] 1990, 19). Note that liberal nationalists draw on Renan's famous expression precisely to show how national identity is rooted in individual consent (e.g. Miller 1995, 22; Tamir 1993, 33). For a more nuanced interpretation of Renan's concept, see Yack (2012, 29).

[42] Miller (2007, 23); Moore (2001, 29); Tamir (1993, 96–102). On the difference between nationality and categories such as class, see Miller (2007, 31–32).

[43] Miller (2000, 29). See also Miller (2007, 118–24).

[44] Miller (2007, 111–34). See also Abdel-Nour (2003); Tan (2008); Thompson (2001, 118).

[45] For a similar point, see Moore (2001, 38–40).

rather than inevitable consequences of fate'.[46] Thus, it makes membership in a national group theoretically changeable at will.

Although appealing, the liberal account of national membership is quite misleading about how such a membership actually works. First, even if I badly want to renounce my national membership and I constantly claim that I do not self-identify with my alleged co-nationals, I may still be positioned into such a category.[47] This is because I may still, unwillingly, display certain traits (e.g. an accent, physical appearance, a style, a gesture, or behaviour) that are *externally recognised* as typical of those who belong to that particular national group. For example, I may deliberately disown my Italian nationality and coherently stop benefitting from, say, the feeling of having such a renowned artistic and literary national heritage. However, my Italian pronunciation may be enough for me to be categorised as an Italian and, for instance, be associated with the corruption that is taken to characterise Italian politics and society.

Second, and relatedly, when some persons who may have already acquired citizenship in a state that endorses a specific national identity heartily wish to become actual members of that nation, they may not be fully accepted as such, because some of their traits are not externally recognised as typical of that nationality. This is the tragic condition experienced by many Italian citizens that are not recognised as Italians because of their ethnicity or race; for example, the appointment of the Italian integration minister, Cécile Kyenge (the first minister of colour in Italian history), in 2013 was questioned by many because, although holding Italian citizenship, she was not recognised as being sufficiently Italian, which also led to several racist attacks even by Italian parliamentarians.[48]

Obviously, liberal nationalists would decry such behaviours and reply that national identities do not need to be based on race or ethnic characteristics;[49] however, the problem is that they often are. Generally, national categories necessitate some 'cultural markers'[50] – that is, mechanisms whereby it is possible to build a shared identity and immediately recognise who is a member of a nation. Nations are constituted by

---

[46] Tamir (1993, 87).

[47] Note that one may still be positioned in a national category even when she has *legally* renounced her nationality to, for instance, become a citizen of a country that does not allow dual nationality. Processes of external recognition can be activated independently of one's legal status because they are initiated in daily interactions or may follow different schemas from those that are used by formal institutions to categorise persons.

[48] Davies (2013). Note that, although former Italian prime minister Enrico Letta deeply criticised these attacks, the parliamentarians who hurled such terrible insults did not resign.

[49] D. Miller (1995, 21).   [50] Moore (2001, 57).

boundaries, and boundaries require that a putative difference be identified between those who can be included within them and those who cannot. The process of *mutual* recognition that, for liberal nationalists, characterises and legitimises national communities is less reciprocal than it may seem. What is necessary and sufficient to grant membership in a national category, especially in daily interactions, is external recognition. To be sure, nations are not fixed and unchangeable entities and norms of membership may become more inclusive over time. However, that membership cannot be universally granted and, in everyday encounters, is still primarily externally determined, even when more encompassing default assumptions are held.[51] In other words, membership in national groups is inherently *structural* in that belonging to groups such as nations hinges upon external categorisation by existing members or outsiders. Therefore, persons suffer from injustices connected to having inherited such an ascriptive national membership even when they do not consider themselves as part of that national group. This is because the moment of conversion plays a much less central role in national membership than liberal nationalists concede.

To strongly distinguish between groups such as nations and other structural groups, liberal nationalists may still argue that the former are perceived as 'encompassing identities'[52] crossing, for example, gender- and sexuality-based categorisations. If nations were not so important for persons, the fact that non-structural collectives that are mobilised around HSGs strive to be acknowledged as part of their respective national communities would remain unexplained. If co-nationals were not, in David Miller's words, 'significant others',[53] why fight to be recognised by them? This line of argument offers only a partial understanding of what 'significance' means in these contexts. It is *not only* because co-national appreciation is vital to persons' self-respect that the public recognition of HSGs is often so heatedly demanded by collective mobilising around the injustice of HSGs. First, since nations represent today one of the most common and effective ways whereby benefits and privileges are distributed, access to the bundle of entitlements that national membership grants (especially when it coincides with citizenship) is a necessity. This is possible only provided that one's externally recognised memberships are proved to be compatible with national loyalty. For example, to be granted the right to marry (and receive its correlated benefits), gay and lesbian persons have to show how categorisation along the

[51] E.g. Canovan (1996, 55); Mason (2000, 25). This important aspect of national membership is usually acknowledged by communitarian scholars (e.g. Walzer 1983, 52).
[52] Margalit and Raz (1990, 448). Similarly, see Kymlicka (1995, 76); D. Miller (1995, 92).
[53] D. Miller (2000, 76).

lines of sexuality does not threaten the national community. In other words, they *need* co-nationals to recognise that their other historical and structural memberships may be easily incorporated into the identity that is supposed to encompass all others (i.e. nationality).

Second, as Hannah Arendt observes, when an ascriptive categorisation is targeted by discrimination and exclusion (e.g. Jewishness), downplaying the salience of this membership in the public sphere is an ineffective strategy for those who are positioned in that category. Conversely, 'one can resist only in terms of the identity that is under attack'[54] because claims abstracting from that identity (e.g. in the name of a shared humanity) are bound to remain unheard within a context that regards such an identity as salient (e.g. an anti-Semitic context). Since it is that putative categorisation that accounts for the experienced discrimination, publicly affirming its value may be, at least in certain cases, an inevitable strategy of resistance. It may be that only when members of the community in which discrimination takes place (which is usually a national community) recognise that bearing a determinate identity does not entail inferiority but may instead even be something to be proud of that members of these groups can improve their condition.[55] This is also the reason why even national self-identification is more easily made and national collectives more effectively constructed or reinforced when persons are discriminated against *because they have been recognised as* members of that nation.[56]

In addition to being *interpretatively* misleading, the insistence on nations as encompassing identities may also be *normatively* problematic. Particularly, this insistence overlooks how the very idea of nations as an encompassing identity has been historically deployed to demand enormous sacrifices to particular categories of co-nationals. For instance, 'at those exceptional moments when the fate of the whole nation is determined collectively',[57] those co-nationals who are recognised as 'women' discover that they may pay a particularly heavy price for what is taken to be their encompassing identity – that is, their national membership. Since 'it is women … who *reproduce* the nation, biologically, culturally, and symbolically',[58] it is quite unsurprising that, during wartime, they are the

---

[54] Arendt (1970, 18). Susan Bickford defends 'identity politics' in a similar vein (1997, 19).
[55] This process of reinforcing one's own identity as a strategy of resistance may be activated even when criteria of exclusion are enforced only at an informal level. See Balibar (1990).
[56] E.g. Berlin ([1979] 2013, 441).   [57] D. Miller (1995, 14).
[58] Yuval-Davis (1997, 2). See also Kandiyoti (1991).

ones who bear the most onerous burden of preserving national identity and being loyal to that identity.[59] This not only exposes women to all sorts of violations during military conflicts but also puts them in jeopardy in the aftermath. For example, after the liberation from Nazi occupation, many countries reserved a particularly harsh and humiliating treatment for female collaborators, such as beating them, shaving their heads and parading them through the streets on the back of a lorry.[60] Even in peacetime, as 'reproducers of the nation', women are the target of many controls on their sexuality, such as natal policies aimed at promoting or limiting population growth.[61] It seems that, although they have been excluded from the body politic for a long time, it was not the case that women historically had no country – contrary to what Virginia Woolf famously argues.[62] Rather, they have been (and still are) overly invested in the destiny of their nation.

The example of women is significant because it shows that, although liberal nationalists argue that nations must equally respect all their members, the idea that nations *should* be regarded as encompassing identities may have deleterious effects, at least when the ways nations actually do place unequal roles on their co-nationals are unravelled. That is, liberal nationalists' suggestion of raising the practice of considering nations as encompassing identities to a normative ideal is likely to worsen the conditions of those co-nationals who are usually (and historically) regarded as fulfilling particular functions within the reproduction and protection of the nation.

The mechanisms whereby membership is granted are not the only characteristic that makes nation-like collectives a type of structural group. Like other structural groups, such as HSGs, these collectives are maintained and reinforced through *relational means* – that is, by the reiteration and reproduction of norms, expectations and habits associated with a particular nation. For example, while special occasions (e.g. sporting events) represent an opportunity to strengthen nationhood, the daily language of media, the sale of national products, and the embodiment of dressing codes and stereotypes of a nation contribute to the ordinary

---

[59] The nation (i.e. the 'motherland') is usually symbolically represented as a 'woman' (e.g. the French Marianne, Mother Russia, Germania, Italia Turrita and Mother Svea). Because the nation is often represented as analogous to the family, women are particularly suited to be the emblem of the nation, as they immediately function as symbolic 'border guards' (Yuval-Davis 1997, 45). Women thus can more easily remind all co-nationals of the exclusionary character of the nation and of the sacrifices national membership requires.

[60] These shameful practices were widespread in post-Vichy France (see Virgili 2002); however, they were also performed in other countries, such as Italy and Norway.

[61] Yuval-Davis (1997, 22–55).   [62] Woolf ([1938] 2006, 129).

enactment of national categories.[63] It is also by this everyday reproduction of structural processes that persons' attachment to national identity is promoted and national categories are entrenched as an effective device to distribute privileges, obligations and status. In other words, through imagination, nations are continuously brought to life.[64]

The fact that groups such as nations are structural collectives does not mean they do not have specificities that make them a particular kind of structural group – that is, one that also has differences from HSGs (and NHSGs). It merely entails acknowledging the structural dynamics that characterise nations (or nation-like groups) as fundamental aspects of what these groups are and how they operate – especially when it comes to analysing the nuances of membership in national groups. For instance, as liberal nationalists argue, groups that self-identify as national communities are characterised by occupying a determinate territory (or, at least, having a homeland) and aspiring to political autonomy,[65] while structural groups such as gay and lesbian persons are territorially dispersed and do not aim at political self-governance. Although the distinctive features of national collectives should be recognised, it is also of paramount importance not to overstress them or take them at face value. As for the idea that nations are politically conscious agents that collectively aim for self-determination, it is worth pointing out that many claims for national autonomy are not necessarily representative of what members of a national group really wish. Often such demands are advanced by political parties and organisations,[66] rather than being the outcome of an inclusive process of decision-making. Moreover, some of these organisations, such as the Kurdistan Democratic Party, which promotes the national self-determination of Iraqi Kurds, tend to be authoritarian and corrupt. At least in these cases, which are neither the norm nor the exception, the fact that claims of political autonomy are representative of the whole nation may be questioned. Additionally, not all groups that self-identify as nations *can* promote their interests in terms of political autonomy or self-determination; sometimes for some national minorities (e.g. Arab citizens of Israel) this is impossible because the surrounding context (e.g. the exclusive identification of citizenship with a determinate religion – Jewishness) does not allow

---

[63] On the 'banal' ways nationality is reproduced, see Billig (1995).
[64] See, famously, Anderson (1991, 224).
[65] E.g. Kymlicka (1995, 11); Miller (1995, 22–26); Moore (2001, 6); Yack (2012, 90–92).
[66] Brubaker (2002, 172).

a similar demand.[67] In these contexts, national groups frame their claims in terms of cultural exemptions (e.g. from military service) and linguistic protection – that is, analogously to how ethnic minorities are usually taken to advance their claims.[68]

Likewise, the assumption that groups must occupy a determinate territory (or have a homeland they might want to return to) in order to be nations can be problematic in that it may exclude some national groups and even reproduce the discursive schemas whereby these groups have been historically discriminated. For example, the nomadic aspirations of Romani people have traditionally undermined their right to nationhood and still represent a major hurdle for the organisations that represent them (e.g. the International Romani Union) to have such a right finally recognised. An international legal system (and an academic debate) putting such an emphasis on the link between territory and nationhood is clearly a hostile context for the Romani people's demand to receive the status of a non-territorial nation.[69]

Groups such as nations are not only structural collectives; like HSGs, they are also historical. In particular, they display a multifaceted historical character. Like HSGs, many nations have been *brought to light through injustices*. For instance, the Igbo, a national minority in Nigeria, became a people as a result of European (and especially British) colonialism – that is, as an effect of and reaction against colonial oppression. Moreover, like HSGs, such collectives would hardly be conceivable without *their particular history*: had its history been different, a nation would have been extremely dissimilar from its present form and might not even exist.[70] Most importantly, as for HSGs, many nations (or nation-like collectives) have suffered from *systematic injustices over history*. Colonialism, slaughters or genocides, slavery, forced assimilation and sterilisation are just a few examples of injustices that some nations were systematically subjected to (often at the hands of other nations).

However, unlike HSGs, nations are structural groups that are historical in another important sense. Nations have been historically regarded as fundamental to organise the international realm, build solidarity and distribute benefits and duties among different populations. This is worth

---

[67] See the Haifa Declaration issued by Palestinian intellectual group Nakba and crafted by a social forum for a statement of the collective national vision of Arabs in Israel (Nakba 2003).

[68] For an influential distinction between rights demanded by national groups (i.e. 'self-government rights') and entitlements claimed by ethnic minorities (i.e. 'polyethnic rights'), see Kymlicka (1995, 27–37).

[69] Goodwin (2004).   [70] Moore (2001, 13).

pointing out for at least two reasons. First, because of the privilege that communities recognised as nations enjoy within international law, the idea of 'nation' constitutes an effective way for peoples seeking protection and independence to plead their cause and hope to be internationally heard. It is unsurprising that, for example, the majority of the Unrepresented Nations and Peoples Organisation (UNPO) members present their case in terms of national self-determination, rather than as an issue of ethnic rights. Moreover, the language of 'nationality' and the construction of strong national communities have provided a vital tool that enabled colonised peoples to resist foreign oppression and recover from colonial dominion.[71] Therefore, overlooking or minimising the significance of national categorisations may backfire on marginalised groups that are trying to advance their claims through the powerful language of nationality.[72]

Second, nations (and nation-like collectives) are historical groups also in that many of their members care about the group existing over time and outliving their own existence.[73] Liberal nationalists are right in pointing out how national membership is an important aspect of many persons' identities, which can create bonds of solidarity among those sharing it. As seen, this per se is not indicative of how membership in a national group is granted; however, the attachment that many persons have for their nation (and the significance of nations internationally) means that such groups would likely also exist independently from the injustices they may be subjected to. Unlike HSGs, whose very existence cannot be easily separated from the historical and present injustices they suffer from, nation-like groups against which systematic injustices were or still are committed would be bound to outlast as a significant way to categorise persons and organise the social world even if such injustices were overcome.

This last point should be read not only as a descriptive observation but also as a *normative* prescription. Because intergenerational networks binding together members of national communities that have historically suffered from injustice have often provided a crucial source of identification and attachment, measures to redress such an injustice should respect and sustain such networks. Redress, in these contexts, cannot entail the disappearance of the group.

In sum, collectives such as nations are groups that are historical in *many* important respects and are characterised by structural dynamics. So far I have identified three types of structural groups and pointed out their differences and similarities, which are usually overlooked within the

---

[71] Rao (2010, 69–104).   [72] Kymlicka (2001, 66).   [73] Gans (2003, 40–49); D. Miller (1995, 23).

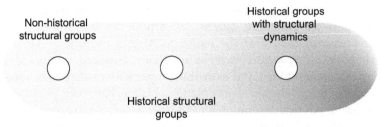

Figure 4.2 The spectrum of structural groups.

literature on historical injustice and by conceptions of structural injustice. What does this mean for how we should think about existing groups and their condition of injustice? To this question now we turn.

4.5   Towards a Spectrum of Structural Groups

The three types of structural groups examined in the previous sections should not be regarded as exhaustive of all the structural collectives that are present within our societies. They should be considered, instead, as three fundamental points of a *spectrum* of structural groups (see Figure 4.2). By being part of a spectrum, rather than being conceived as mere separate categories, NHSGs, HSGs and HGSDs can be analysed in their commonalities without suppressing their differences and reducing a type of group to one of the others. Moreover, the idea of the spectrum provides a way to conceptualise the range of structural groups that exist in our societies, transnationally and internationally, in a fluid fashion. This is because, although many actual groups displaying structural elements do not fit precisely into one of the three large categories identified, they can still be placed within the spectrum in relation to such categories. In other words, by analysing the relation (if any) between history and (in)justice characterising a determinate group, it is possible to collocate it within the range of structural collectives.

To exemplify how the idea of the spectrum works, consider the case of African Americans. Within the literature on groups, there is a general discomfort with identifying the precise collective in which the group of African Americans should be included.[74] Unlike national groups (traditionally conceived), African Americans do not ask for political autonomy. To be sure, black political separatism has been a strand of the African

---

[74] E.g. see Kymlicka (1995, 24–25).

American emancipation movement advocating the creation of separate institutions for American citizens of African ancestry, independence from European society or the return to African countries.[75] However, black political separatists have been heavily criticised within African American communities, and even those organisations that most forcibly argued for such goals, such as the Nation of Islam, have been progressively considering political separation and independence as a last resort if freedom, justice and equality are not achieved by other means.[76] Nor do African Americans ask for exemptions or special protection of cultural practices as some national minorities that are unable to demand self-determination do.

On the other hand, African Americans present numerous strong affinities with HSGs; most importantly, they have suffered from serious systematic injustices over history (e.g. slavery and de jure segregation during the Jim Crow period) that are now formally rejected by American society. They underwent all three kinds of past injustices from which many HSGs have been created; by means of racist discourses and theories aimed at showing their 'inferiority' and 'abnormality', African Americans were denied the right to vote and were excluded from paid employment or relegated to servile occupations. In this respect, African Americans represent a paradigmatic case of an HSG as US citizenship has been defined in opposition and in relation to their status as second-class citizens.[77]

Nevertheless, unlike many HSGs (e.g. women and gay men), African Americans are concentrated in a bounded territory, and they have been formed by the systematic violations experienced within that determinate context.[78] Comparatively, African Americans have built more extensive and resistant networks of solidarity and belonging, and have developed a strong, although complex, community precisely in virtue of that history

[75] E.g. Moses (1988); Robinson (2001).

[76] Black political separatism has been traditionally criticised as a form of black supremacism and racism (see, famously, King [1967] 2010, chapter 2). Importantly, it should not be confused with forms of black solidarity whereby African Americans try to organise to protect and promote their interests in a society fraught with racial injustices (see Shelby 2007).

[77] Shklar (1991, 22).

[78] To be sure, I do not claim that HSGs such as gay men are not formed by a particular history or within specific contexts. As we will see in the following chapters, by focusing on 'women', identifying the specific ways women have been systematically subjected to injustices becomes crucial to understanding how such a group is contextually reproduced and how their unjust condition can be overcome. My point is merely noticing how the category 'African American' (as different from mere 'blackness') plays a crucial role in the structures that regulate US society but is not particularly significant outside the US boundaries (see § 3.1), whereas categories such as 'women' and 'gay men' are historical and structural groups at a global level that then are locally specified.

of injustice.[79] In particular, while the link between unjust history and structural injustice is crucial for the present condition of both African Americans and other more mainstream HSGs, persons who are recognised as African Americans tend to be more aware of being part of an inter-generational group and of having inherited an unjust history. In a way similar to what usually happens to members of nation-like collectives, for many African Americans such a history is an important part of their *personal* identity (i.e. how they think of themselves). This is not to suggest that *all* members of other HSGs do not regard their membership as a fundamental component of who they are or that they have no historical consciousness about the structural group they are positioned in. Here I am simply stressing a difference in degree resulting from the specific context in which the position of African Americans has been created and is repro-duced, which should be considered if we want to fully grasp the character-istics of such a group.[80]

In other words, the idea of the spectrum of structural groups helps collocate African Americans vis-à-vis the relation between history and injustice that characterises their condition. Rather than being considered as a puzzling collective entity or anomaly within a classification of groups, African Americans can be coherently seen as a part of a broad range of structural collectives, one that displays important similarities to other groups that are historical and structural. At the same time, the fluidity of the spectrum does not reduce them to a sort of national minority or treat them as analogous in every respect to women and gay men, for example. Through the idea of the spectrum, the particular history of African Americans can be conceived in relation to how other structural groups have been affected by the interconnection between history and injustice while also acknowledging how the distinctiveness of this history bears on the characteristics of this group.

Another interesting case, which proves how thinking about structural groups in terms of a spectrum is fruitful, is represented by the group of prisoners and ex-prisoners. Unlike NHSGs (e.g. the homeless and veter-ans), many convicts and ex-convicts suffer from lawful discrimination and have their rights restricted in ways that are very similar to how HSGs have

---

[79] On the importance of these ties for African Americans' emancipatory project, see Shelby (2007).

[80] For instance, redressing the HSI suffered by African Americans needs to tackle the new reproduc-tion of the historical injustice that is linked to being recognised as an African American – i.e. to a historical-structural position – *without* severing those sources of belonging (e.g. intergenerational networks of solidarity and cultural affiliations) that have played (and still do so) a crucial role in African Americans' identification with that position.

been systematically subjected to injustice in the past. In many countries, such as the UK and the US, prisoners are disenfranchised and, when released, ex-convicts suffer from various discriminations, some of which are legally enforced (e.g. housing and employment discrimination, and ineligibility to public assistance). However, while for HSGs such a formal discrimination is in the past (even though it endures by other informal means), for prisoners and ex-prisoners it is a present reality – that is, a reality that is largely recognised as legitimate and an effect of just processes, like imprisonment itself.[81] Thus, like NHSGs, the group of convicts and former convicts does not technically have a history of injustices or, at least, one that is largely and publicly recognised as having been characterised by systematic injustices. Even in the case of (ex-)prisoners, it would be a mistake to think they can be reduced to NHSGs or to HSGs (at least for now) as this would offer a misleading account of their peculiar condition, which is characterised by structural dynamics but also by a *present* reality of legal discrimination and exclusion.[82]

In sum, the idea of the spectrum of structural groups avoids drawing draconian distinctions between collectives displaying structural dynamics and avoids merely reducing a group or category to another.[83] Indeed, it shows how thinking about the analogies and differences between the types of structural groups is decisive to understand the situation of those groups displaying structural features that exist within our societies and the kind of injustices they suffer from. In particular, the idea of the spectrum broadens the range of groups to be considered when dealing with historical injustices and their present normative relevance. Once past injustices have been framed in terms of HSI (§ 3.2), all groups displaying *both* structural and historical features should be regarded as potentially affected by an unjust

[81] One may say that prisoners and ex-prisoners are actually not a structural group because membership in that category is not ascriptive but largely voluntary as it results from the choices made by particular individuals (i.e. breaking the law). Although I cannot defend an account of convicts and former convicts as a structural group here, I hope my brief account of the treatment reserved to ex-prisoners at least hints at the extent to which societal structures (that include but are not limited to institutions) have a role in creating a disadvantaged position within society.

[82] Obviously, I do not want to suggest that because the legal discrimination against (ex-)prisoners is recognised by societies and formal institutions as just, this means that it is actually so (see, e.g., Hoskins 2014). I emphasise that the injustice of prisoners has not (yet) been acknowledged as a history of injustices because, as seen in Chapter 3, it is when societies change and recognise certain treatments as unjust that (historical) injustices are reproduced through other means. This also entails that if we want to overcome the unjust condition of (ex-)convicts, the first necessary move would be to end their systematic *formal* discrimination and exclusion.

[83] It is noteworthy that the notion of the spectrum of structural groups is more encompassing than Young's suggestion to conceive of ethnic and national groups as forming a *continuum* (Young 1997b).

past that still structures the present. I cautiously say such groups *potentially* suffer from HSI because such a determination hinges upon an analysis aimed at identifying and establishing whether unjust history is newly reproduced into the structures of the present.

The conception of HSI has a twofold implication for the account of groups that should be endorsed in the debate over historical injustice. First, such a conception brings to the forefront groups that are not traditionally included in mainstream theories of historical justice, namely HSGs. Indeed, groups that can be described as HSGs should be at the centre of any theoretical and normative attempt to discuss the significance of unjust history. This is precisely because HSGs have been created by a history of systematic injustices and are reproduced by the structural presence of that history, and thus represent paradigmatic cases of the complex ways the unjust past endures over time. Because of the scant attention generally paid to HSGs within the literature on historical injustice, the following chapters (Chapters 5, 6 and 7) will be devoted to providing an account of one such group – namely, women – and its condition of injustice.

Second, while expanding our traditional understanding of which kinds of groups should be considered in normative discussions about history and (in)justice, the conception of HSI also casts new light on those groups that are already a concern to scholars of historical injustice – namely, HGSDs such as nations. It does so by emphasising how these collectives exhibit structural characteristics that cannot be neglected. Such structural dynamics make it possible for history to be newly reproduced, even for those HGSDs against which injustices were committed in the past. This turns out to be fundamental when reflecting upon what is owed to these groups from the perspective of justice and upon the types of remedies that are necessary to overcome the present condition of injustice such groups suffer from. As we will see in Chapter 8, recognising the historical and structural dimensions of the injustice towards a group entails acknowlededging the force of reparations claims while also recognising that redress cannot be obtained if the unjust history is not revealed *and* its new structural reproduction is not tackled. As I will argue, this should significantly change our attitude towards the institutions and structures that regulate our societies (and the transnational order) (§ 8.3).

CHAPTER 5

Defining Women as a Group

Conceiving of historical injustice as historical-structural injustice (HSI) leads not only to conceptualising structural groups as forming a spectrum but also to broadening our understanding of which groups suffer from unjust history and its new reproduction. As already mentioned, women may be considered one such group and a particularly interesting case to illustrate the encompassing character of a conception of HSI because it has been largely neglected by the literature on historical injustice.[1] The following three chapters thus will be devoted to exploring some dimensions of the structural reproduction of unjust history of women in egalitarian contexts (Chapter 6) and reflecting on how they should be tackled (Chapter 7). To do so, an account of women as a historical-structural group (HSG) should be provided. This is the aim of this chapter.

Defining women as a group is recognised as particularly challenging by feminist scholars.[2] On one hand, because any definition of women* may erase important differences and consequently significant power asymmetries (e.g. along lines of class, race, sexuality, ability) among women, it may be tempting to avoid defining women*.[3] On the other hand, feminists have also argued that feminism as a movement precisely hinges upon the existence of women* – that is, an oppressed group around which feminism can organise and mobilise.[4] Without a precise subject, feminism would be not only ineffective but also futile as it would lack the underlying reasons

---

[1] As already mentioned, in her recent work, Catherine Lu observes that 'women' should be regarded as a group suffering from enduring injustice (Lu 2017, 161). However, she does not provide a fully fledged account of how the group of women should be defined, and, as we will see, the task of defining 'women' is not so straightforward and requires an engagement with serious theoretical and political concerns raised in feminist theory. Nor does Lu explore how the condition of 'women' in formally egalitarian contexts can be conceived as the new reproduction of an unjust history, as, instead, I will do in the next chapter.

[2] Unless stated otherwise, in this chapter, women* will refer to the *group* of women.

[3] See, famously, Butler (1990, 9).

[4] E.g. Frye (1996a, 991); Haslanger (2000); Stoljar (1995, 262); Stone (2004, 136); Young (1997a, 17–18).

for its actions.[5] Therefore, the enterprise of defining women* is not so escapable.

Although within the feminist tradition there are many interesting endeavours to define women*, this chapter focuses on 'structural accounts' of women* by critically engaging especially with Young's conception of seriality.[6] This is because my attempt to define women* shares in their political project of defining women* in order to understand and fight women's oppression and (as with Young) of identifying women* as one paradigmatic case of injustice. In this respect, my account, which conceptualises women as an HSG, can be read as an attempt to offer an improved version of structural conceptions of women*, which relies on and helps construct a theory of *historical* injustice in which women* figure as a paradigmatic case. In doing so, this chapter also aims to defend the significance of structural accounts of women* in analysing gender injustices. Defining women as an HSG explains what being categorised as a woman entails – that is, how this external categorisation operates in determining the set of constraints that those who are recognised as women can potentially encounter. It shows how it is possible to hold a structural account of women* without erasing significant differences among women. Importantly and relatedly, by focusing on unjust history, such an account highlights how the set of constraints women can encounter is determined by how power structures have *historically* intersected.

5.1 Young's Account of Women*

5.1.1 Women as a Series

Structural accounts of women* are characterised by a specific orientation in addressing the question as to whether women can be considered a group. Precisely, in answering that question, structural accounts do not want to solve the ontological problem of sexual difference by delving into the issue of whether the distinction between a (biological) sex and a (social and cultural) gender is neat and defensible.[7] Nor do these accounts aim to interrogate whether we should develop a 'positive' definition of womanhood that is

---

[5] Young (1997a, 16). For a recent refutation of the necessity of a detailed account of women* for feminist politics, see Mikkola (2016).

[6] For other structural accounts of women*, see Gunnarsson (2011) and Haslanger (2000).

[7] For famous and compelling critiques of the sex/gender distinction, which stress how even 'sex' (i.e. the division of human beings into two sexes) is a cultural and social construct, see Butler (1990, 10) and Gatens (1996, 85).

freed from patriarchal meanings for emancipative purposes.[8] They only intend to develop an account of women* which can examine and denounce the conditions of oppression and disadvantage linked to being a woman while being successfully used to combat them.[9] To wit, structural accounts of women* pursue a profoundly critical goal, namely understanding what the category of women* *does*, how it operates in persons' lives and in the regulation of societies, what happens to those who are included in it *in relation to* those who are not, and how this inclusion is connected to oppression and domination.

Before examining Young's account of women*, it is thus important to note what Young is trying to achieve in conceptualising women as a group. For Young, women* denotes a group that suffers from a specific type of injustice (i.e. structural injustice), which, as seen, occurs when a group of individuals is systematically positioned in a disadvantaged position vis-à-vis other groups as the outcome of the accumulation of many agents' routinised actions over time (§ 4.3). She aims to reveal the injustice of women* and point out the dynamics that structural injustice displays. Moreover, in presenting women as a group, Young intends to make a case in favour of group political representation, specifically for the inclusion of members of groups suffering from structural injustice in democratic institutions, as something crucial not only for democracy but also to overcome injustice. It is important to bear these two distinct yet interconnected aims pursued by Young in mind because, as I show below, some shortcomings of Young's account of women* stem from an unexplored tension between the conception of groups underlying the idea of structural injustice and her case for group political representation.[10]

By drawing on Jean-Paul Sartre's concept of seriality, Young argues that women* should be better conceptualised as a 'series', rather than an interest- or identity-based collective. A series

> is a social collective whose members are unified passively by the objects their actions are originating around and/or by the objectified results of the

---

[8] For this position, see, e.g., Frye (1996a, 998).

[9] Haslanger (2000). Note that my distinction is merely analytical; i.e. it aims to clarify the specific concerns driving structural approaches. It does not mean that reflections about the sex/gender distinction and 'positive' definitions of womanhood are not also motivated by a profound critique of the social order or that structural accounts do not have implications for the other issues mentioned.

[10] The existence of these two aims in Young's attempt to define women* appears particularly evident in her *Inclusion and Democracy* (2000), when she builds on her previously developed idea of gender as seriality (1997a) to show that women* is one significant case of oppressed structural groups calling for political representation.

material effects of the actions of the others . . . The unity of the series derives from the way that individuals pursue ends in respect to the same objects by a continuous material environment, in response to structures that have been created by the unintended collective result of past actions.[11]

For Young, women* is a series because individuals are 'positioned as feminine' by being oriented in their actions towards certain objects (e.g. public bathrooms) and social practices (e.g. make-up) whose meanings and rules are defined by specific structures. Such structures are (1) 'enforced heterosexuality', which refers to the institution of heterosexuality as the norm with which individuals are expected to comply, and (2) the 'sexual division of labour', which amounts to the division of tasks and labours between the two sexes.[12] For Young, although the particular connotations of these two structures significantly vary worldwide and over time, enforced heterosexuality and the sexual division of labour *universally* organise social reality to *determine* the constraints women* encounter.[13] Importantly, the series of women is formed, maintained and reproduced by these structures, which put individuals not only in relation to others who are similarly collocated but also to those who are differently positioned within these same structures (i.e. the series of men).

Young argues that individual women's identities are not determined by membership in the series of women: saying someone is a woman 'predicts nothing in particular about who she is, what she does, how she takes up her social positioning'.[14] Individual women have their own interests and embody the gendered structures in which they are positioned in a different way, although their actions (whatever they may be) are both enabled and constrained by such structures.[15] Thus, the series of women cannot be regarded as a self-conscious group whose members are 'united by actions that they undertake together',[16] share common goals and mutually recognise one another as co-members. Obviously, from the series of women many self-conscious groups are established and 'arise on the basis of and in response to the serialized condition [of "women"]'.[17] Feminist movements and organisations are a particular type of self-conscious group stemming from the series of women as they organise around the common goal of changing the structures

---

[11] Young (1997a, 23).   [12] Young (1997a, 28–29).
[13] Young (1997a, 28–30). In a later essay, Young adds 'hierarchies of power' as a third structure that creates the series of women. This structure refers to how societies organise the distribution of status and authority (e.g. within the military, state institutions, corporate boards), i.e. by positioning women in a subordinate position vis-à-vis men (Young 2002, 425).
[14] Young (1997a, 32).   [15] Young (1997a, 29).   [16] Young (1997a, 23).   [17] Young (1997a, 34).

through which women are serialised.[18] However, for Young, every women's self-conscious group, feminist collectives included, are always 'partial in relation to the series' of women as their goals cannot embrace the 'totality of the condition of women as a series'.[19]

That said, Young maintains that, in virtue of their similar social positioning, members of the same series have a particular social perspective, which amounts to having 'similar kinds of knowledge about the workings of society or similar kinds of routine experiences'.[20] This aspect is fundamental to Young's more general theory of injustice and inclusion. Indeed, it is on the basis of women's social perspective that Young argues for women's representation in the body politic.

Let me take a step back and briefly present Young's case for group representation. Young criticises the ideal of abstract citizenship for not recognising how allegedly universal and impartial decisions tend to express the partial preferences and reflect the particular experiences of privileged groups.[21] The inclusion of marginalised groups in political processes of decision-making therefore becomes fundamental to legitimately reach democratic decisions and to face and remedy the structural injustices from which members of these groups suffer.[22] Because of the unavailability of direct democracy in contemporary politics, the inclusion of marginalised groups can be promoted only through mechanisms of political representation.

Young advances a sophisticated theory of democratic representation, according to which the process of representation should be considered as a 'differentiated relationship' between representatives and the represented.[23] For our purposes, it is sufficient to stress how, for Young, each person should be represented in three crucial and separate aspects of her existence: her interests, which are instrumental to the achievement of her goals; her opinions, which form the basis of her political judgements; and her *perspective*, which stems from the particular social position she occupies within societal structures.

What is a social perspective, and why should it be represented? Young contends that 'structural social positions ... produce particular location-relative experience and a specific knowledge of social processes and consequences'.[24] Sharing a social perspective with those who are similarly positioned within social structures does not mean agreeing upon a specific interpretation of issues, because this orientation of the sight 'conditions

---

[18] Young (1997a, 34).   [19] Young (1997a, 36).   [20] Young (2000, 102).   [21] Young (1998, 408).
[22] Young (2000, 141).   [23] Young (2000, 125–28).   [24] Young (2000, 136).

but does not determine what one sees'.[25] Nor does it define the interests one may pursue. However, social perspectives give to those who occupy them a particular outlook on and knowledge of how society works that are unavailable to persons who are not located in such a position. Because of the importance social perspectives play in persons' lives, a person can feel fully represented in the body politic if at least some of the elected representatives share her social perspective – that is, if some representatives occupy her social-structural position. It is now clearer why Young stresses how individuals who are serialised as women have similar knowledge of how societies work and similar routinised experiences. She argues in favour of the inclusion of more women (i.e. more representatives that are serialised as women) into political institutions and decision-making bodies on the basis of the fact that members of the series 'women' share a social perspective.

*5.1.2   The Problems with Young's Account of Women**

Arguably, Young's account of women* as a series has considerable merits. Particularly, it avoids presuming that all women qua women share an identity and thus avoids identifying a range of features (e.g. social, behavioural, psychological) women display as women. Moreover, such an account points to the relation women* has with men as a group in that not only is the former positioned within societal structures in connection with the latter but, one may observe, the very social structures through which women are serialised (i.e. enforced heterosexuality and the sexual division of labour) also serialise men in a position of advantage vis-à-vis women*.[26]

However, as it stands, this account reveals some shortcomings. The first flaw lies in *the pre-identification* of those structures creating the constraints that women as women* face. Although Young importantly observes that the specifications of these gendered structures vary contextually, she still maintains that enforced heterosexuality and the sexual division of labour are universally the structures that determine constraints on women's actions. Nevertheless, the pre-identification of gender structures is problematic as it misses the opportunity to theorise how the constraints certain women encounter in being serialised as women *in a determinate context* can

---

[25] Young (2000, 139).

[26] This is not to deny that some *individual* men may suffer more disadvantages than some individual women. Differences in structural positions between women and men refer to the *series*, not to specific individuals.

be reduced to neither of the structures that have been pre-identified by Young. Other structures also need to be factored in.

To see how this is the case, let me return to an example that draws on the current situation in Italy and with which I opened this book. Although Italy has in place a good legislation granting women the right to abortion (the 1978 Law 194), it has become particularly difficult to have an abortion. This is because the majority of Italian doctors (80–90 per cent of gynaecologists in many regions) are conscientious objectors and thus refuse to terminate pregnancies. As seen, this means many women have to go abroad to have an abortion or, more often, resort to clandestine (and thus incredibly dangerous) means. The situation is so dramatic that some women in hospitals are left without assistance even after the procedures for the abortion have started if, for example, the doctor who initiated the procedure finishes her shift and a conscientious objector takes her place.[27]

Which are those formal and informal structures that create this severe constraint faced by women* in Italy? Such structures cannot be only reduced to the enforced heterosexuality and the sexual division of labour that arguably organise Italian society. To understand why the actions of those who are serialised as women in Italy are so limited in relation to the possibility of having an abortion (and thus exercising their rights), one also needs to look at *other* structures that regulate social relations in Italy. Specifically, one has to consider the enormous influence the Catholic Church exerts not only on Italian politics but especially on Italians' professional lives. In Italy, Catholic faith is not so much a private issue but is primarily a matter of 'public respectability';[28] despite what many think, Italians tend not to be particularly practising Catholics in the private sphere. However, when it comes to professional bodies (e.g. the medical establishment), 'public respectability' means acting as a Catholic – that is, according to the Catholic Church's precepts. For a gynaecologist, violating this informal norm has serious consequences for her career, social status and sometimes physical safety.[29] This example shows that if we want to fully understand what happens when women are serialised as women (i.e. what the category of women does to women's lives in constraining their actions), pre-identifying the structures that create the injustice suffered by women* is problematic as it is bound to neglect other structures that – in the specific context of analysis – are crucial factors in analysing the restraints imposed on women's actions.

---

[27] Pasolini (2014).   [28] Conti (2013).   [29] Bia (2016).

One may object that the sexual division of labour does actually explain the constraints women face in the Italian case as that situation can be interpreted as an attempt by the Catholic Church (and a quite successful one) to control women's reproductive freedom. Certainly, this explanation captures the rationale behind the pressure exercised by the Catholic Church on this matter; however, my point is that to understand how women as members of women* are constrained in their actions in this case, we cannot simply limit our analysis to the Catholic Church's motives, which have obviously to do with the sexual division of labour. We need to factor in another structure, which is constituted by the norm informally regulating 'public respectability' in Italian professional life and is not directly related to the role of women in reproduction. Indeed, it is reasonable to think that, because of how 'public respectability' is constructed in Italy, Italian citizens (independently of their position in the sexual division of labour) would also face this de facto serious hindrance to the exercise of their legal right to self-determination should physician-assisted suicide be legalised.[30] This is not to say the two structures identified by Young are unimportant within societies (e.g. in Italy), but simply to point out that, in many cases, the constraints faced by women as women* in a determinate context cannot be explained by referring only to them.

The second shortcoming revealed by Young's account of women* as a series is that every woman (as a member of women*) is presumed to be constrained by gendered structures (i.e. enforced heterosexuality and the sexual division of labour), although the ways individual women act upon these structures are different. What remains unclear is *how* such constraints operate in women's lives. Some women may claim they are not subjected to, say, the normative expectations of enforced heterosexuality. Although arguably remote, it is still worth considering this possibility not so much because of its empirical likelihood but for the theoretical reply that it has received from structural accounts of women*, which I think is unsatisfactory. Famously, Sally Haslanger responds to the theoretical challenge that 'non-oppressed' women posit by arguing that a structural account of

[30] For instance, in the tragic, famous case of Eluana Englaro – a woman who lived in a vegetative state for seventeen years after a car accident and eventually died in 2009 after the removal of her feeding tubes – the Catholic Church vehemently interfered with her father's long legal battle to satisfy the desire not to be kept alive under such circumstances that Eluana had expressed before the accident. Even though this case involved only suspending feeding (and not proper physician-assisted suicide), doctors were pressed to conscientiously object to the procedure by the Catholic Church and, in fact, many hospitals refused to take Eluana on, thereby turning her father's pain into an ordeal (see McVeigh and McVeigh 2009).

women* applies only to those who are '*systematically* subordinated'[31] because they are marked as women. Only those women who are systematically subordinated as women count as women in the relevant – that is, structural – sense.[32] Although thought-provoking, this reply is not only counterintuitive, as many women who are not systematically subordinated as women are still commonly seen as women.[33] More importantly, this answer misses significant mechanisms whereby the category women* operates. Being categorised as a woman does not necessarily entail being systematically oppressed as such; it means being in a position in which the occurrences of certain unjust constraints and abuses (e.g. rape) are both extremely *more likely to occur* and condition someone's life. In other words, using a Koselleckian terminology, by being recognised as women, persons occupy a particular (i.e. disadvantaged) position within those societal structures that are the conditions of possibility for certain events to happen. One does not have to be systematically subordinated by the sexual division of labour to be a woman in the relevant sense; by merely being recognised as a member of women*, she is placed in a position within the structure of, say, the sexual division of labour that makes it extremely more likely for her to be affected by certain expectations (e.g. becoming a full-time parent) than for someone who is not recognised as a woman. Recognising how someone who is considered as a woman but is not systematically subordinated (or may not even actually experience gender oppression) is still a woman thus is important to fully grasp the complex ways in which the category women* works in women's lives.

The third weakness of Young's account is that, although anti-essentialist in its intentions, it still maintains that women qua women have a *common* social perspective, thereby essentialising them. In feminist theory, essentialism generally refers to 'the view that there are properties essential to women, in that any woman must necessarily have those properties to be a woman at all'.[34] Now, it may be that the seriousness of the charge of essentialism has been exaggerated in feminist theory.[35] It is also likely that, by trying to identify what makes women a group, any definition of women* will inevitably contain some residuals of essentialism. However,

---

[31] Haslanger (2000, 39, my italics).
[32] One different reply may be that although some women do not subjectively feel constrained by gender structures, they are objectively so. Without wanting to deny that socialisation, including a gendered one, works by making persons perceive oppressive structures as non-oppressive, I do not consider this reply because simply labelling women's feelings and opinions as the result of false consciousness or adaptive preferences is controversial from a feminist perspective.
[33] Mikkola (2010, 571).   [34] Stone (2004, 138).
[35] See, e.g., Alcoff (2006, 153); Schor (1994, 42).

such residuals become problematic when (and insofar as) they neglect some important differences among women, which are important to understand their experience and oppression. Indeed, accounts of women* have historically served to mobilise the feminist movement around the concerns and experiences of only certain (privileged) women by supposing that 'the womanness underneath the Black woman's skin is a white woman's, and deep down inside the Latina woman is an Anglo woman waiting to burst through an obscuring cultural shroud'.[36]

To be sure, Young is careful in specifying that an individual woman's identity (i.e. how she defines herself and how she acts) does not necessarily depend on her being serialised as a woman; for example, someone who is a woman and a Catholic may construct her identity only on the basis of her religious faith and therefore express, say, conservative opinions about women's sexual reproductive freedom. However, for Young, in being serialised as a woman, she still has a similar kind of knowledge about the workings of society and similar routine experiences to an atheist woman. In other words, because of their common social perspective, women have a similar outlook on certain (gendered) aspects of society, experience similarly routine (gendered) events, and acquire a particular direct knowledge. However, the idea that it is somehow possible to identify a 'woman part'[37] that all women share is what many feminist critiques of the very concept of women* doubt. This is because it seems that there is no 'golden nugget of womanness' in women that can be separated from the other structural components of women's lives (e.g. race, ability, sexuality).[38] Although acknowledging important differences among women, Young's account still posits a nugget that all members of the series women share – that is, a certain routine experience and local knowledge that women qua women have. This is problematic because it fails to fully take into account how it is because women can have different routine experiences (and different knowledge of the workings of society) that they may react to similar events in a different fashion.

To clarify, consider an episode that became notorious in the context of South Africa Truth Commissions, namely the violence inflicted on Ms Yvonne Khutwane. Ms Khutwane, an anti-apartheid activist from Zwelethemba, was arrested and sexually abused in a police car by two policemen much younger than her. By reading the transcripts of the painful interview with Ms Khutwane, it is clear that the sexual assault she suffered was experienced as humiliating and traumatic not because of

[36] Spelman (1988, 13).   [37] Spelman (1988, 133).   [38] Spelman (1988, 159).

the sexual violation per se. Ms Khutwane felt ashamed, mortified and injured especially because her violators were as young as her children; for someone who was used to living in a context in which respect for the elderly is a fundamental norm, that intrusion was unbearable.[39] It was because Ms Khutwane's routine experiences did not include sexual harassment that she experienced the abuse in that way. In other words, her experience of that traumatic event did not only depend on how she took up her multiple social positions. It was also filtered by her specific knowledge of the workings of society where she lived, a society where those who are both old *and* women are not sexually molested.

Interestingly, during the interview and when the testimony was reported, Ms Khutwane's experience was interpreted (including by feminist scholars) exclusively along gendered lines as one example of the many gendered crimes and violations committed during Apartheid.[40] Ms Khutwane's experience of the abuse was neglected or misread in favour of those interpretative processes that were more familiar to interlocutors and scholars.[41] The discrepancy between Ms Khutwane's feeling of what happened to her inside the police car and the interpretation given by the majority of feminist scholars is probably due to their different knowledges of society. For such scholars, sexual harassment is part of women's routine experience and thus the violations suffered by Ms Khutwane are an obvious case of such nefarious, and yet standard, practices. Conversely, for Ms Khutwane, her shock and humiliation ('As [one policeman] reached for my panty, I became frightened, *not knowing what he was going to do*')[42] was due to the fact that sexual harassment was not a component of her routine experience.[43] According to her knowledge of society, her multiple position as an old woman should have spared her from similar outrages. Obviously, this does not change the gravity of what happened to her. Nevertheless, it does show that persons serialised as women do not necessarily have common routine experiences and knowledge of a society – that is, a similar social perspective. This is because women's outlooks on and knowledge of society, which explain (at least partially) how women react

[39] For the transcription of Ms Khutwane's interview, see the Truth Commission Special Report (1996).
[40] Most notably Minow (1998, 84).
[41] See Ross (2003, 87–93) for a comprehensive analysis of Ms Khutwane's case.
[42] Truth Commission Special Report (1996, my italics).
[43] Conversely, for some women, rape or sexual harassment is such a daily component of their routine experience that they deal with it with resignation or even by carefully preparing for this violence. For instance, many Mexican women migrating to Northern states, knowing they will almost certainly be raped as a price for their border crossing, start using birth control pills when the date of the illegal departure approaches (Martínez, quoted by Falcon 2001, 34).

towards what happens to them, do not depend on gender alone but also on how gender *intersects* with other structures in which women are positioned (e.g. age). Insisting on the existence of a social perspective that women, by being serialised as women, share thus is misleading when we try to understand the injustice women* suffer from and what kind of impact being categorised as a woman has on women's lives.

This is not to say that persons similarly positioned within structures (i.e. serialised as women) cannot share routine experiences and knowledge of how society works. Consciousness-raising groups, in which women gathered together to discuss their experiences, played a crucial role in the development of feminist liberation movements in many countries (especially in the 1960s and 1970s). It was precisely by recognising that they had similar experiences that many women started becoming aware of gendered oppression and being feminists.[44] However, acknowledging that many women have similar routine experiences – that is, a social perspective – is more useful in understanding how feminist groups are created from the series of women than in theorising women as a structural group because it risks missing the complexity of women's social *perspectives*.[45] It leads to an underappreciation of the ways in which 'multiple, co-constituting ... categories are operative and equally salient in constructing ... lived experiences'.[46] As I will show below (§ 5.3), the intersection of different yet mutually constructed structures (e.g. race and gender; gender and age) is also fundamental to theorise the kinds of constraints the category women* places in women's lives.

In sum, although valuable in many respects, Young's account of women* as a series turns out to miss important mechanisms whereby the category women* operates. Does this mean we should reject structural accounts of women*? Such a move would be too rushed and counterproductive as structural accounts provide crucial insights about the group of women – for example, the fact that this group is based on serious and real

[44] In her memoir of the 'feminist revolution', Susan Brownmiller, for example, explains how she turned into a feminist by listening to the similar experience of postpartum depression shared by women in her consciousness-raising group: 'In that one forty-five-minute period I realized that what I'd been blaming myself for ... was a combination of physiological things and a real societal thing, isolation. That realisation was one of those moments that *makes you a feminist forever*' (1990, 152, my italics).

[45] This is not to deny that knowledge is situated and that oppressive positions may produce standpoints from which usually neglected aspects of the social world can be seen (e.g. Code 1993; Collins 2000, 269–90; Haraway 1988). My point simply challenges the idea that we should postulate the existence of a common perspective that all women have qua women in a structural account of women*.

[46] Carastathis (2014, 307).

injustices. To show that we should revise rather than abandon structural conceptions of women*, in the next section I critically analyse the serious problems a non-structural understanding of women* – namely, Alison Stone's idea of 'genealogy' – reveals.

5.2   Women* as a Genealogy

Criticising Young's concept of seriality as essentialist, Stone puts forward an alternative account of women*, which is meant to maintain the importance of such a category. For Stone,

> Women always become women by reworking pre-established cultural interpretations of femininity, so that they become located – together with all other women – within a history of overlapping chains of interpretation.[47]

Stone builds on Judith Butler's and Moira Gatens's suggestion that women* should be an open-ended concept and that we should aim to construct a 'feminist genealogy of the category of women'.[48] However, for Stone the genealogy of the meanings the concept of women* has had over history cannot be drawn without reconstructing first the genealogy of 'women themselves' – that is, of how women's 'experiences and psychologies [have been] shaped in overlapping and historically interconnected ways'.[49] By drawing on Nietzsche's original formulation of genealogy, Stone argues that women* is not only a genealogical history of the concept of femininity but also a genealogical history of how women themselves have become women by taking on and reinterpreting already existing meanings of femininity according to their particular condition. By embarking on this interpretative enterprise, 'each woman becomes located within a historical chain of women, a chain composed of all those who have successively engaged in reinterpreting the meaning of femininity'.[50] For Stone, women*, thus, becomes an intergenerational 'ongoing chain of practice and reinterpretation' in which individual women are 'into complex filiations with one another' over time.[51]

Stone's sophisticated account of women* tries to show how, although women do not have a common attribute – a nugget of womanhood – they still can be said to form a distinctive group on the basis of being located in this entangled genealogical history of 'multiple, overlapping threads of interpretation'.[52] Such an account offers an engaging understanding of

---

[47] Stone (2004, 137).   [48] Butler (1990, 5); quoted in Stone (2004, 136).   [49] Stone (2004, 136).
[50] Stone (2004, 136).   [51] Stone (2004, 136).   [52] Stone (2004, 136).

'subjectivity' – that is, of how women *actively* become women in their embodied and lived experience by reinterpreting what being a woman is (for them). In this respect, Stone's open-ended notion of women* gives everyone who identifies as a woman – that is, participates in the genealogical chain of the meanings of femininity – membership in women*. Thus, for instance, in Stone's account male-to-female transgender persons, who may not be recognised as women by society yet self-identify as such by reworking existing interpretations of femininity, would count as women.

That said, Stone's concept of genealogy cannot be a convincing substitute for Young's account. This is because Stone fails to incorporate one of Young's (and feminist structural theorists') crucial insights about the category women* – that is, that this category is related to the injustices from which women suffer. It may be important to understand how interpretations of femininity change and persist, and how subjects enact them; however, Stone's account does not explain whether (and how) being recognised as a woman may be normatively problematic. Even if we could establish that some meanings of femininity are more controversial than others, which Stone's conception of genealogy does not attempt to do, we would still be left with the question as to why these meanings are *unjust*. For instance, why should we be concerned with unjust interpretations of femininity that conceive of women as merely sexual objects when women themselves (and I agree with Stone on this) do act upon these interpretations and rework them? What is not included in Stone's account and, instead, is central in Young's conception of women as a series are those unjust structural factors that condition persons' lives when they are serialised as women. By being entirely focused on how individual women take on and adjust existing definitions of femininity, Stone's account of women* overlooks how being located in the chain of women* is not only enabling but also profoundly constraining within societies. Moreover, Stone does not theorise how interpretations of femininity are intrinsically related to understandings of masculinity and how this relation is a hierarchical one.

One may object that Stone's conception of a genealogy of women* is a powerful tool for justice for those, such as male-to-female transgender persons, who fight for being considered as women within societies that do not serialise them as such. Through the idea of genealogy, not only are they included in the category they self-identify with but also their contribution to the ongoing chain of the meanings of womanhood can be acknowledged. Be that as it may, Stone's conception of women* is also problematic in these cases as it cannot fully account for the injustice male-to-female transgender persons face. To be sure, not having one's own gendered identity recognised by the surrounding society is a crucial component of that injustice. However, the injustice from which trans* suffer is more complex and cannot be fully comprehended without also providing an account of the constraints they encounter when (1) they are recognised as trans* in a society hostile to that identity or (2) they are serialised as women. I will touch upon (1) in the next section while discussing my account of women*. To see how (2), instead, is the case, consider the opposite example of female-to-male transgender persons and their descriptions of how their conditions have been significantly improved when they started being recognised as men. This is not just because they were given the gendered identity they self-identify with but also because they started being conferred those privileges that are associated with being serialised as men – for example, being more respected in the workplace.[53] To give an account of the acquisition or loss of gender privilege experienced by trans* after transition, one has to focus on those structures that distribute privileges and disadvantages according to membership into gendered groups – which is exactly what Stone's analysis casts aside.

Stone's idea of genealogy is unable to pursue a central aim that Young tries to achieve in conceptualising women as a group, namely the theorisation and normative criticism of what the category of women* does in persons' lives. The history of women is not merely a history of how women have reinterpreted what being a woman means; it is *a history of injustices*. It is by starting from this consideration that I will offer a revised account of Young's concept of women as a structural group, which can overcome the flaws revealed by the notion of series without abandoning its important project.

5.3   Women* as an HSG

As argued in Chapter 4, there is a particular type of structural group – that is, the HSG – which is formed by the unjust interconnection between history and structures. As contended, such groups have been the object of overt and legal discrimination in the past, which is now decried by contemporary societies. Nevertheless, their discrimination, though no longer legal, is newly reproduced through, for instance, informal and subtler means. In other words, for such groups past injustice has become what I defined as HSI.

---

[53] Schilt (2010).

I also argued that to identify HSGs one has to look at collectives that were targets of serious injustices in history, and I identified three possible (but not exhaustive) kinds of past injustices against groups that are bound to lead to HSI: (1) denial of the right to vote and to participate in the body politic; (2) legal exclusion from paid work or relegation to menial occupations; and (3) public recognition of being abnormal or inferior, which legitimised abuses and exclusion or sustained the enforcement of legal discrimination.

When we consider the treatment that women qua women received *within 'Western' societies* over history, it is quite undoubted that they were the object of serious injustices. First, women were denied the right to vote and to political participation (1); for example, the US and the majority of European countries conceded women's suffrage only at the beginning of the twentieth century and some countries, such as Italy and France, enfranchised women only after World War II.[54] Moreover, (white) women were generally denied the right to work or to have paid employment, especially after they got married. Even when allowed (or constrained by force or necessity, as in the case of African American women in the US and working-class women) to enter the labour force, they were confined to servile occupations; for them, access to servile work was a way to enforce legal subordination (2).[55] Usually such legal exclusion and discrimination were justified through philosophical, moral and pseudo-scientific arguments concerning women's allegedly inferior nature (3); women were typically depicted as infantile, unsophisticated and naïve subjects who were not suited for political and intellectual life and who instead should have been 'protected' from it. When not described as silly or candid 'angels of the heart', women were represented as demoniacal creatures apt to deceive men and lead them astray.[56] In both cases, women were deemed to be too irrational, childish and passionate compared to the (male and white) rational norm.

Today, (at least so-called liberal and democratic) societies have rejected their dark history by, for example, adopting anti-discriminatory laws and endorsing equality of opportunity as a value. However, women seem to suffer from many constraints by virtue of their membership in women* and many significant dimensions of inequality between women* and men endure within these societies, as we will see in Chapter 6. Importantly, the

---

[54] Notably, some countries in Europe, such as Switzerland and Liechtenstein, granted women's suffrage only in very recent times (i.e. in 1971 and 1984, respectively).

[55] On the case of the domestic sphere and African American women in the US, see § 6.3.

[56] For a seminal analysis of women in Western political thought, see Okin (1979).

specification of the historical injustices from which women suffered over history differs according to the context and the particular position of women within other historical structures that regulated societies (e.g. race). Similarly, the specific ways inequalities between women* and 'men' persist vary across countries and within societies. What I want to highlight here is simply that women* names a collective against which many injustices were committed over history and that is still put into a position of disadvantage vis-à-vis 'men'; thus, women* can be regarded as an HSG. Specifically as an HSG, women* can be defined as

> a particular category that is rooted in *past* legally enforced discrimination and exclusion, and whereby society still groups persons so as to differently distribute *expectations, norms and social roles*.[57] *By being recognised* as women, persons are located into a particular position of disadvantage within certain societal structures and in relation to 'men', who, instead, are located in a position of advantage. In virtue of being structurally positioned as women, persons can *potentially* encounter a set of constraints, expectations, stereotypes and abuses which in a specific context is associated with the position women*.

Therefore, X is a woman if she is recognised as a member of the HSG 'women'. By being externally recognised as a woman and being categorised as such, X is likely to encounter or to have previously encountered a set of constraints associated with her ascriptive membership in women*. Importantly, the set of constraints that women* and specific women can potentially encounter in a determinate society depend on both the particular structures that regulate that society and how these structures have historically intersected with each other. In other words, the specification of the structures that constrain women's actions varies between and within societies.

Let me now spell out the characteristics of the conception of women* as an HSG and, in so doing, show how it may be an improvement over Young's account. As argued, Young's account reveals three flaws: (1) it assumes that all women are constrained by the structures that serialise persons into women, which may lead to include in women* only those who are systematically subordinated as such; (2) it pre-identifies those structures that serialise persons as women (i.e. enforced heterosexuality and the sexual

---

[57] Here I use the term 'society' broadly – i.e. including not only public (e.g. political, social and economic) institutions but also the family and the intrinsic interplay of the 'public' and the 'private'. For instance, the interaction between medical institutions and the family is fundamental to understanding how it is that many persons are recognised not merely as female but as women for the first time (Karraker, Vogel and Lake 1995).

division of labour), thereby neglecting structures that, in a specific context, are crucial to understand the constraints women* face; and (3) it maintains that women have a common social perspective, thereby overlooking important differences in women's experiences.

According to the account of women* as an HSG, for a person to be a member of women*, it is not necessary that she be systematically subordinated as a woman and thereby regularly experiencing the set of constraints associated with being a woman. Nor is it necessary that she has been *actually* subordinated as a woman or that she is experiencing some of the constraints linked to women*. Conversely, it is sufficient that, by *being recognised* and categorised as a woman, she can *potentially* experience some (or all) of these constraints.[58] This shift from the systematic subordination and actual experience of constraints associated with the category of women to the potentiality for such a subordination and experience does not imply that the ascriptive membership in women* is less limiting. Indeed, comprehending one's likelihood to experience a determinate set of constraints, which are connected with one's own known or discovered ascriptive position, may be as conditioning as having to actually face them. For example, knowing that, as a result of her membership in women*, she is likely to become a mother and shoulder the burden of domestic work, one person may be tempted to renounce a brilliant full-time career, independently of the fact that these prospects are already (or will be) a reality.

Focusing on the potentiality of being constrained and subordinated, rather than on the actuality of subordination, is crucial not only because it allows one to include in women* even those persons who are not (or do not feel) oppressed as women and yet are recognised as such, thereby avoiding counter-intuitive implications. Most importantly, it explains how the category women* operates in persons' lives: it is *the very external recognition of someone as a woman* that places her into a disadvantaged position within societal structures which distribute benefits and burdens (e.g. the division of domestic labour) and are the condition of possibility for certain wrongs to systematically happen (e.g. rape). It is in this sense that all women (i.e. all those who are recognised as women) suffer from the injustice of women*, although for some of them the actualisation of the set of constraints associated with that category may not systematically occur.

---

[58] Note that my argument about the conditions under which someone can be said to be a member of the HSG of women is consistent with the claim made in Chapter 4 about HSGs being groups that have systematically suffered from injustice over history. The fact that injustices have systematically been committed to a group does not entail that individual members must systematically experience subordination because of their group membership to be considered its members.

The stress on external recognition as a ground for membership in women* may seem problematic as it excludes from the account those women who self-identify as women but are not recognised as such by society. Two observations are in order. First, my account does not aim to be the only conception of women* that feminist theory and practice should endorse. It simply wants to capture a specific yet important form of injustice that women, as an HSG, suffer from – that is, HSI of women*. It may well be that feminism should also deploy (at least in certain contexts and for certain political purposes) an additional concept of women as a 'lived identity', which would fully respect persons' self-identifications.[59] Second, without factoring in the role that external recognition plays in structuring women*, one 'pervasive threat in the daily lives of trans people' would remain unexplained: what Talia Mae Bettcher defines as 'reality enforcement'.[60] 'Reality enforcement' occurs when someone who has presented herself as, say, a woman is not seen as such (or is 'discovered' not to have, or to have not always had, female genitalia).[61] Needless to say, this has traumatic and often fatal consequences for trans*, especially when those enforcing reality transphobically feel themselves to have been 'deceived' as in the infamous murders of Gwen Araujo and Angie Zapata. Now, it is precisely because external recognition prevails over self-identification in determining membership in women* that reality enforcement can take place. As seen (§ 4.1), those enforcing reality are (unjustly) those who have the authority (in that determinate context and moment) to recognise a transgender woman as a woman.

Another important feature of the account of women* as an HSG is that it avoids identifying in advance those structures that can constrain women as women*. It remains deliberately vague on these structures and the substantive content of the set of constraints created by them, leaving to a contextual analysis the task of identifying what these structures and such content exactly amount to. To be sure, this account does not neglect the importance of structures of enforced heterosexuality and sexual division of labour in understanding the injustice of women*. However, it does not regard them as the only structures that universally determine the condition of women*. This is not only because, as Young acknowledges, the meaning of these structures changes cross-culturally but also because it may be that, within certain societies (e.g. Italy), those who are recognised as women encounter further constraints as women (e.g. having to resort to a clandestine abortion even though they have a right to abortion) by

---

[59] Jenkins (2016).   [60] Bettcher (2014, 392–93)   [61] Bettcher (2014, 392–97).

being positioned within structures that can be irreducible to enforced heterosexuality or the sexual division of labour (e.g. the influence of the Catholic Church over the respectability of doctors). In other words, while maintaining that the injustice of women* is structural because it is produced by both domestic and transnational structures, the account of women* as an HSG remains open to how those structures within which women are positioned are historically reproduced and thus it abstains from singling out universal structural sources of women's subordination.[62]

Moreover, unlike Young's, this account remains silent on the social perspectives, routine experiences and knowledge of societies that persons recognised as women are supposed to share in virtue of their structural position as women, thereby avoiding to neglect important differences among women's experiences. Assumptions about (or even reference to) these aspects are not necessary to understand how women* is formed and affects women's lives. What matters is that societies categorise persons as women and this categorisation puts the recognised subjects in the position of being likely to encounter a set of constraints associated with this categorisation itself.

One may wonder how exactly the process of recognising someone as a woman takes place and whether that process always somehow entails identifying common features that all women share. For instance, drawing on Wittgenstein's notion of family resemblances, Natalie Stoljar conceptualises women* as a 'cluster concept' in that it is formed by a cluster of various (e.g. bodily, emotional, behavioural) features. Thus, for a person to be recognised as a member of women*, she must display only enough of these features.[63] Stoljar offers a plausible way of describing how societies and individuals within societies identify certain persons as women. However, the account of women* as an HSG places what happens after the (external) recognition at the forefront. What should be a concern for justice is that, whenever and however the process of recognition has taken place, the person recognised as a member of women* can potentially encounter the set of constraints that are socially associated with this historical-structural membership.

By avoiding both presuming a common social perspective among women and pre-identifying the structures in which women are located as women, this account can recognise how not only women's routine

---

[62] On the importance of not identifying a single source of women's subordination, see also Yuval-Davis (1997, 6).

[63] Stoljar (1995, 282).

experiences but also the *constraints* on women's actions stem from the *intersection* of the different yet interconnected structures in which women are positioned. In particular, according to such an account, to analyse the potential set of constraints that persons who are recognised as women are likely to encounter by being included in the HSG of women, we need to consider the ways whereby the structures in which they are positioned have been *historically* constituted in a *mutual* fashion.

To illustrate this point, let me give some examples of the unjust constraints that those structurally positioned as African American women are bound to face in the US. Since the introduction and enforcement of mandatory-arrest policies in cases of domestic violence in the US in order to promote a more aggressive response to domestic violence complaints, African American women have become vulnerable to unjust constraints that white women are significantly less likely to encounter. These policies are generally detrimental because they increase the risk of an escalation of violence (and even death) for victims of domestic abuses; however, in the case of African American women, they also allow for the real possibility of being arrested. This is mainly because police officers interpret self-defence behaviour 'through the lens of stereotypes [of African American women] as overly aggressive'.[64]

Similarly, compared to white girls, African American girls tend to be more harshly punished by teachers at school and get suspended more often because they are perceived as overly talkative, aggressive and assertive. In other words, they are stereotypically seen as not being able to comply with norms of (white) femininity (e.g. submission and passivity), which is precisely how African American women have been historically depicted.[65] Being suspended at school may have dire consequences, such as dropping out and subsequently being unemployed or finding only low-paying occupations. Finally, quitting education puts young persons in a position in which they are more likely to be involved in criminal activities (i.e. the so-called school-to-prison pipeline).

When facing an abuse that even white women are likely to suffer from, such as rape, African American women are likely to deal with other specific constraints on their actions. These constraints stem from the ways racial and gender structures have historically intersected in the US. For example, when the rapist is recognised as black, women may face pressure from their black communities that, in the name of internal loyalty or to avoid strengthening racist stereotypes about

---

[64] Crenshaw (2012, 1455).   [65] Blake et al. (2011) and Crenshaw, Ocen and Nanda (2015).

black men's sexuality, can compel them not to report the crime.[66] Or, as for a white rapist, they are potentially vulnerable to the historically rooted stereotyping (on the part of police officers) of black women as inherently sexualised and immoral, which undermines their credibility as victims of violence.[67]

These few examples show how to understand the kinds of constraints that those who are recognised as African American women are likely to face. We need to look not only to the structures of both race and gender but also to the *history* of the intersection of these structures. Particularly, rather than simply adding race to the gendered structures constraining African American women's actions, we have to consider how these structures have historically been mutually constitutive in (re-)producing in the US those background conditions within which persons interact with one another.[68]

It is important to highlight how the improvements on Young's concept of series which I have carried out are made possible by bringing the *unjust history* of women to the forefront. By defining women* as an HSG, we can point to the interplay between past overt discrimination and contemporary categorisation as fundamental to understand the unjust set of constraints that those who are recognised as women are likely to encounter. This means being more sensitive to the different ways whereby this unjust history has developed and remains present. One may object that an account of women* as an HSG seems to presume that formal oppression against women is universally a thing of the past, thereby neglecting how in many countries those who are recognised as women are still subjected to overt legal discrimination and exclusion. My account does not want to overlook this significant point; however, it is explicitly constructed to conceptualise the HSI of women* – that is, how in societies formally committed to women's rights and equality, women's history of legal discriminations and exclusions is still newly reproduced in different

---

[66] The persisting myth of the black rapist (of white women) is one of the paradigmatic 'controlling images' of African American men's sexuality, one which has been central in the development of unequal interracial relations in the US (e.g. Davis 1983, chapter 11).

[67] Crenshaw (1991, 1271).

[68] This is why theorists of intersectionality emphasise that the intersection of structures cannot be conceived in additive terms, because it is simultaneous (Carastathis 2014, 306; Cho, Crenshaw and McCall 2013, 787). The intersection of structures does not result in what Jonathan Wolff and Avner De-Shalit define as a 'cluster of disadvantage', i.e. a situation in which persons are disadvantaged in different respects (e.g. race and gender) (Wolff and De-Shalit 2007). It creates a set of constraints that can be comprehended only when the ways the structures have been developed historically together are revealed.

ways.[69] In this respect, the deliberative specificity of the conception of women* as an HSG aims to capture a widespread (yet not universal) type of injustice.

It is now time to examine such an HSI by concentrating on some of its dimensions and analysing how they can be fully theorised (and subsequently tackled) when the structural reproduction of unjust history is revealed.

---

[69] This is not to suggest that the condition of women* in societies that banned legal discrimination is not qualitatively different from how women are treated in contexts in which discrimination is still formally endorsed.

CHAPTER 6

Women and the Reproduction of Unjust History in Egalitarian Contexts

In Chapter 5, I argued that women should be regarded as a historical-structural group (HSG). What does this tell us about the condition of women within liberal democracies? In this chapter, I examine how the framework of historical-structural injustice (HSI) developed in Chapter 3 can (1) show how the unjust history of women is reproduced in formally egalitarian societies (e.g. Nordic countries) and (2) cast light on some enduring dimensions of gender inequality within egalitarian societies – namely violence, occupational segregation and the division of domestic labour.

Two preliminary observations are needed. First, the aspects I focus on in this chapter should be considered as neither encompassing all the dimensions of gender inequality nor exhaustive of how history is reproduced in the condition of women within egalitarian contexts. Nevertheless, such aspects are at least indicative of how the unjust past suffered by the HSG of women is structurally reproduced within societies that endorse equality of opportunity and adopt anti-discrimination legislations. Second, this chapter makes some generalisations about the unjust history of women and their present condition within egalitarian societies. This may seem inconsistent with many arguments offered in the book and the very framework of HSI developed here, which underline the significance of context, the specificity of histories and the importance of examining how structures (e.g. of gender and race) have historically intersected. The inevitable generalisations made here do not undermine the core of my theory of historical injustice or the claim that a contextual and intersectional analysis is a crucial aspect of a historical and structural approach to injustice. Particularly, they do not endorse 'colour-blind intersectionality'[1] – that is, carrying out an analysis that takes being privileged along certain dimensions (e.g. race) as a default assumption. These generalisations, which are

[1] Carbado (2013).

partly due to length constraints, instead aim to show how the structural reproduction of the unjust history affects all women, although in importantly different ways.

Why is unravelling the reproduction of unjust history important to theorise gender inequality? As for violence against women, this chapter aims to show that that radical injustice is sustained by what I described as the banal presence of unjust history, which refers to those daily scripts made up by, for example, stereotypes, expectations and norms whereby persons interact (§ 3.2). Moreover, I argue that considering unjust history and its reproduction explains why, even in a strongly egalitarian context, gendered occupational segregation and gendered division of domestic labour would still be normatively troubling. This is because the difference they create is bound to reinforce those stereotypes, expectations and norms that constitute important dimensions of the banal presence of unjust history. Certain different outcomes between women and men would still be worrying, even if women were not materially worse off than men, because of the systematic history of group-based inequality and the ways such a history is reproduced into the fabric of egalitarian societies.

6.1 Violence

Violence against women (VAW) is recognised as a form of discrimination and a violation of human rights that causes serious domestic and international concerns about public health. According to the World Health Organisation, about 35 per cent of women worldwide have experienced intimate-partner violence or non-partner sexual violence.[2]

Hardly anyone would claim that VAW should not be considered as a particularly serious problem, even in formally egalitarian societies. Nevertheless, understanding what lies at the root of this problem is not straightforward. In this section, I explain the advantages that approaching VAW from within a paradigm of HSI may have both generally and particularly for some of its specific forms within liberal democracies.

Before proceeding, let me justify the specific definitions of women and violence this section endorses. Following the account of women provided in Chapter 5, VAW should be considered as violence against those persons who have been recognised as members of the HSG of women, independently of what we think a woman is (or should be).

[2] Garcia-Moreno et al. (2013, 2). For some country-based prevalence data, see UN Women (2013).

Regarding the problem of defining 'violence' per se, in this section I endorse the definition of VAW provided in the Protocol on the Rights of Women in Africa (PRWA), according to which VAW encompasses

> all acts perpetrated against women which cause or could cause them physical, sexual, psychological, and economic harm, *including the threat to take such acts*; or to undertake the imposition of arbitrary restrictions on or deprivation of fundamental freedoms in private or public life in peace time and during situations of armed conflicts or of war.[3]

This definition has at least three advantages. First, instead of equating women with gender, it addresses the problem of VAW as one affecting 'women' – that is, a particular gendered HSG. Second, by considering threats as a form of violence, it seems well suited to capture the dimension of potentiality that is characteristic of what it means to be recognised as a woman (§ 5.3). Third, the definition provided by PRWA includes acts (or threats to perform acts) that are not generally identified as forms of violence, namely acts pertaining to the economic sphere. Violence has an economic dimension not only because it affects women's employment opportunities[4] but also in that it assumes economic and financial forms, from economic deprivation (e.g. refusal to provide necessary food and medicines) to unequal access and control of household resources. Therefore, this definition can show how many abuses in the private sphere relate to patterns of historical-structural inequality between HSGs within societies at large, a point to which I now turn.

There is a widespread conviction that formal equality between men and women would translate into a decrease in violence. The story of progress suggests that once discrimination is outlawed and equality of opportunity is legally endorsed, violence should be on the verge of extinction. However, it suffices to glance at the rates of VAW in liberal democracies to see that this is not the case. The prevalence of intimate-partner violence (IPV) is particularly striking. In the US, twenty-two million women have been raped in their lifetime, and 63.84 per cent of women who have reported being raped, physically assaulted or stalked since age eighteen have been victimised by a former or current husband, cohabiting partner, boyfriend or date.[5] In these contexts, it is tempting to conceive of VAW as a temporary backlash against the achieved progress and to believe thus that liberal democracies have come to terms with their past but that some

---

[3] PRWA, Article 1(j) (my italics).   [4] Secretary-General UN Women (2006, iii).
[5] Black et al. (2011).

individuals cannot accept it.[6] Following this narrative, it is only a matter of time before formal equality translates into freedom from violence; no particular course of action, besides enforcing existing laws, is necessary. This is a simplistic understanding of the relation between history and (in) justice which does not consider how unjust history structures the present. By examining the dynamics of IPV within liberal democracies, it becomes clear that violence not only systematically contributes to the endurance of the historical injustice against women but also is significantly interconnected with the more banal forms of its reproduction.[7]

Within liberal democracies, IPV is largely characterised by 'an ongoing ... pattern of coercive and controlling behaviour that causes a range of harms in addition to injury'.[8] Physical violence is complemented by such a continuous and subtle strategy of monitoring the daily aspects of women's lives that by the time violence escalates into assaults, battering and sexual abuse, women have already been seriously harmed.[9] Within liberal democracies, what makes IPV a dimension of the HSI women suffer are (1) its particular *forms* and (2) the *conditions for its very possibility* as a strategy for men to dominate known women.

IPV operates through a capillary regulation of 'everyday behaviours associated with stereotypic female roles'.[10] For example, by continuously controlling women's income, taking all the important financial decisions and persuading women to quit their work to devote themselves to the household, men re-establish an unequal division of roles that was previously enforced by discriminatory laws. By evaluating activities women are expected to undertake daily – such as cooking, cleaning, ironing and child care – and measuring women's value on the basis of their performance in these routine and underrated tasks, men 'keep ... women in their "proper place"'[11] – that is, where they have been legally confined to over history. The particular forms IPV takes within liberal democracies are closely connected with those inferior roles to which women in the past were unjustly assigned through lawful exclusion from citizenship, property and 'meaningful' work, and through the moral, religious and scientific justification thereof. IPV becomes a means to reproduce unjust social

---

[6] Taylor and Jasinski (2011, 346).
[7] By building on CEDAW (Article 5), Serena Parekh (2011) also points to the link between VAW and structural inequalities. Nevertheless, her analysis focuses on how governments should be held responsible for the structural injustice underlying VAW, rather than exploring in what sense VAW is indicative of the structural reproduction of unjust history.
[8] Stark (2007, 100). See also Johnson (2008, 25–29).   [9] Stark (2007, 218).   [10] Stark (2007, 5).
[11] Hattery (2007, 3).

processes that started in the past but are no longer legally enforced; in this sense, it contributes to new reproduction of the HSI of women.

On one hand, IPV as a daily microregulation of women's lives according to predetermined female roles is possible insofar as equality before the law is endorsed.[12] If discrimination on the basis of membership in the HSG of women was ratified and enforced by law, there would be no need for such a capillary control. Obviously, this is not to say that within formally sexist societies IPV is not present.[13] Nevertheless, *the particular forms* IPV takes within liberal democracies would be less attractive because women's subordination in the private realm would already be sanctioned de jure – for example, by legal exclusion from citizenship and the labour force. When discrimination of one group to the advantage of another is formally recognised as an injustice, subtler means are devised to reproduce historical injustices de facto.

On the other hand, IPV as a form of continuous coercive control is effective *because* unjust history is structurally reproduced within societies at large. As Evan Stark notes, IPV 'proceeds by exploiting and targeting persistent inequalities'[14] between the HSG of women and that of men. The more apparently banal forms of women's HSI, which, as previously argued in general terms, constitute important elements of the scripts whereby persons interact with each other (§ 3.2), provide IPV with the background conditions for being operative. Within liberal democracies, it seems IPV largely targets roles that those who are recognised as women are expected to perform in virtue of their historical-structural membership – for example, being attentive and capable ladies of the house. IPV, in the particular form of coercive control, deploys stereotypes, expectations and habits that are bound up with unjust history as a source of inspiration, thereby reproducing it. It also becomes a sign that history is still structurally present. In other words, it is possible to recur to violence as a micromanagement of women's traditional roles because certain expectations and norms still affect persons' lives by, for example, establishing the criteria whereby women's value should be assessed. It is because the expectation that women (and not men) would be able to prepare at least a decent meal

[12] Stark (2007, 194).

[13] Nor is this to suggest that IPV did not exist in the past when discrimination against women was sanctioned by law as, for instance, the works and life of Mary Wollstonecraft show. Here, I only point out that the *role* IPV plays in contemporary liberal democracies and its *forms* can be understood only if the dynamics between history and structure are considered.

[14] Stark (2009, 1514).

and take care of their house is still deep rooted within societies that women can be humiliated and denigrated for not cooking well or not living up to the standards of cleanliness that have been set (by society, partners, family members and women themselves).

To see this, consider the following counterfactual: Would it make sense, within our societies, to mortify and demean a man by criticising his way of baking a cake or doing the washing? Would it be effective to deploy a man's performance in household chores or his caring skills as a criterion for his own value? Would it make sense to emotionally and psychologically control a man's life by capillary monitoring and assessing his activities as a homemaker? Arguably, these strategies would be largely ineffective. This is because, within liberal democracies, IPV as a coercive micromanagement of *women's* lives builds precisely on these taken-for-granted aspects of the historical injustices towards women that continue to structure societies. The banal presence of history makes the radical reproduction of historical injustice also possible within those societies that have seemingly come to terms with their unjust past.

The problem of IPV (and, more generally, VAW) in Nordic countries well exemplifies the importance of framing violence in liberal democracies as a dimension of the HSI of women. Nordic countries usually stand out in international appraisals of the condition of women worldwide.[15] In particular, the almost equal political representation of women and the gender-friendly parental-leave policies are taken as indicators of the outstanding level of gender equality displayed by such countries. Therefore, focusing on Nordic countries will point out most forcefully the historical-structural character of VAW, which is rooted in forms of injustice that seem to be long gone.

Within Nordic countries, the undoubted improvement of women's condition has not resulted in a significant reduction of the level of VAW, and particularly of IPV. A recent survey carried out by the European Union Agency for Fundamental Rights determined that Nordic countries present the highest rates of women who have experienced violence since the age of fifteen (e.g. 52 per cent in Denmark, 47 per cent in Finland, 46 per cent in Sweden), in large part inflicted by current or former partners.[16] Thus, although some of these countries were among the first in the world to ratify the UN Convention on the Elimination of all Forms of Discrimination against Women (e.g. ratified in Sweden in 1980 and enforced in 1983) and have arguably implemented an advanced legislation on VAW and

---

[15] Hausmann et al. (2017, 10).   [16] European Agency for Fundamental Rights (2014, 28).

protection of women's integrity (e.g. the Kvinnofrid law),[17] VAW and IPV are still prevalent.[18]

The significant rates of VAW within Nordic countries thus show that although pursuing an equal-opportunity agenda is necessary, it is not sufficient for overcoming one of the radical forms of the HSI of women.[19] As already noticed, it is important to recognise that, within liberal democracies, VAW in its specific forms may (unconsciously or not) represent a means to reproduce unjust history while also acknowledging that this strategy is possible because other unjust structural dimensions persist. In other words, the more banal ways societies and interpersonal relations are still informally organised through roles, expectations and attitudes that are bound up with unjust history make violence, in its specific forms, a rational and viable device. The narrative of progress is ill suited to fully capture the banal radicality of the reproduction of unjust history. By focusing mainly on the achievements and conceiving of the past as a legacy that will be overcome in the near future, a progressive conception of history fails to grasp the more structural relation between (unjust) history and justice. In the case of Nordic countries, such a narrative is particularly powerful as it maintains their worldwide supremacy in terms of gender equality.[20] The international image of Nordic countries as having successfully come to terms with their unjust past makes it more difficult to accept and deal with the complexity of the endurance of VAW.

The narrative of progress has far-reaching implications for the way the problem of VAW is framed within Nordic countries in at least two respects. First, these countries tend to adopt a neutral framework to approach the problem by describing violence as 'an interactional problem between two equally situated parties'[21] or an issue within low-income and socially impoverished families.[22] By treating the problem as mainly due to particular individuals or particularly harsh situations, this approach avoids

---

[17] Amnesty International (2010).
[18] The gap in VAW rates between Nordic countries and other European countries (e.g. Poland) results also from the fact that the former has a higher proportion of reported cases than the latter. However, barriers to disclosure to relevant authorities also persist in Nordic countries; in Iceland, for example, 77 per cent of episodes and patterns of violence remain unreported (Iceland Ministry of Welfare 2012, 11). Moreover, the pervasiveness of VAW and IPV in such countries would remain quite striking even if the sum of the reported and unreported cases turned out to reduce the gap between Nordic and other European countries.
[19] Amnesty International (2010, 3); Sørensen (2001, 840); Eriksson and Pringle (2005, 1); Ertürk (2006, 6).
[20] Enander (2010, 21).   [21] Keskinen (2005, 32). On Finland, see Hearn and McKie (2010).
[22] Elman (2001, 50).

calling into question the historical-structural roots of violence that persist within society at large. In this way, the prevalence of VAW can be reconciled with the belief that an unjust history of women's legal subordination to men's protection and their exclusion from the body politic, the labour market and the holding of property has been superseded by the present commitment to anti-discrimination and egalitarianism.[23]

Second, and relatedly, the narrative of progress offers a misleading picture of the typical profile of those women who suffer from IPV and of their perpetrators; while women (especially mothers) who remain in abusive relationships are depicted as feeble, already socially deprived and having had a violent childhood, male perpetrators are imagined as deviant, addicted to alcohol or drugs, immigrants, unemployed and mentally ill.[24] These beliefs remain widely held within Nordic countries, notwithstanding the fact that the data indicate that they are very much mistaken.[25] Besides offering a misguided account of the problem, this narrative has serious effects on those who are perceived as the exception to an otherwise realised progress. In particular, since women who suffer from violence are assumed to live in a society that has successfully empowered them by providing opportunities and exit options, victims of IPV tend to regard their situation as a personal failure.[26] This situation resonates with what generally happens within liberal democracies to many high-income or well-educated women who have difficulties with disclosing their experiences with IPV because they perceive it as particularly shameful.[27] This is because the dominant narrative tends to focus on material resources and formal opportunities as being sufficient to overcome IPV. Therefore, when individual women have these means, the only explanation they find available to understand their situation is in terms of their own weakness, which is a source of personal humiliation. What remains hidden is that, as argued in Chapter 3, stereotypes, expectations and norms bound up with historical injustices still regulate social and interpersonal relations between HSGs and also that these historical-structural processes are profoundly interconnected with the prevalence of IPV (and VAW in general), as seen above. In Nordic countries, this neglect is reinforced by the prevailing view that

---

[23] For example, in Sweden, women's suffrage was obtained only in 1921, and until 1920, families were organised around a patriarchal model that gave fathers exclusive custodial rights to children (Nordborg 2005, 111).

[24] Elman (2001, 50); Gottzén (2013, 207).   [25] On Sweden, see Lundgren et al. (2002, 74).

[26] Enander (2010, 21). I use the term 'victim' here to stress how this 'progressive' narrative undermines women's opportunities to become 'survivors'.

[27] Weitzman (2000).

these societies have substantially achieved gender justice and the fact that this attainment is a source of national pride and international esteem.

Likewise, the narrative of progress has an impact on the perception and self-understanding of abusive men. By explaining their behaviour as episodic, random and due to individual pathologies, stress or economic disadvantage, perpetrators fail to conceive of their violence against their partner as a systematic control that is grounded in the reproduced injustice women suffer from. Moreover, when VAW is described as exceptional and committed by others, men who do not resort to violence avoid questioning whether their own stereotypical assumptions, expectations and actions contribute, in a more banal way, to the HSI of women, of which violence is a radical manifestation.[28] Therefore, the story of progress makes the banal radicality of the reproduction of unjust history more difficult to unravel at both a societal and (inter)personal level, thereby sustaining HSI.

The account of HSI developed in Chapter 3, which focuses on the new reproduction of (unjust) history within the different structures of societies, instead offers a theoretical and normative framework to understand VAW in three respects. First, it provides a conception of (historical) injustice that resonates with the explanation of VAW given by international treaties and activists. VAW is conceived as being grounded in 'historical and structural inequality in power relations between women and men, and [seen as persisting] in every country in the world'.[29] HSI conceptualises this inequality by arguing that the injustice suffered by the HSG of women is due to unjust social-structural processes that started in the past and, although they may appear superseded, are still reproduced and deeply affect persons' lives in relation to their ascriptive membership. Without understanding how the injustice women have suffered over history through legally enforced mechanisms of exclusion and discrimination is reproduced, VAW may seem a random and individualised phenomenon. Conversely, persons who are recognised as women can potentially encounter violence because of the HSI of women. VAW is both a means by which HSI is perpetuated and a consequence thereof.[30] Thus HSI offers a framework to understand why VAW has not been eradicated in egalitarian contexts, such as in Nordic countries.

The utmost importance of generally conceptualising VAW as interconnected to the HSI of women does not mean violence takes the same shape worldwide. Indeed, context-based analyses are crucial to understand the

---

[28] Gottzén (2013).   [29] CSW, Article 10.   [30] Secretary-General UN Women (2006, 29).

prevalence and the forms of violence within determinate societies.[31] In this regard, by highlighting the role of history in (certain) structural injustices, the framework of HSI is sensitive to the specific ways women have been excluded and discriminated against within particular contexts over time. Contextual analyses of the different histories of injustice characterising women within different societies are needed not only to identify the prevalence and the specific forms of VAW but also to grasp how such violence is publicly framed, justified, condoned or explained and how agencies and individuals react to it.[32] Although the significance of context is often recognised when culture-based forms of violence (e.g. dowry-related violence; female infanticide; female genital mutilation and cutting; 'honour killings'; forced marriage) are considered, it would be misleading to regard the structural relation between history and (in)justice as something that concerns only certain cultures. This is because, as showed above, that relation is crucial to understand the forms violence widely takes in liberal democracies (and in majority groups within them).

Second, HSI casts light on particular aspects of VAW by offering a new understanding of some of its dimensions. For instance, VAW is considered as affecting women across their life cycle and, more precisely, even 'before [their] birth'.[33] This is usually meant to identify particular forms of violence girls suffer from before they come into the world, such as prenatal sex selection, alongside those that they experience during childhood (e.g. female infanticide, sexual abuse and early marriage).[34] Nevertheless, from within the framework of HSI, the fact that women are affected by violence even before their birth assumes a different, and more general, meaning, which can hold even in those contexts in which practices such as sex-selective abortions are rarely performed. Indeed, as seen, members of HSGs should be considered as structural descendants because they inherit a social (and transnational) position originally constituted through legal discrimination and reproduced by informal (both banal and radical) means (§ 4.2). In this sense, violence affects women even before they are born in that it is part of the historical-structural position of women, which is occupied by different persons over time and inherited by them when they are recognised as members of such an HSG. So reconceived, VAW is thus an issue of intergenerational (structural) injustice.

---

[31] For example, the Beijing Declaration and Platform for Action, adopted by 189 countries at the Fourth World Conference on Women in Beijing in 1995, called for more contextual analyses of VAW.

[32] Dobash and Dobash (1998, 9).   [33] Secretary-General UN Women (2006, 42).

[34] Secretary-General UN Women (2006, 45).

Third, by endorsing the framework of HSI, it is possible to reply to a challenging objection directed to gender-based accounts of VAW. According to this objection, establishing whether the rationale behind individual cases of male-on-female violence is discrimination against someone as a woman is not a straightforward task. For example, personal motives may appear as the main causes of an eruption of violence against an individual that happens to be a woman. This objection tends to neglect how personal motives – such as jealousy, stress, unemployment and addiction – which are often used to explain violence at an individual level, are likely to hide structural factors. This does not mean all episodes of violence experienced by women are grounded on their historical-structural membership. However, as already noticed, we must be aware of widespread beliefs about the occurrence of violence and the background of victims and perpetrators in that such beliefs not only turn out to be dangerous myths once data are examined closely but also provide misleading rationales for violence.

Another version of the objection against gender-based accounts of VAW suggests that violence may stem from other forms of prejudice, such as racial, class and ethnical intolerance.[35] As Jasminka Kalajdzic contends, the emphasis on discrimination against women as the underlying cause of, for example, sexual violence 'can obscure other characteristics of a woman's identity that determine which women are raped ... Sexism and racism, therefore, operate in conjunction'.[36] This is an important objection to which two replies can be made. The fact that the target of violence is, in any case, persons who are recognised as women confirms that violence becomes a means to perpetuate historical injustices, even within liberal democracies. When the systematic historical injustices suffered by indigenous peoples in the US and Canada are considered, it is not surprising that indigenous women are, respectively, 2.5 and 3.5 times more likely to experience violence than women who are not indigenous.[37]

Moreover, and relatedly, as argued, the framework of HSI is not only able to incorporate the insight that those who are recognised as members of many disadvantaged HSGs (or historical groups with structural dynamics; see § 4.4) are in a particularly precarious condition. Most importantly, it can also show how the particular set of constraints these persons potentially face and the specific forms of violence they are likely to encounter are

---

[35] Edwards (2010, 21).   [36] Kalajdzic (1996, 477–78).
[37] Native Women's Association of Canada (2011, 3); Amnesty International USA (2007, 2). These already striking ratios are likely higher because of the large number of unreported cases and the governments' reluctance to seriously investigate violence against indigenous women.

linked to the history of the intersection between the different structural groups to which they belong and the history of the relations between such groups and those that have been historically constituted as in a position of advantage vis-à-vis them (i.e. non-indigenous persons and men) (§ 5.3). In the US and Canada, indigenous women experience particularly cruel forms of violence, such as femicide, sexual violence and torture, quite often from non-indigenous men. By focusing on history, it is possible to see the connection between the specific forms of violence indigenous women can encounter today and the injustices they legally suffered over history: from the use of sexual violence as a tool of conquest and colonisation by settlers (e.g. during the Trail of Tears and the Long Walk)[38] to late twentieth-century forced sterilisation.[39] In this sense, these specific forms of violence can be interpreted as means whereby unjust social-structural processes that started in the past and are no longer legally enforced can be newly reproduced. Furthermore, even in the case of indigenous women, that violence is enabled by the fact that *that* unjust history structures societies, from the complex ways in which the jurisdiction over tribal peoples undermines survivors' access to justice and perpetrators' accountability[40] to even more banal mechanisms such as women's 'historical [strained] relations with federal and state government agencies'[41] and historical stereotypes such as the already discussed binary 'princess/squaw' (§ 3.1).

To wit, approaching VAW from within the paradigm of HSI is crucial because by focusing on history and its structural reproduction, we can understand how VAW operates within determinate societies and the forms of violence women experience. As for indigenous women, the cruelty of the violence they suffer from is bound up with the unjust history of colonialism; we also saw that for other women within liberal democracies too, violence (and especially IPV) is interconnected with the historical injustices committed against women. As I will show in the next chapter, concentrating upon the structural interplay between history and present

---

[38] Amnesty International USA (2007, 16); McGillivray and Comaskey (1999, 22–52); Smith (2005); Weaver (2009).
[39] Lawrence (2000); Torpy (2000).
[40] As an example, consider the US Supreme Court decision *Oliphant v. Suquamish Indian Tribe*, which ruled that tribal nations lack the authority to punish crimes committed by non-Indians (Deer 2004, 22). This decision's devastating effects on violence against indigenous women have been countered only recently by the passage of the Violence Against Women Reauthorization Act of 2013, signed into law in 2013 and implemented in 2015; it gives tribal courts the right to prosecute non-indigenous men who commit violence against indigenous women.
[41] Amnesty International (2007, 5).

violence is fundamental to identifying those discourses and policies on VAW that are more apt to stop history from being reproduced.

Before doing so, let me turn to two other aspects of women's condition within liberal democracies that should be approached by considering the structural reproduction of unjust history: women's occupational segregation and the gendered division of domestic labour.

6.2   Occupational Segregation

When we look at the presence of women in the waged labour force within contemporary liberal democracies, it is difficult not to emphasise radical changes. It is well known that, after a rise in women's employment during World Wars I and II mainly due to higher demands of production and men's conscription, from the second half of the twentieth century onwards women have increasingly entered the labour force. In the UK, for example, notwithstanding the recession, today two-thirds of women aged sixteen to sixty-four are working – an increase of 14 per cent compared to the rates in 1971 which was driven by the endorsement of anti-discrimination legislation and the rise of the service sector, in which women tend to be traditionally employed.[42] The high percentage of women in paid employment in liberal democratic countries seems to support the narrative of progress by pointing to a real revolution in gender relations. Nevertheless, when the characteristics of women's presence in the waged labour force are more closely examined, this narrative appears quite misleading. Indeed, women tend to work part-time and in less remunerative occupations, are paid less than men for equal work and perform traditionally female jobs.[43] In the labour market, women and men are segregated in different occupations and women are largely concentrated in particular occupations.[44]

In this section, I mainly focus on women's concentration in traditionally female jobs. This is because I argue that, from within the framework of HSI, this concentration would still remain normatively problematic even if other dimensions of the overall gendered occupational segregation were tackled. To start with, let me briefly explain exactly what constitutes

---

[42] Office for National Statistics (2013, 1).
[43] In the UK, for example, 42 per cent of women are employed part-time, whereas 88 per cent of working men are in a full-time job (Office for National Statistics 2013, 1). Women are concentrated in traditionally female occupations, which are also low paid; women constitute 82 per cent of those employed in caring and leisure types of occupations, and 77 per cent of workers in administrative, secretarial and sale/customer jobs are female (Office for National Statistics 2013, 12).
[44] For the difference between segregation and concentration, see Blackburn and Jarman (2006, 290).

occupational segregation. To clear conceptual confusion, sociologists Robert M. Blackburn, Jude Browne, Bradley Brooks and Jennifer Jarman contend that the overall segregation in the total given labour force has two orthogonal properties: 'vertical occupational segregation' and 'horizontal occupational segregation'. While the former measures the correlation between the distribution of occupations by sex and by pay, the latter refers to the extent of the difference in occupations between men and women without entailing a difference in pay.[45] Obviously, the two properties are usually interrelated; women tend to concentrate in quite low-paying jobs, which are undervalued and not economically profitable because they have been traditionally occupied by women.[46] Nevertheless, the vertical and horizontal properties of occupational segregation are distinguished by sociologists to stress that it is the former that measures inequality, whereas the latter indicates difference without inequality. That is, we can have a highly horizontally segregated labour market in which women and men concentrate in different occupations but in which everyone is paid the same. In this case, the labour market would present difference but not inequality.[47]

To support this claim, Blackburn and Jarman point to the occupational segregation in the labour force of Nordic countries.[48] These countries have undertaken measures to tackle the gender wage-pay gap and the glass ceiling, which prevents qualified women from advancing upward in their organisation into management-level positions. As already seen, Nordic countries are renowned for their commitment to gender equality. However, their labour forces are still highly segregated along the horizontal dimension, even compared to less egalitarian countries.[49] For example, in Denmark, while significant changes in vertical occupational segregation have occurred, the concentration of women (and the near absence of men) in the pink-collar ghetto has remained the same over the last decade.[50] Similarly, in Sweden, low-paying or middle-paying jobs, which were traditionally female dominated, continue to be largely performed by women, and men are overrepresented in typically male-dominated

---

[45] Blackburn et al. (2002, 514); Blackburn and Jarman (2006, 290–94); Browne (2005, 3–7).
[46] Folbre (1994, 101); Rhode (1999, 10).   [47] Browne (2005, 5).
[48] Blackburn and Jarman (2006, 294). For a comparative study, see Charles (2003).
[49] Note that in Nordic countries, some differences between women and men in the labour force along the vertical dimension remain; on Iceland, see Jafnréttisstofa (2012, 16). However, it is worth stressing that, although Nordic countries' attempt to tackle the vertical dimension through important policies and initiatives (e.g. quotas for women in corporative boards, acts on equal pay for equal work), addressing the horizontal dimension has proven to be even more challenging.
[50] Bloksgaard (2011, 6).

occupations, such as computer technician and carpenter.[51] For Blackburn and Jarman, the high level of horizontal segregation in these egalitarian contexts should not be regarded as particularly puzzling. It merely confirms that the horizontal dimension measures difference, and not inequality, in occupation.

However, such a difference is not unproblematic. Indeed, it can reinforce the process of structural reproduction of unjust history, which, in turn, is correlated with radical injustices against women, such as IPV. Consider a hypothetical country in which women have suffered from a systematic unjust history; they have been denied the rights to vote, participate in politics and own property, and they have been legally excluded from paid work or relegated to menial occupations. These systematic injustices were justified through official scientific, moral and philosophical discourses on women that depicted them as inferior and subordinate to men. In this country, not only are these injustices now outlawed and anti-discrimination legislation endorsed but also women's history is publicly recognised as unjust. Imagine that many other changes happened in the country over time that led to the creation of a socialist society in which power is held by a socialist party and a strong socialist ethos is internalised by the majority of citizens.[52] Regarding its labour force, this country does not appear vertically segregated; women and men are equally paid for the same job across all occupations. Moreover, no differential in income exists among workers. However, the labour market in this country is highly gender segregated along the horizontal dimension; women concentrate in traditionally female-dominated occupations, while men continue to perform typically male jobs. Considering the unjust history and the ways it is structurally reproduced, would we say that the difference in occupation, although not entailing economic inequality, is normatively unproblematic?

From within the framework of HSI, we have strong reasons for thinking this should not be the case. As argued in Chapter 3, HSI should be conceived as unjust social-structural processes that started in the past and, although they may appear concluded, are reproduced in different ways and still deeply affect persons' lives in relation to their membership in groups that are both historical and structural. Unjust history is reproduced at a structural level by nourishing, for example,

---

[51] Sweden Population Statistics Unit (2012, 62–63).
[52] This example differs from the present and past reality of many socialist or communist countries, such as the German Democratic Republic (Sørensen and Trappe 1995).

stereotypes, expectations and norms which provide the daily scripts whereby persons interact. In the case of women, as seen in the previous section, within egalitarian contexts radical injustices such as IPV are significantly correlated with women's unjust history. Particularly, IPV builds precisely on those taken-for-granted aspects of the presence of history that continue to structure societies and interpersonal relations. Even in the hypothetical case sketched above, the horizontal segregation of occupations between women and men remains normatively problematic because *that* difference is bound to reinforce those stereotypes, expectations and norms that constitute important dimensions of the banal reproduction of unjust history. For example, the great concentration of women in occupations to which women have been legally confined in the past or whose tasks are somehow associated with the roles women had to perform (e.g. nursing and caring) is likely to perpetuate stereotypes, expectations and norms that continue to affect women's lives. This difference can spill over into grave inequalities, such as IPV, by contributing to the reproduction of the banal presence of the unjust past whereby radical injustices operate.

This connection is important also with regard to those existing egalitarian countries mentioned by Blackburn and Jarman. As previously seen, VAW is a serious and enduring matter even in Nordic countries, a matter that has not been successfully tackled by conventional progressive means. Thus, it may be that addressing the *difference* horizontal occupational segregation expresses can provide a starting point to combat violence. To be sure, the problem with horizontal gender segregation is also compounded by those economic inequalities I have abstracted from in my hypothetical case. Not only are women not paid the same within one occupation but also they earn less across various occupations. In particular, since stereotypically female jobs tend to not be remunerative and women usually concentrate in them, what in our imaginary case was a problematic difference is in reality correlated with economic inequalities.[53] Nevertheless, my point is that when we approach the issue of horizontal gender segregation from within the framework of HSI, along with considerable worries about the distribution of income and resources we may have additional reasons for concern. These reasons stem from the

---

[53] In Sweden, for example, two of the most low-paid (and traditionally pink-collar) occupations – cleaners and personal care – are highly dominated by women (i.e. 79 per cent and 86 per cent, respectively) (Sweden Population Statistics Unit 2012, 72–73).

particular banal ways unjust history is structurally reproduced and is at the roots of radical injustices.

As Susan Moller Okin observes, 'Wage work has a history of extreme segregation by sex that is closely related to the traditional female role within marriage'.[54] In this sense, it seems that housekeeper remains the most gender-segregated occupation. Why is it a problem the fact that men and women do not share housework?

6.3   The Gendered Division of Domestic Labour

Arguably, one of the most enduring features of the relations between women and men is the gendered division of domestic labour (hereafter GDDL). Nordic egalitarian countries are no exception. In Sweden, for example, although men and women share housework more than in other countries, women still shoulder the bulk of it.[55] The persistence of GDDL is particularly puzzling considering the huge transformations households and families have undergone in the last fifty years. As a result of economic and social changes, the once common model of family constituted by the male breadwinner and the female caregiver has been progressively substituted in the majority of liberal democracies by that of the dual-earner couple, thereby prompting a modification of the gender order.[56] Alternative family arrangements, such as same-sex unions, have presented significant challenges to the traditional family by questioning the unequal gendered division of roles that was once believed to be constitutive of the family.[57] Nevertheless, the unequal GDDL is still a predominant feature of the majority of households in egalitarian countries.[58] Generally, there seems to be a weak link between persons' opinions and views on gender equality and their respective practices in the households.[59] This is not to say conservative men and women tend to share caring and domestic chores more equally than progressive heterosexual couples; however, the latter do not necessarily arrange their domestic lives according to their own values.

Within feminist scholarship, GDDL represents a leitmotiv of the struggle for gender equality. Although, as black feminists highlight, not all

---

[54] Okin (1989, 141).
[55] Evertsson and Nermo (2004); Sweden Population Statistics Unit (2012, 39).
[56] See, famously, Fraser (1997b, 42). For a historical analysis of the emergence of the dual-earner family in the UK, see Waite and Nielsen (2001).
[57] E.g. Calhoun (2002, 102–31); Dalton and Bielby (2000); Malone and Cleary (2002); Moore (2011); Roseneil and Budgeon (2004); Ruspini (2013, 1–28, 93–116).
[58] Scott and Plagnol (2012, 198).   [59] Poeschl (2008, 75).

women were confined to the unpaid private sphere,[60] caring and domestic services have largely been a prerogative of women based on their stipulated role in society. Thus it is not surprising that feminists have declared that without a transformation of GDDL, the revolution in gender roles is still incomplete.[61] Some claim that it is precisely because of the persisting division within families that the feminist revolution has stalled.[62] Why is GDDL within contemporary households still so problematic? And why is such a division so resistant to changes within society at large?[63] I argue that, in a way similar to the issue of horizontal occupational segregation, one of the main reasons GDDL should be worrisome is *the particular difference* it creates. Moreover, I contend that GDDL is such a persistent feature of egalitarian societies because of its peculiar capacity to reinforce the traditional roles women and men have occupied over history. Additionally, in turn, it is supported by the daily scripts of stereotypes, expectations and norms whereby the unjust past is reproduced.

Feminists fiercely argue that GDDL disadvantages women. In the last two decades, this disadvantage has been largely described through the powerful image of the 'double shift': in addition to working outside the home, women seemingly have to shoulder the burden of all the work involved in maintaining a family (e.g. caring for children and the frail elderly, and doing domestic chores). They are doing more than men, and, so the argument goes, they are not even compensated for what, in terms of hours and energy, resembles an additional working shift.[64] Finally, besides being overburdened with work and stress, women enjoy less free time and thus can participate less in political and social life.

As influential as it may be, this line of argument about the disadvantage GDDL produces and the very metaphor of the double shift is misleading. Time-use surveys have recently shown that when all the productive hours are summed up, women and men actually work almost the same amount of hours. In Sweden, for example, they both spend roughly 7.5 hours per day doing productive work.[65] Similarly, in the UK, on average women work only sixteen minutes longer per day than men – a difference that cannot be

---

[60] Davis (1983); hooks (1982, 21–24).   [61] Espin-Andersen (2009).

[62] See, famously, Hoschschild [1989] (2012, 12).

[63] Note that the GDDL is a characteristic of many family arrangements, and not only of heterosexual couples, such as the practise of 'othermothering' performed within African American communities. Indeed, many of these caring networks sharing caring and domestic work are still largely formed by women. I will turn to the importance of these alternative networks in the next chapter (§ 7.2).

[64] For a recent restatement of this line of argument, see Gheaus (2012, 4–5).

[65] Sweden Population Statistics Unit (2012, 38–39).

defined as a proper second shift.[66] Thus, in terms of total working hours, the disadvantage women suffer seems not so considerable. Insisting on the double shift as indicative of why GDDL is problematic may lead some to reply that, given that men and women actually work the same amount of hours, because men already do their fair share they do not perform caring and domestic chores.[67] This is misguided, and it may backfire on the achievement of historical-structural justice for women as it misidentifies the reasons for men's noncooperation. Thus feminists are right in saying GDDL should be addressed in order to achieve gender justice; however, equality of time may not be the best argument to support this claim.[68]

Other feminist scholars contend that the main problem with GDDL lies in the economic disadvantage women are likely to experience as a result of unequal private arrangements.[69] In fact, although women and men are working the same amount of hours, the majority of women's productive work remains unpaid; while men are usually employed full-time outside the home and thus spend the bulk of their productive hours doing paid work, women tend to be in part-time occupations and devote the rest of their working time to housework,[70] thereby not earning any income from the largest number of hours they spend doing their share of productive work. This means that, on average, heterosexual cohabitants have unequal economic resources, which translates into unequal power within the household.[71] The importance of this argument should not be underestimated as unequal income and power have a serious impact on women's lives; for example, they make it harder for women to exit abusive relationships. Nevertheless, as with the issue of horizontal occupational segregation, for GDDL, too, economic equality should not be the only concern. Imagine that caring and domestic labour were remunerated through, for example, generous weekly allowances, making gender economic inequality, although probably still existent, less substantial or at least not such a severe constraint for those who want to leave an abusive partner. In this

---

[66] For some data on time spent on paid and unpaid labour by women and men in OECD countries, see https://stats.oecd.org/index.aspx?queryid=54757 (accessed 3 July 2018).

[67] Notably, see Hakim (2010).

[68] Note that time surveys do not usually consider an important and constraining aspect of unpaid care, namely 'supervisory care' – i.e. a carer's being 'on call' and ready to interrupt her own activities to provide care (Folbre and Wright 2012, 4). By drawing on the findings of time-use surveys, I intend to suggest that equal time, although significant, is not the only reason why GDDL matters for questions of justice.

[69] E.g. Okin (1989, 154).

[70] https://stats.oecd.org/index.aspx?queryid=54757 (accessed 3 July 2018).

[71] Okin (1989, 156–59).

case, would GDDL still be a problem? As we will see (§ 7.2), many feminists argue that cash payment is not a solution for GDDL because it would incentivise women to remain at home and not enter full-time employment. Nevertheless, why is the fact that women would eventually be more tempted not to participate in the labour force a problem, even when leisure time and economic resources were more equally distributed?

The answer lies in the worry that this would reinforce the banal presence of unjust history. Care and housework are activities associated with the roles women had to perform over history and the sphere that either they were confined to or they had to work in as servants. The domestic sphere was so invested with the function of defining what women should be that, for example, in the US one way to establish the more 'inferior' status of African American women during slavery was to deny them a 'room of their own'.[72] By being forced to work in slavery plantations or in masters' houses, produce children as masters' property, and nurse the masters' children instead of their own, African American women not only were excluded from public life but also were prohibited from having a private sphere, what was deemed to be the 'natural' place for 'proper' – that is, white – women.[73] This example is given just to suggest that domestic activities have a symbolic meaning linked to the historical injustice towards women – a meaning that cannot be neglected. The disadvantages of GDDL, even when mitigated by a more equal distribution of economic and time resources, would consist in its potential to reinforce those stereotypes, expectations and norms whereby unjust history is structurally reproduced.

One may object that since, as showed, other dimensions of women's condition are bound to perpetuate the unjust past, it is not clear why we should focus on GDDL. If we can tackle the HSI of women without interfering with such a private matter as domestic arrangements, why should we concentrate on that? To be sure, the sceptic does not deny that interference in the private sphere is required under grave circumstances – for example, violence; however, she thinks that because GDDL is too discretionary and not sufficiently harmful to authorise state action, we should simply focus on more public domains, such as occupational segregation. At least two responses can be offered to this objection. First, as feminists argue, 'the domestic sphere is created by political decisions' and is profoundly and unavoidably interconnected with what happens at a public level.[74] This means that how the private sphere is demarked, what its role

---

[72] Collins (2000, 46).   [73] Collins (2000, 47).
[74] Okin (1989, 111). See also Olsen (1985, 837, 842); Schwarzenbach (2009, 221).

and function are, and which citizens can legitimately share a common private sphere together depend on public decisions, which in turn are historically contextual. Thus the private and the public cannot be easily separated not only because they mutually impact each other but also because the former is constructed by the latter in many often unacknowledged ways.[75]

Second, the role GDDL plays in reinforcing HSI cannot be neglected. Evidence of this is provided by cases in which women earn more and work a larger number of hours than their male partners. Under these circumstances, we would expect the bulk of domestic labour to be shouldered by men. Nevertheless, sociological research suggests that even in these contexts it is still women who are mainly responsible for household chores and caring.[76] In particular, perpetuating GDDL becomes a highly effective way to maintain, especially at a symbolic level, what is consciously or unconsciously regarded as one's position in society. In other words, though in other respects women and men seem to have broken with the past, GDDL remains a crucial means to reproduce history. This is partly because the private sphere is a dimension in which inequalities can be more easily negotiated.[77] However, most importantly, maintaining that division becomes an effective strategy because, as previously argued, it is strongly associated with the injustices from which women have suffered over history. In these cases, men's resistance to share caring and domestic chores cannot be motivated by the belief that they are already contributing equally to the household. It is driven by the still-considerable power that establishing an unequal domestic arrangement has to preserve or reactivate those different roles and expectations that women and men have historically occupied and held. GDDL represents so powerful a symbol of women's subordinate status that, as seen, within liberal and democratic countries, IPV is conducted by monitoring exactly those activities that women were (and still are) supposed to perform within the household.

Therefore the significance of GDDL as a site where and whereby HSI can be reproduced cannot be overlooked. Achieving historical-structural justice for the HSG of women entails addressing GDDL and, as we will see, revaluing the activities performed within the domestic sphere in such an effective way that everyone, regardless of their ascriptive memberships, can feel the expectation to undertake them (§ 7.2).

---

[75] Pateman (1989, 118).
[76] E.g. Bertrand, Kamenica and Pan (2015); Bittman et al. (2003); Ridgeway (2011, 141–45).
[77] Stark (2007, 191).

Moreover, in egalitarian societies, GDDL not only constitutes a way to reproduce unjust history. It is also a sign that that unjust history is still structurally present. That is, it is because certain stereotypes, expectations and norms still regulate societies at large that sharing domestic chores represents an exceptional condition. By providing the daily scripts whereby persons interact and societies are organised, the banal presence of unjust history maintains GDDL.[78] In this respect, we cannot expect that a system of formal equality of opportunity and equal rights would translate into similar paths for the two mutually constitutive groups in the long run, because unjust history is structurally and newly reproduced within egalitarian contexts. This means women (and men) are still likely to encounter different types of constraints on the basis of their gendered ascriptive memberships that set for them different expectations and norms and regulate their interpersonal interactions. Standard measures are not sufficient to achieve historical-structural justice for women; we need, as we will see in the next chapter, more 'transformative' actions.

In sum, in this chapter I showed how unjust history affects the HSG of women within egalitarian contexts through complex and intertwined mechanisms. The reproduction of stereotypes, norms and expectations associated with the roles women were supposed to undertake over history explains persisting differences between women and men, such as occupational segregation and the unequal division of domestic labour. These differences in turn reinforce the banal reproduction of unjust history by confirming stereotypes, conforming to norms and meeting expectations which stem from the historical injustice towards women. Moreover, that banal reproduction lies at the roots of what are (rightly) considered radical injustices from which women still suffer, such as VAW, by providing the strategies and the background conditions whereby violence is exercised. Violence in turn becomes (consciously and unconsciously) a means to reproduce unjust history. In this sense, HSI operates as a sort of *gearbox* whose components mutually reinforce one another. Recognising that women are a group that suffer from the structural reproduction of history thus proves to be crucial to understand not only the origins and workings

---

[78] In contemporary liberal democracies, a component of unpaid domestic labour has been shifted on female (often temporary) migrants, which is the result of neo-liberal policies and governments' direct encouragement of hiring migrant care workers through cash allowances for home-based care provision and specific migration programmes. Although I cannot discuss this crucial issue here, it is important to observe that the hiring of female migrants as care workers within households is an important mechanism of the new reproduction of GDDL in such contexts rather than a challenge to it. I examined the interplay between the reproduction of GDDL and temporary labour migration within the European Union in Nuti (2018); see also Lutz (2011).

of present forms of injustice and inequality between women and men but also the reasons why certain types of differences would be normatively problematic even if inequalities in resources were overcome.

To effectively address the condition of women in liberal democracies, the mechanisms whereby the unjust history is structurally reproduced should be deactivated. To do so, two steps are necessary. First, as attempted by this chapter, problems such as violence, occupational segregation and GDDL must be addressed from within the HSI framework so as to avoid misidentifying their roots and the normative challenges they present. Second, actions to disable the reproduction of unjust history should be carefully devised. This further step is the focus of the next chapter.

CHAPTER 7

The Policy of the Unjust Past

In the previous chapter, I showed how the historical injustice from which women suffered remains structurally present even in egalitarian societies. Moreover, I argued that the theoretical and normative framework of historical-structural injustice (HSI) can illuminate some dimensions of the relation between history and injustice characterising the historical-structural group of women – namely, violence against women (VAW), (horizontal) occupational segregation and the gendered division of domestic labour (GDDL). Particularly, HSI helps explain why these dimensions are problematic and identifies their roots in the structural interplay between (unjust) history and (present) injustice.

This chapter aims to illustrate how the conception of HSI offers a framework in which policies addressing the previously discussed dimensions of the HSI of women can be assessed and developed. My goal is not to provide a critical analysis of all the proposals undertaken or developed to face these problems, which would be impossible. Instead, I aim to offer a conceptual tool to understand why certain actions are more apt than others and to suggest some routes that can be followed. Particularly, I argue that the most promising policy proposals, which I call 'transformative measures',[1] are those that directly tackle the banal reproduction of unjust history (e.g. stereotypes, norms and expectations bound up with historical injustices towards women). These measures attempt to intervene on the relation between individual agency and structural reproduction – that is, the ways historical structures are reactivated in daily interactions through individuals exercising their agency while also being the background conditions that enable and constrain that agency.

In this respect, the chapter aims to stress *the significance of policy making* in redressing unjust history. On one hand, when history is reconceived as being newly structurally reproduced, policy making aimed at addressing

---

[1] I borrow this term from Fraser (1997a, 23).

present inequalities may leave intact or even reinforce the complex ways whereby history is reproduced if it does not fully factor them in. Consider the already mentioned example of mandatory-arrest policies in cases of intimate-partner violence (IPV) that are implemented in a context such as the US in which race has historically intersected with gender (§ 5.3). Such policies are extremely counterproductive because, by failing to heed how the police works under historical stereotypical assumptions about African American women's aggressive behaviour, they often result in the arrest of 'racialised' women. On the other hand, precisely because history is structurally reproduced even in daily interactions, policy making that is sensitive to such dynamics constitutes an important device to channel individuals' agency in different directions and deactivate the daily reproduction of history.

7.1 Intimate-Partner Violence Prevention and the Bystander Approach

As seen, VAW, and particularly IPV, is pervasive within egalitarian societies and operates in these contexts in specific ways (§ 6.1). Policies aimed at addressing VAW are usually grouped in three categories according to their specific goals: (1) protective measures (e.g. refuges and sanctuary schemes), which shelter abused women, make them safe in their homes and help them exit the abusive relationship; (2) restorative measures (e.g. perpetrator programmes; counselling and confidence-building programmes for survivors), which attempt to change the behaviour of abusive partners or help survivors build their lives after the relationship ends; and (3) preventive measures (e.g. campaigns, self-defence classes, men's mentoring programmes, bystander approach), which are directed at stopping violence from happening in the first place. While (1) and (2) try to protect women from already existing violent relations and to restore these broken ties, respectively, (3) intervenes at the beginning of the process by endeavouring to prevent violent relationships from being established.

Although protective measures are crucial to increase women's options, an exclusive focus on protection is insufficient to tackle VAW. Specifically in the case of IPV, protective measures should be implemented very carefully because it is when women try to exit from abusive relations and seek shelter that they risk the most serious injuries, including death.[2] Paradoxically, precisely because of the dynamics of IPV such measures

---

[2] Gauthier and Bankston (2004); Kurz (1996).

might not fully protect women. Some also voice scepticism about restorative programmes aimed at abusive men as they 'cannot hope to address men's violent practices in general',[3] although they may provide an opportunity for behavioural change to *some* participants. This is because many men join these programmes under external (e.g. legal or police) imposition or (more or less consciously) to regain their partners' trust,[4] rather than to change their attitudes and behaviour. Moreover, such programmes target abusive men who have already been reported, which means many violent men against whom no charges have been pressed (let alone men who have not been hitherto abusive) cannot benefit from them.

Preventive measures, which are usually underfunded, attempt to overcome the limits of both protective and restorative actions. They aim at preventing the creation of violent relationships by focusing on their enabling conditions and by targeting not only violent men. Within the framework of HSI, prevention is crucial and it means changing those historical structures that constitute the background wherein abusive relationships are built. But what kind of preventive actions should be undertaken and prioritised?

Traditionally, preventive measures against VAW have been constituted by *self-defence classes*, which teach women how to increase their safety and defend themselves against attacks. Although self-defence classes are usually conceived as a way to empower women and enhance their confidence,[5] they are also criticised because they might convey the problematic message that women are the ones responsible for controlling men's urges and preventing violence, thereby normalising men's violence and failing to question societal norms.[6]

The framework of HSI can help show how the specific ways women have been formally discriminated against over history compound those effects that insistence on self-defence class as a preventive measure can have in particular societies. In societies such as Italy in which ('good') women have been depicted as feeble creatures in need of men's protection, and therefore denied political, civil and economic rights, self-defence classes, when properly framed, may counter the still-regulative stereotype (and ideal) of the psychologically and physically passive woman.

Conversely, there are contexts in which self-defence classes may be particularly deleterious. In Nordic countries, the normative model of womanhood is the independent, autonomous, self-assured woman who is able to

---

[3] Hearn and McKie (2010, 149).   [4] Hearn (1998, 193).   [5] Ullman (2002, 140).
[6] Banyard, Plante and Moynihan (2004, 65).

immediately exit an abusive relationship 'at the first slap'.[7] This contemporary model is bound up with the traditional image of the responsible and strong mother-woman that has represented the ideal of womanhood in Nordic countries and has played a fundamental role in the historical development of modern welfare states.[8] Women were not necessarily excluded on the grounds of their putative weakness, but they were constructed as publicly praiseworthy only when willing to protect their families (and themselves). That is, historically in Nordic countries the state and religious associations have considered women responsible for ending violence within families.[9] Today, when women remain in abusive relationships and do not defend themselves, they fail to conform to the normatively constructed image of womanhood, thereby becoming (self-)blameable.[10] In such contexts, reliance on self-defence classes, which revolve precisely around building an image of strong womanhood, is likely to reactivate a pernicious historical social norm which has a serious impact on how the problem of IPV is perceived in Nordic countries. As seen, a normative emphasis on the independent woman, especially in societies that consider themselves as gender egalitarian, results in misconceptions about the dynamics of IPV (§ 6.1). Particularly, it promotes an individualist understanding of IPV as a personal failure and does not recognise how IPV is instead connected to historical-structural injustices reproduced within societies at large.

The above-mentioned examples show that when prevention of IPV is approached from within the framework of HSI, it becomes possible to evaluate the desirability of certain policies precisely by looking at the particular ways women have been excluded over history and the specific interplays between history and structure in different societies.

In addition to self-defence classes, preventive measures have increasingly included *programmes exclusively directed to* (non-abusive) *men.* One of the first and most renowned of these programmes is the Mentors in Violence Prevention (MVP) programme, which aims to develop charismatic (male) mentors who can inspire their male peers to refrain from violence and teach

---

[7] Enander (2010, 20). See also Wiklund et al. (2010, 223).

[8] Hautanen (2005, 72). Interestingly, in Finland, the normative model of the responsible and strong mother-woman was reinforced by the 1980s women's movement, which used it to claim citizenship rights and the inclusion of (this kind of) women in the political and economic sphere (Hautanen 2005, 72).

[9] For example, Finland's largest religious body, the Evangelical Lutheran Church of Finland, still quite recently issued a publication on how women should handle a violent husband and act as responsible mothers (Hautanen 2005, 74).

[10] This situation is exacerbated when women suffering from IPV are also mothers (Keskinen 2005, 39; Hautanen 2005, 74).

them how to intervene when other men interact violently with women.[11] This programme has been conceived for and implemented in contexts usually dominated by a strong masculinity culture, such as sports teams, college fraternities and the military.[12] Programmes such as MVP seem to be promising; for instance, they require men to examine their own potential for violence and consider themselves as 'the main doers of violence',[13] and they show how it is possible to be male without resorting to violence. Nevertheless, precisely in doing so, MVP (and similar programmes) still risks positing men as the ones who *can* decide whether to deploy violence. Men are taught that their strength can be used in other ways, and, in so doing, their privilege is not challenged. For example, MVP usually intends to teach its participants that men can be manlier when they direct their force to shield and defend women who are in a dangerous situation. In such programmes, for instance, participants are shown the effects IPV and sexual violence have on women who experience them. Although this is usually done to build a sense of empathy towards victims (or potential victims) of men's violence,[14] it is likely to display women as vulnerable and powerless subjects in need of (male) protection. To wit, when the message of how men can refrain from violence is coupled with the goal of women's protection, male privilege seems to be reinforced rather than dismantled. This is because opposition to VAW is not uniquely a feminist issue but also a patriarchal leitmotiv: strong men do not prove their masculinity by beating women but by protecting them.[15] These programmes thus may provide a more subtle resource for the historically rooted norm that takes men as the protectors of women, a norm that, as many feminist scholars argue, also has far-reaching and problematic racial implications.[16] Rather than analysing how 'men' is a group historically constructed *in relation to* that of 'women', these programmes may position men as the main agents who are rightly at the centre of power but simply need to know how to use their power in a better fashion. This is not to say these kinds of programmes should be outright dismissed, but that we need to be aware of

---

[11] Katz, Heisterkamp and Fleming (2011, 685).

[12] The Fraternity Violence Education Project, aimed at fraternity leaders, and Men Can Stop Rape are other important examples of these programmes, alongside preventive (male) campaigns, such as the White Ribbon Campaign (i.e. a public education campaign to help men stop VAW) and the #AllMenCan hashtag lately spread on social networks such as Twitter, which urged men to show how they *can* be feminist.

[13] Hearn (1998, 6). See also Berkowitz (2002, 165).

[14] Berkowitz (2002, 170); Langhinrichsen-Rohling et al. (2011, 746).   [15] Stark (2007, 370).

[16] E.g. Davis (1983, chapter 11).

their possible effects so as to avoid a reactivation of an unjust history that still structures societies.

One of the limits of both self-defence classes and MVP is that they are mainly directed only to women and men, respectively. However, as seen, IPV (and VAW) concerns two groups that are mutually constituted and stems from a complex web of relations between these groups and the historical structures within societies at large. Therefore, it calls also (and mainly) for *relational measures* – that is, measures tackling these relations and the structures in which they are established. To wit, these measures should be holistic and relational by being aimed at both groups and the surrounding context. The so-called *bystander approach*, one of the newest and most promising preventive measures, incorporates, at least in principle, these intuitions.[17] The bystander approach endorses a holistic view on VAW in that it directly engages with communities at large by bringing to the forefront the role all community members should play in preventing violence.[18] Indeed, Sarah McMahon and Victoria Banyard define 'bystanders' as

> third party witnesses to situations where there is high risk of . . . violence and who by their presence have the ability to do nothing, to make a situation worse by supporting or ignoring the perpetrator behavior, or to make the situation better by intervening in prosocial ways.[19]

The bystander approach encompasses a variety of voluntary programmes that are usually offered in universities but that can also be devised for schools and workplaces. Unlike self-defence classes and programmes such as MVP, bystander approaches seem more promising as they focus on the relational dimension of VAW. In particular, they recognise the importance of working with both men and women through the combination of single-sex and mixed sessions in which participants can feel safe to disclose their personal experiences while also being pushed to exit their comfort zone.[20] Although this approach has been developed to tackle sexual violence (especially on college campuses), it has been recently applied, with

---

[17] MPV-like programmes are usually considered as bystander approaches because one of their goals is teaching men how to become active bystanders by intervening when a friend, colleague, family member or stranger is at high risk (Langhinrichsen-Rohling et al. 2011, 745). However, I distinguish such programmes from bystander approaches to show how the latter, when directed to women, men and society at large, are more promising than the former.

[18] E.g. Potter and Banyard (2011, 680); Banyard, Plante and Moynihan (2004, 71); McMahon and Banyard (2012, 3).

[19] McMahon and Banyard (2012, 3).

[20] On the importance of involving both women and men in prevention of VAW, see Jewkes, Flood and Lang (2015).

encouraging results, to IPV prevention.[21] IPV presents an even-harder challenge to the involvement of bystanders because it usually happens in the 'private' sphere, which tends to make the abuse more concealed, and because, more importantly, that sphere is still regarded by many as a dimension in which third parties should not interfere, as we will see below. Yet since IPV is intertwined with societal historical structures and their daily reproduction (see § 6.1), bystander approaches are needed to prevent this widespread form of VAW.

That said, the majority of existing accounts of the bystander approach display some problems. First, many accounts explicitly consider the main contribution of bystander approaches to be the responsibility that *communities* (and community leaders), rather than societies, have to prevent violence.[22] Such a strong emphasis on community is problematic for at least three reasons. In contexts characterised by historical structures along racial, ethnic and class lines, an exclusive stress on community responsibility would likely single out certain disadvantaged ethnic, racial and class groups as particularly sexist and violent, thereby neglecting how IPV is pervasive within society at large and precisely reinforcing historically rooted stereotypes against these groups.

Moreover, when it is precisely community norms that need to be changed to prevent violence, an excessive focus on community leaders is questionable in that it may reduce violence by paradoxically strengthening those norms that are at its roots. As for programmes such as MVP, it is important to remember that the fight against VAW is not exclusively a feminist theme but also a conservative and patriarchal one. When the emphasis is merely on communities and their leaders, there may be a decrease in (and a prevention of) violence for the wrong reasons. In other words, more (male) bystanders may become more active and intervene in cases of IPV not as a result of a change in community norms but because they conceive of themselves as protectors of women precisely through such community norms. To be sure, male feminist community leaders and male feminist role models (e.g. charismatic teachers and respected peers) are fundamental to reach out and involve other men in bystander programmes because of their access to networks unavailable to women.[23] Also, bystander programmes should obviously be devised by considering the particular communities in which they are implemented.

---

[21] McMahon and Dick (2011).
[22] See Banyard, Plante and Moynihan (2004, 73) and Potter and Banyard (2011, 680) on the centrality of communities to bystander approaches.
[23] Casey, Carson and Bulls (2016, 235).

Because the aim is to challenge social norms that assume particular inter-pretations in different contexts, contextual sensitivity is paramount.[24] However, the difference between bystander approaches that overstress community responsibility and context-sensitive preventive strategies is that the former do not necessarily challenge community norms, whereas the latter are aimed precisely at this. This difference comes down to devising programmes that are tailored to specific contexts and histories but avoid reactivating historical stereotypes and norms intertwined with IPV.

Second, bystander approaches focusing extensively on community responsibility tend to endorse gender neutrality, rather than gender equal-ity, as a value. This is the case with the Green Dot programme, one of the most influential bystander approaches, originally developed by Dorothy Edwards at the University of Kentucky to prevent violence on college campuses.[25] Such programmes are undoubtedly more attractive to partici-pants because, by framing violence as a couples/family problem, they avoid making men feel blamed. Nevertheless, their appeal lies precisely in the fact that participants are never asked to question their own position in the societal historical structures in which VAW is rooted, thereby leaving community and societal norms unchallenged.[26] By portraying violence as gender-neutral, these programmes offer a misguided diagnosis of the problem and consequently provide a misdirected solution to it. This is not to say that *outreach* activities aimed at men should not draw on 'positive' messages and refrain from portraying all men as potential perpe-trators. However, during the programme a progressive switch in frame-works is necessary to theorise (1) the contribution of men to the historical structures enabling (and reinforced by) IPV and (2) the relation between the historically co-constitutive groups of women and men.

Third, as some scholars observe, participants in bystander programmes tend to be significantly more willing to intervene when they see blatant forms of violence and in situations in which the victim and the perpetrator are not related.[27] This makes current bystander models more difficult to apply to IPV, in which abuse is usually more complex to identify and, by definition, the victim and the abuser are in an intimate relationship.

---

[24] Oliver (2000).
[25] On the Green Dot programme, see Coker et al. (2011); Katz, Heisterkamp and Fleming (2011, 690); Langhinrichsen-Rohling et al. (2011, 745).
[26] In § 6.1, I showed precisely the serious shortcomings of gender-neutral ways of framing VAW, which individualise an injustice bounded up with the reproduction of historical structures.
[27] McMahon and Banyard (2012, 7); McMahon, Postmus and Koenick (2011, 126).

Rather than dismissing the potential of this promising approach to violence prevention, these problems call for a reformulation of the bystander model, which is possible through the HSI framework. As seen, VAW and IPV should be conceived as part of the HSI suffered by women as a group (§ 6.1). IPV draws on and is enabled by the banal structural reproduction of unjust history: those stereotypes, norms and expectations whereby history is structurally reproduced within societies, which form the day-to-day scripts in which persons interact and constitute the background conditions in which IPV happens while also nourishing the abusive strategies adopted. Approaching violence prevention through the lens of HSI offers a gender-based understanding of IPV (and VAW) that both focuses on society as a whole and is sensitive to different contexts in that it shows how IPV is an injustice that can be fully captured only when the specific interplays between history and structures are considered.

The conception of HSI can also highlight the importance of correcting bystanders' unwillingness to intervene in cases of subtler abuses and when perpetrators are in a relation with their 'victims', and it is able to offer an explanation thereof. Such unwillingness can be seen as resulting from the combination of two factors. First, bystanders fail to become active participants when the abuse is covert or in circumstances of low risk (e.g. in the presence of sexist jokes, discriminatory language or chauvinist expectations) because these problematic circumstances are quite widespread and normalised. This means that this kind of engagement would probably prompt participants to question their own daily practices, thereby encouraging self-criticism that not many are willing to undertake. Second, the very idea that abuses between (especially intimately) related persons is a matter concerning only those directly involved (i.e. an individualised problem) is one of the most pervasive interpretative frames structuring egalitarian societies. This frame stems from the unjust myth of the private/public division, which played a key role in the history of the injustice suffered by women and is reactivated precisely in the dynamics of radical injustices such as IPV.

Thus, integrating the bystander model of VAW prevention with the HSI framework looks promising; however, in practice it would require at least a threefold modification of the majority of mainstream bystander approaches. It would be necessary to include *continuous moments of self-reflection* as part of the implementation of the programme. Participants need to interrogate their own position within those historical structures present within societies that are at the roots of violence. They have to reflect on how, in their day-to-day practices and interactions, they contribute to the banal reproduction of the unjust history that enables IPV by, for instance, relying on stereotypes of how a woman is expected to behave (e.g. as perfect homemakers) or by embodying norms on gender roles (see § 6.1). This can be more easily done when the bystander approach is implemented in an interactive way, such as through participatory theatrical representations, because participants can explore the relation between their own practices and violence by directly 'acting' on it.[28]

Moreover, when the bystander model is approached from within the HSI framework, a broader account of bystanders should be endorsed. Since not only high-risk situations but also daily practices and normalised historical structures need to be addressed, bystanders are not only those who witness abuses; *everyone* is, with different responsibilities and capacities, a bystander. Because we exercise our agency within these structures and we reinforce them with our actions (or inactions) every day, different patterns of actions and relations can contribute to deactivating unjust structures. Also, by engaging with others and, for instance, calling them out when they make sexist jokes and rely on problematic assumptions, stereotypes, norms and expectations, we can stop normalising them.[29]

Finally and relatedly, bystander programmes should make participants aware that their own position in historical structures underlying IPV is *intersectional*. This means that some of our proactive behaviours may have the effect of reinforcing unjust long-term structures (e.g. racial ones) which have historically intersected with gendered structures underlying IPV (and sexual violence). For instance, in the case of a white American male bystander who stands up to intervene when an African American man makes a sexist comment, failure to interrogate one's own intersectional position in deciding how to act may turn out to perpetuate the stereotype of black men as inherently violent and hyper-sexual, which has played a crucial role in governing interracial relations in the US.[30]

---

[28] Peer theatre groups employing a bystander approach based on participatory theatre include the interACT Performance Troupe at California State University, Long Beach; the Voices Against Violence Peer Education Group at the University of Texas at Austin; and the Interactive Theatre project at the University of Colorado (Ahrens et al. 2011; Mitchell and Freitag 2011).

[29] The fact that, through the exercise of our agency, everyone is a potential bystander does not mean we all share the same responsibility because of that. I will return to the problem of present responsibility within unjust structures in § 9.2.

[30] One crucial mechanism whereby African American men's sexuality has been regulated in the US over history is the (persisting) myth of the black rapist (of white women) (e.g. Davis 1983, chapter 11).

In sum, the framework of HSI not only shows which preventive measures are more apt but also offers new insights into how to improve the most compelling measures.

7.2 The Gendered Division of Domestic Labour and the Mandatory Caregiving Service

As seen, GDDL is a fundamental dimension of the HSI suffered by women; it reproduces and is enabled by historical structures and is deeply interconnected with IPV and other radical injustices (§ 6.3). Addressing it is thus crucial. In this section, I mainly focus on two different policies, namely equal parental leave and the idea of a mandatory caregiving service, arguing for the comparatively more transformative potential of the latter. What these policies have in common is the attempt to dismantle GDDL to change the background conditions of inequality between women and men.

In this respect, they differ from what Nancy Fraser calls 'affirmative' measures proposed or implemented to improve women's condition in the household which 'aim at correcting unequal outcomes of social arrangements without disturbing the underlying generative framework'.[31] Affirmative measures include proposals for wages for domestic labour, a caregiver stipend, and, at least to a certain extent, a basic income. As some feminist scholars observe, these measures are bound to backfire on gender equality; they may turn out to be 'hush money', by offering a financial reward to women for their domestic work while expecting that women would not demand more substantial changes.[32] They are also likely to incentivise women's withdrawal from the labour force.[33] Such measures would provide women with some safety net against poverty and reduce their economic disadvantage, but they would not change the historical-structural background in which relations between men and women are established. Women would still be expected to do the bulk of domestic labour, although they would be remunerated for their contribution. Nevertheless, as argued, GDDL is problematic not only because it is unpaid labour but also because of the *difference* it reinforces – that is, its enormous capacity to sustain the banal reproduction of unjust history (§ 6.3). Therefore, we need to devise policies that, unlike affirmative measures, target that difference by, for example, creating a society in which the model of a universal caregiver is the norm[34] – that is, in which both men and women are expected to perform

---

[31] Fraser (1997a, 23). [32] Robeyns (2000, 122). [33] Gheaus (2008, 4–5); Robeyns (2001, 103).
[34] See, famously, Fraser (1997b).

caring and domestic labour. This is what transformative measures, such as equal parental leave, aim for.

Many conceive of 'equality-promoting'[35] *parental leave* or 'daddy quotas',[36] which try to motivate fathers to spend time away from work to take care of (usually infant) children, as strong egalitarian measures whose ultimate goal is eliminating GDDL and transforming gender relations in an egalitarian fashion.[37] Much of my criticism, in this section, is general as it intends to challenge the idea that these schemes (however they are devised) constitute the best measure to address both GDDL and the HSI that is at the root of GDDL yet is reinforced by it.[38] As a tool to change relations between men and women and redress the HSI suffered by women, equal parental leave presents at least three interrelated shortcomings.

First, it risks normalising heterosexual coupledom by neglecting other forms of family arrangements and caring networks and by reinforcing other historical-structural injustices (e.g. along the lines of race and sexuality), which intersect with those committed against the group of women. This can be seen by looking at some of the strongest and most novel proposals which deploy the 'behavioural and normative power of defaults'.[39] By prescribing that by default fathers are expected to take a certain amount of leave from work for childcare purposes, these proposals intend to convey a strong normative message, namely that society expects childcare to be a concern not only of mothers but also of fathers. These proposals are regarded as potentially very effective because, as behavioural studies show, persons experience general (e.g. time, financial, psychological, normative) costs in opting out from default options already set for them, which means that, in this way, many fathers would take parental leave.[40]

However, equal parental-leave schemes are not usually tailored to non-nuclear families. Apart from households composed of single mothers, other family and caring arrangements not conforming to the (often heterosexual) coupledom seem not to benefit from these policies. Non-nuclear families not only involve divorced or separated parents but also many other ties. For

---

[35] Brighouse and Wright (2008); Gheaus and Robeyns (2011).   [36] Barclay (2013).

[37] Barclay (2013, 168); Brighouse and Wright (2008, 363); Gheaus and Robeyns (2011, 184).

[38] This is not to suggest that equal parental leave is undesirable and should not be provided. I only intend to show that, when the HSI framework is endorsed, other measures should be seen as more apt to tackle GDDL and become a priority.

[39] Gheaus and Robeyns (2011, 183). See also Browne (2013, 153).

[40] Gheaus and Robeyns (2011, 184). Default parental leave seems thus well suited to overcome standard implementation issues with parental leave, such as fathers' low uptake even in egalitarian contexts (e.g. Nordic countries). See Barclay (2013, 168); Bekkengern (2006, 149); Browne (2013, 152).

example, enlarged families constituted by three or more persons (e.g. a bisexual person separated from her former partner and cohabiting with someone else) would have to choose only one designated carer to take advantage of the leave. Such non-nuclear family arrangements are particularly widespread among LGBTQ+ networks and characterise other groups, as with the practice of 'othermothering' performed within some African American communities.[41] These networks implicitly endorse a different (and, as I argue below, potentially transformative) view on caring and parenting duties which conceives of them as shared responsibilities among many persons, rather than obligations that only those directly tied to children (e.g. biological and foster parents) have to fulfil. By starting from the assumption of the nuclear family, equal parental leave does not support these non-mainstream and historically marginalised arrangements. When amendments to default parental leave are proposed to *include* these networks (e.g. by opening up the leave provision to multiple designated carers),[42] their *exclusionary* effects are even more troubling. Precisely because defaults are powerfully normative and nonconformity to them is costly, allowing non-nuclear families to enter parental-leave schemes by opting out of the default option would paradoxically reinforce the expectation that the (sharing) nuclear family is the norm. To wit, to achieve more equality between men and women, default parental leaves either leave unscathed or risk to reinforce historical patterns of marginalisation of groups along the lines of sexuality and race.

Second, equal parental-leave schemes overlook the encompassing character of unpaid domestic labour and its impact on GDDL. Not only do they exclude important caring networks but also they seem to reduce the unpaid caring work that women are expected to perform, and that men are asked to share, to child raising. As significant as child raising may be, it is not the sole dimension of care constituting GDDL. For example, women are usually supposed to take care of the frail elderly, the sick and the disabled – all crucial caring labour that is not covered by parental-leave schemes. Many women are caught in what has been termed 'sandwich care', which refers to multiple caring commitments.[43] Like child raising, all these other forms of caring involve various tasks: (1) 'interactive care activities', in which the carer and the recipient interact (e.g. spending time with an old father); (2) 'support care' – that is, activities that make interactive care possible (e.g. cleaning the old father's house and preparing

---

[41] Collins (2000, 193–211).   [42] E.g. Browne (2013, 163n12).
[43] Bianchi, Folbre and Wolf (2012, 49).

his meal); and (3) 'supervisory care', which requires being available to provide care (e.g. being ready to leave the workplace to assist the old father).[44] Moreover, daily housework (even when it is not instrumental to caring tasks) is unaddressed, although it has been historically (unpaid) labour expected (only) from women. Conceiving of parental leave as the best measure to address GDDL seems to neglect how GDDL involves much more than parental duties.[45] If we aim at eliminating GDDL, we cannot mainly rely on parental-leave schemes as they are, at the very least, limited in scope.

Third, supporters of equal parental-leave schemes tend to mistake involved fatherhood for gender equality. The mere idea of men spending time at home with their children – caring for and playing with them and becoming engaged in their lives – is seen as a 'real and enduring gain for equality'.[46] This expected outcome of parental leave is regarded as changing the 'social ethos' and working towards the creation of an egalitarian society.[47] Nevertheless, what supporters of equal parental leave seem to overlook is that being an involved father does not amount to being a gender-egalitarian man. As Lisbeth Bekkengern argues, it is possible to construct a masculinity in which raising one's own children is a fundamental part of what being a man means while not challenging the role men are expected to play in other areas of the household and in society in general.[48] The construction of this kind of masculinity, which equal parental-leave schemes promote, does not ipso facto translate into eradicating GDDL and transforming relations between men and women. Men can start thinking about childcare as expected from them without also regarding all other caring and domestic responsibilities women are supposed to shoulder as such. To wit, men's involvement in childcare is a necessary but not sufficient condition for transforming relations between men and women as groups.

On the whole, a major problem with the equal parental-leave discourse comes down to underestimating the pervasiveness and dynamics of the banal reproduction of unjust history. As seen in Chapters 3 and 6, within formally egalitarian contexts, unjust history is structurally reproduced in subtle ways in that it nourishes those stereotypes, expectations and norms that provide the day-to-day scripts whereby persons interact and in turn

---

[44] Folbre and Wright (2012, 1–4).
[45] As Nancy Folbre observes, 'Support for family labor need not be defined simply in terms of support for raising one's own children' (Folbre 1994, 115).
[46] Barclay (2013, 168); Browne (2013, 154).   [47] Gheaus and Robeyns (2011, 186).
[48] Bekkengern (2006, 154–57).

reactivate that history. The fact that such a reproduction is subtle makes it even less identifiable and more difficult to transform because it tends to occur even when some significant changes have been brought about. Thinking that through equal parental-leave schemes, *'with a bit of luck,* we may ... move ... closer to a society in which care is at the same time valued as it should be and distributed more justly',[49] GDDL is eliminated, and equal relations between men and women are successfully established underestimates the historical-structural nature of the injustice at stake.

To address GDDL, other measures are necessary – measures that intersectionally acknowledge the encompassing character of care and the ways unjust history is reproduced. One such measure is the proposal for a *mandatory caregiving service,* which prescribes that societal members serve a period as caregivers.[50] A mandatory caregiving service realises Fraser's normative model of the universal caregiver by making 'the performance of care ... part of what it means or what is implied by being a member of a political community'.[51] From within the HSI framework, a mandatory caregiving service becomes a crucial measure to turn what has been historically an expectation unjustly placed only on women into an obligation everyone is required to assume.

It is worth pointing out that a mandatory caregiving service can be justified also through different rationales. For instance, Cécile Fabre conceives of it as a sufficientarian duty to help the needy, which arises from the acute shortage of staff in hospitals and social-care services within many societies. Under these circumstances of emergency, in which many persons in need are left unassisted, everyone is expected to do her fair share as a cooperative member of society.[52] However, the importance of grounding the idea of a mandatory caregiving service in an obligation of historical-structural justice (rather than sufficientarian distributive justice) lies in the goals this measure is meant to contribute to achieving. A mandatory caregiving service should endeavour ultimately to enable the transformation of the relations between men and women by tackling GDDL. This means that even within a society in which public care was efficiently provided and there was no demand for caring personnel, a mandatory caregiving service would still be necessary. Although in such a society the sufficientarian duty to help the needy may be met, until unpaid caring and

---

[49] Gheaus and Robeyns (2011, 188, my italics).
[50] Bubeck (1999). Note that also Ingrid Robeyns defends a 'care experience programme', which is similar to the measure I defend below, in a short essay (2000), but she does not theorise its potential vis-à-vis equal parental leave.
[51] Bubeck (1999, 423).   [52] Fabre (2008, 56–58).

domestic labour is mainly undertaken by women, we would still have to implement measures to incentivise the de-gendering of such labour in order to overcome the problematic difference reinforced by GDDL.

Let me now specify further what a mandatory caregiving service should entail. This service is meant to produce both symbolic and pragmatic outcomes. Symbolically, it aims to change societal gendered expectations around caregiving and housework. Pragmatically, it intends to offer a 'school for carers'[53] to every societal member so as to provide them with the practical and empathetic skills necessary to perform care. To achieve these outcomes, the caregiving service should be preceded by an adequate compulsory training, explaining the rationale behind the service and teaching how to appropriately perform caring and housework tasks. This is because while everyone can, for example, bathe a frail old person, doing so respectfully is not straightforward. Ideally, caregiving service should be spent at different workplaces (e.g. kindergartens, hospitals and nurseries) to appreciate the multiple dimensions of care. Because gendered norms start regulating relationships from an early age, caregiving service would be more apt for teenagers, rather than adults, and could be implemented as the last component of a programme run in collaboration with schools, which should also include home economics classes starting in primary school and tailored at the different stages of students' education. Importantly, some exceptions can be made under particular circumstances. Those teenagers who are already performing caring tasks (e.g. taking care of their younger siblings or an ill parent) should be exempted from the service to avoid encumbering them further. By already performing caring activities, such teenagers are already likely to learn the importance of care and the skills caregiving demands. However, since understanding the rationale behind the mandatory caregiving service is paramount to transform relations, they may still be required to attend the compulsory training and the rest of the programme.

A mandatory caregiving service is bound to be received with resistance; should those teenagers who refuse to perform it be exempted from it? Can they appeal to a sort of 'conscientious objection' as in the case of mandatory military service? After all, proponents of mandatory caregiving service often defend it precisely through an analogy with the obligation to serve in the military.[54] Even assuming that military service is a requirement of citizenship – which I doubt – when considering conscientious objection, the parallel does not hold. Objection to military service is usually grounded

---

[53] Bubeck (1995, 260).   [54] Bubeck (1999).

on an arguably unproblematic value, namely refusal to commit violence. Conversely, it is difficult to come up with a justification for a value-based objection to caregiving service that does not rely on the different roles women and men have been expected to occupy over history. A mandatory caregiving service precisely aims to signal such a difference as normatively troubling and address it, thereby challenging the very grounds on which refusal is based. Granting exceptions on the basis of 'conscience' would thus be self-defeating.

The proposal of a mandatory caregiving service so reconceived would overcome the shortcomings of equal parental-leave schemes. Unlike parental leave, it recognises the encompassing character of care, and it does not confuse good fatherhood with gender equality by not limiting the service to child raising, offering participants the opportunity to understand the various tasks and activities involved in caregiving and providing a rationale grounded on the necessity of transforming relations between men and women.

Moreover, a mandatory caregiving service (justified in terms of historical-structural justice) attempts to eradicate GDDL by avoiding the reinforcement of other 'intersecting' injustices. In not treating (heterosexual) coupledom as the norm, this measure not only recognises the existence of alternative caring networks but also enables them. Consider the aforementioned case of 'othermothering', a practice traditionally performed within African American communities. By sharing parental and caring (informal) obligations among many members of a community, othermothering endorses a broader conception of caring responsibilities which extends them beyond intimate partners and biological or foster parents.[55] By transforming caring (in all its dimensions) into a task everyone is expected to perform, a mandatory caregiving service praises and normalises practices such as othermothering while revising them in more egalitarian terms. While othermothering is still a female-dominated practice (i.e. a practice African American *women* tend to undertake), a mandatory caregiving service promotes what may be called an 'othercaring' – that is, a caring both men and women are expected to do. That is, this measure endorses some potentially innovative aspects of othermothering by de-gendering it.

The realisation of a mandatory caregiving service is the first necessary step towards eradicating GDDL, although it may obviously not be enough. Other measures, such as equal parental leave, are needed too – for example,

---

[55] Card (1996, 17–18); hooks (1984, 144).

to resist employers' pressure on nontraditional caregivers (e.g. men) to undertake caring duties.[56] Similarly, a mandatory caregiving service must not support the privatisation of care and thus be a substitute for state-regulated measures enabling a more reasonable work-family balance, such as public provision of care (e.g. the establishment of child centres) and reduction in work time.[57] Nevertheless, these measures are more likely to channel persons' actions in different (i.e. de-gendered) directions when they are designed and implemented within societies that run the proposed mandatory caregiving service. For instance, public provision of childcare certainly increases women's options but does not lead per se to a transformation of the relations between women and men since it does not require any change in the expectations of what the latter should do. Thus, a mandatory caregiving service should be regarded as the *precondition* for other measures to become more transformative. It can also have the interrelated effect of revaluing activities and tasks traditionally associated with the role women were (unjustly) expected to play because it de-genders them. Nevertheless, tackling the banal reproduction of unjust history and thus transforming relations between women and men would also require tackling (historically rooted) differences in another interconnected domain: the occupational sphere.

7.3 Occupational Segregation and (Horizontal) Affirmative Action

As seen, from within the HSI framework, the horizontal dimension of occupational segregation – the concentration of women in the pink-collar ghetto – should be considered as problematic independently of its vertical component. That is, it would remain normatively questionable even if

---

[56] However, the structural constraints preventing fathers from taking time off work to look after their children should not be overstressed. Arguing for equal parental leave on the assumption that the majority of fathers are precluded from taking leave only because of others' practices and employers' expectations regulating the workplace (see, e.g. Browne 2013, 164) is problematic because mothers suffer from significant constraints too (e.g. the 'mommy track') but do take parental leave (Bekkengern 2006, 151). Moreover, this argument seems to overlook how unjust history is structurally reproduced within egalitarian contexts. Fathers may not publicly endorse inegalitarian gender views but may perpetuate them in private (or even at a more unconscious level). Thus, although the decision not to take parental leave may be justified in pragmatic terms or by referring to the hostile environment, other (historically structural) norms may be also at play. As seen in Chapter 6, this is particularly true for those who live in countries that are internationally appraised for their gender equality. A full recognition of the banal reproduction of unjust history points at the interaction (and mutual reinforcement) of workplace structures, persons' actions and societies. I thank Jude Browne for discussions on this point.

[57] E.g. Gornick and Meyers (2005).

traditionally female jobs were not as poorly remunerated as they tend to be (§ 6.2). Once justice is de-temporalised and, thus, unjust history is conceptualised as structurally reproduced in the fabric of society, horizontal occupational segregation should be interpreted as both signalling that history is structurally reproduced and contributing to its reproduction. In this section, I defend affirmative action (and preferential hiring), one of the most discussed and controversial measures designed to counter overall occupational segregation, and apply it specifically to the horizontal dimension.

Before proceeding, let me briefly indicate what I mean by affirmative action. Affirmative action is 'any policy that aims to increase the participation of a disadvantaged group in mainstream institutions'.[58] Outreach programmes that simply inform disadvantaged groups about job opportunities and invite them to apply are often included as a type of affirmative action. In the context of horizontal occupational segregation, such measures are certainly desirable. For instance, in 2015, the UK Department of Work and Pensions launched the social media campaign #NotJustforBoys to encourage girls and young women to take up careers in traditionally male-dominated fields, such as science, technology and engineering.[59] Since outreach programmes are usually less controversial than preferential hiring measures because they do not deploy group membership as a relevant *selection* criterion, I focus on the latter to show how they can be justified to tackle (horizontal) occupational segregation on the basis of the interplay between history and structure.[60]

A further preliminary clarification is needed. Affirmative action has usually targeted two groups – namely, African Americans and women. In this section, I concentrate only on the latter. This importantly means that my defence of affirmative action and especially my proposal of horizontal affirmative action apply to the specific case of women. Therefore it may be the case that affirmative action would not constitute a transformative measure as far as other groups displaying historical and structural dynamics are concerned (including those groups that supporters of affirmative action usually consider, such as African Americans).

---

[58] Anderson (2010, 135). See also Sterba (2003, 200); for an earlier defence of affirmative action, see Thomson (1973).

[59] www.gov.uk/government/news/notjustforboys-leading-businesses-back-women-as-captains-of-ind ustry (accessed 3 July 2018).

[60] For instance, Robert S. Taylor argues that while 'outreach' affirmative action would be allowed under non-ideal conditions by a Rawlsian conception of justice, that conception would rule out preferential affirmative action such as soft and hard quotas (2009, 491–98).

How should affirmative action be justified in the case of gender segregation in the labour market? Although there are different rationales for
affirmative action, the most promising model is the one recently advanced
by Elizabeth Anderson – that is, the 'integrative model'.[61] This is because
this model, which Anderson applies to the case of the 'black-white' divide
in the US, argues that affirmative action is needed to tackle the roots of
enduring forms of group-based injustices.[62] Such injustices do not merely
involve the actual discrimination that members of disadvantaged groups
experience in the job market. They also stem from the fact that historical
injustices still hinder present equality through the division of persons into
different yet interdependent ascriptive groups to which particular roles and
expectations are conferred.

Applying the integrative rationale to the case of women, affirmative
action is required to place members of this group into occupations that
were closed to them in the past and still remain largely precluded to them
because of how the banal reproduction of unjust history regulates societies
at large and the workings of employment institutions in particular.
Affirmative action not only intends to prevent the likely discrimination
some women can encounter in the selection processes of certain employment organisations. It also aims to integrate women into occupations once
formally and now informally restricted to men so as to challenge those
stereotypes, expectations and norms bound up with unjust history that
provide the scripts of persons' interactions. The integrative model thus
does not temporalise justice as it recognises that some unjust histories
endure structurally.[63]

Nevertheless, in the case of women, the HSI framework pushes the
integrative model further in two significant respects. First, unlike what is
generally assumed by its advocates, affirmative action is due and justified

---

[61] Anderson provides an illuminating classification of different models of affirmative action: compensatory, discrimination blocking, integrative and diversity. As she points out, unlike the others, the
diversity model, which stresses the epistemic desirability of having institutions and organisations
whose members have different social backgrounds, is not grounded in a theory of (in)justice
(Anderson 2010, 142–44).

[62] Anderson (2010, 149).

[63] The other models of affirmative action, instead, temporalise justice. The 'compensatory model',
which argues that affirmative action is owed to members of disadvantaged groups, such as women,
because of past discrimination and exclusion, is mainly backward looking and thus separates past
and present injustices. The 'discrimination-blocking' model, which is aimed at those institutions
that are still discriminating against members of disadvantaged groups by blocking actual discrimination when it occurs, grounds affirmative action only on the present discrimination suffered by
certain individuals and thus fails to theorise the relation between past and present. See also Anderson
(2010, 137–48).

not only for particularly prestigious (and remunerative) professional fields (e.g. politicians, corporate leaders and professionals in STEM fields). It should also be implemented for other kinds of jobs, which are comparatively less well paid and enjoy a lower status within societies but have the expressive power to contribute to and thus reinforce the banal reproduction of unjust history. As previously argued, occupational segregation not only is constituted by a vertical component, which measures inequalities in pay, but it also displays an interrelated yet distinctive horizontal property, which amounts to the different concentration of men and women in occupations. Within societies in which women suffered from formally sanctioned discrimination and exclusion, the horizontal property becomes crucial because the concentration of women (and men) in traditionally female- (or male)-dominated jobs creates a problematic *difference* – one that nourishes those stereotypes, norms and expectations whereby history is structurally reproduced (§ 6.2). In addition to (vertical) affirmative action, which aims to include women in particularly well-paid and valued professions, *horizontal affirmative action* is needed to integrate women into jobs that, by virtue of their connection to the unjust history of women, are symbolically salient (e.g. construction and repairing workers; drivers; firefighters).

Second, this type of affirmative action should not be limited to women; rather, it should be directed at *both* women and men, thereby recognising how historical-structural injustices are relational in character. By reserving a preferential treatment to women in the hiring process for, say, construction jobs and to men in occupations such as nursing, child education and secretary, horizontal affirmative action would try to tackle the banal reproduction of history, which is reinforced when certain jobs are dominated by women or men. The increase in the *presence* of members of the group that is not commonly associated with a determinate occupation can contribute to breaking the pernicious link between that occupation, group membership and expected roles. Horizontal affirmative action would also have the potential effect of revaluing traditionally female occupations by integrating those who have been reluctant to apply for these jobs (e.g. because of the putative inferior status of such jobs) into these occupations.

To be sure, this integration may not be sufficient to reconsider undervalued occupations and one may worry that it would worsen existing inequalities. Here the concern is that the majority of men applying for female-dominated jobs and thus targeted by horizontal affirmative action would be from worse-off backgrounds or migrants from developing countries. In this respect, integration may turn into segregation as it would reinforce class or ethnic inequalities by confining already disadvantaged men to poorly paid jobs.[64] This is an important concern, but not one that should lead to a rejection of horizontal affirmative action. It simply points out the need to supplement it with other measures aimed at revaluing occupations in the pink-collar ghetto (especially paid caregiving), such as increases in pay.[65] Moreover, it is noteworthy that many issues faced by men in traditionally female occupations are also related to the fact that such occupations are largely perceived as 'female', which makes it more difficult for male workers to negotiate their working activities with the role assigned by society to them. However, when traditionally female tasks, such as caregiving and domestic chores, are de-gendered (e.g. through the implementation of a mandatory caregiving service), and more men are employed in traditionally female jobs (e.g. through horizontal affirmative action), these problems may become less serious.

One may object that affirmative action is problematic because its recipients are not the same persons who have originally suffered from the discrimination.[66] This long-standing objection seems to be particularly challenging when groups such as women are considered; while an argument based on the intergenerational inheritance (from ancestors to descendants) of disadvantages can be available for groups such as African Americans, 'being female is not passed on from generation to generation'.[67] The problem with this objection lies in its narrow understanding of 'descendants'. As seen, when justice is de-temporalised and the interplay between history and structures is fully considered, descent should be conceptualised not only along family lines but also along structural-positional lines. In this sense, beneficiaries of (horizontal) affirmative action are in a particular and normatively significant relation to those who were formally discriminated against and excluded over history. They are not mainly (or only) their biological heirs; they are their structural descendants. As argued (§ 4.2), contemporary members of groups that have both historical and structural features – such as that of women – should be

---

[64] On the problems encountered by men in female-dominated jobs, see Sarti and Scrinzi (2010).

[65] Similarly, horizontal affirmative action should not be seen as a measure to tackle the vertical dimension of occupational segregation. It may be, as it actually tends to be, that when professions become more female dominated, inequality in pay between women and men increases. This simply shows that, although interconnected, the two dimensions of gendered occupational segregation require different solutions and, thus, as argued, they should be conceptually and practically separated. Here I simply put forward a proposal to counter the horizontal dimension of such segregation, which becomes particularly problematic per se when it is approached through the lens of HSI. I thank Jude Browne for pressing me on this point.

[66] E.g. Sher (1979, 81).   [67] Wolf-Devine (2005, 61).

conceived as structural descendants because they have inherited a social (or transnational) position constituted through injustices over history and maintained by the reproduction of such history through different means (e.g. stereotypes, informal norms, expectations). Thus, although being a woman is not a property transmitted through family lines, it is a (structural) position that is handed down from one generation to another within societies.

Some may also critically observe that affirmative action benefits only qualified members of disadvantaged groups – that is, individuals who are already well off in societies.[68] Usually supporters of affirmative action restrict such schemes to candidates who have all the credentials required for the job so as to avoid the 'underachievement problem'.[69] If unqualified applicants from disadvantaged groups were hired through affirmative action, they would perform poorly and this would have far-reaching consequences not only for them but also for other members of the groups by reinforcing the idea that they cannot properly execute certain tasks because of their group membership.[70] Only the preferential selection of qualified applicants can hope to overcome this problem. This, however, increases the concern that affirmative action benefits the already advantaged. Horizontal affirmative action, which I argued should supplement existing accounts of the integrative model when it comes to gendered occupational segregation, is less open to this criticism. Although it maintains the qualification requirement, horizontal affirmative action is not mainly directed at individuals who are already well off. Rather, it extends the benefits of gender integration to society at large by targeting 'symbolically salient' jobs that, although not particularly remunerative, play an important role in reproducing historical structures. Moreover, horizontal affirmative action is relational in character in that it is directed to both women and men. Therefore, even those that may feel excluded from standard (vertical) affirmative action programmes can benefit from it. This point is significant. Indeed, some men who would like to choose a career in a pink-collar occupation (e.g. child worker and primary school teacher) feel discouraged from doing so because of widespread and pervasive gendered stereotypes and expectations attached to such jobs.[71]

---

[68] Fishkin (1984, 88–89); Goldman (1976, 190–91); Simon (1974, 315–19); Sher (1979, 81–82).

[69] E.g. Anderson (2010, 151); Browne (2014); Sterba (2003, 233, 261).

[70] Murray (2000, 251–57) quoted by Sterba (2003, 260). On the problem of underachievement in the context of affirmative action in universities, see Sander and Taylor (2012).

[71] Cameron (2001). Stereotypes about men in traditionally female occupations are indeed pervasive, as showed by the infamous recent case of the UK MP Andrea Leadsom's comments about how men

7.4 Policy Making and Redress

In the previous sections, I analysed some measures devised to address the three dimensions of the HSI suffered by women, which were discussed in Chapter 6 (i.e. violence, GDDL and occupational segregation). All the measures defended share important features, which should be seen as general desiderata of policy making in the context of injustices that are both historical and structural. Policy making should devise and implement transformative measures, which directly tackle the banal reproduction of unjust history. Such measures have a deconstructive function as they should try to deactivate the workings of historical structures regulating societies and unequal interpersonal relations. Simultaneously, they also have a constructive goal because they should attempt to channel persons' actions in different directions so as to create new structural conditions for equal relationships to emerge.

Which are the general desiderata of transformative policy making? First, transformative measures should be *relational* – that is, they should recognise how HSI is constituted by the interactions between groups that have been mutually constituted over time (e.g. women and men). In the case of the men-women divide, this can be obtained when, for example, measures engage both groups. As seen with respect to horizontal occupational segregation, affirmative action should target not merely women but also men by increasing the number of men in pink-collar jobs and thus de-gendering them. As for VAW (and IPV), measures targeting only men or women, such as self-defence classes and men's programmes, are less apt than those including both groups, such as the bystander approach. By being relational, transformative measures not only offer the opportunity to tackle the relational character of the injustice at stake but also show how historical-structural justice can be achieved only when everyone becomes aware of their own structural position.

Second, policy making should be *intersectional* – that is, sensitive to the other injustices that have historically intersected with that of the group in question. Policies, such as equal parental leave, that do not consider how race and sexuality-based HSI intersect with the HSI suffered by women are bound to leave intact or reinforce these injustices.

Third and relatedly, policy making should proceed from a *full awareness of how a specific unjust history is structurally reproduced*. This means it should

---

should not be hired to look after children because they could be potential paedophiles (see Stone 2016).

be context dependent to avoid reactivating the particular structures of the injustice through the perpetuation of those stereotypes, norms and expectations whereby a specific history is recreated. For instance, as argued, the especially serious implications that certain policies, such as self-defence classes, have in certain countries stem from their potential to reinforce stereotypes, norms and discourses that have historically served as a justification for discriminating against and excluding women. Awareness of the banal reproduction of unjust history also entails recognising its pervasiveness. Unlike equal parental leave, transformative actions need to consider how an unjust history is reproduced also in subtle ways – that is, ways that are difficult to detect and counter.

In sum, once justice has been de-temporalised, policy making becomes a crucial component of redress. Not only does policy making have to be sensitive to historical structures to avoid reinforcing them but also it has the potential to contribute to transforming such structures because it can intervene in individuals' daily interactions, channel individual agency in new directions and thus create different – more egalitarian – norms and expectations. Although this chapter has illustrated this point by looking at some dimensions of the injustice suffered by women, the insight into the importance of policy making as a tool of redress applies to all injustices that are historical and structural. Neglecting the relation between policy making and historical injustices underestimates the dangers policy making can cause when it is insensitive to historical structures and deprives us of an important instrument to change such structures.

In contemporary politics, however, struggles for historical justice usually take different forms – most notably, reparation claims. While this and the previous chapters (6 and 7) have shown how my account of HSI casts light on the condition of women in a formally egalitarian context and the ways to address it, the next chapter will consider how the framework of HSI can help us understand the significance of historical injustice in contemporary political struggles such as reparation claims (but also importantly beyond them).

CHAPTER 8

The Politics of the Unjust Past

In contemporary politics, the unjust past is at the core of several struggles for social and global justice. In particular, since the Federal Republic of Germany established a compensation scheme for survivors of Nazi persecution and reached a reparations agreement with Israel in September 1952 for the Jewish Holocaust, demands for reparations of past injustices have gained momentum in emancipatory politics.

This chapter aims to show what de-temporalising injustice entails when we look at the 'politics of the unjust past', which is exemplified by (but importantly not limited to) claims for reparations. To do so, I focus on the case of the history of racial injustice in the US, which has rightly received lots of attention by scholars of historical injustice and reparations and is still at the centre of contemporary activists' quest for racial equality. Specifically, I argue that historical injustices (of even a distant past) that have been reproduced over history press *backward-looking* demands on certain powerful contemporary agents because of the significant role these agents have played in the reproduction of these injustices over time. Such agents owe what I will call 'a structural debt'. By reconceiving accountability for historical injustice in structural terms, I show that 'reparative justice' – that is, establishing 'what ought to be done in reparations for injustice, and the obligation of wrongdoers, or their descendants or successors, for making this repair'[1] – is a crucial component of de-temporalising injustice. In defending reparations, I also make a case for approaching reparations in a participatory way to minimise the risk of excluding certain viewpoints and social positions from the pursuit and design of repair.

A backward-looking normative evaluation of accountability is necessary for de-temporalising injustice. However, I also contend that reparations do not exhaust what *redressing* an unjust history that has been reproduced

---

[1] Thompson (2002, xi).

through changes should amount to.[2] We also need to question the workings and the very desirability of our existing background conditions, including our institutional set-up. This is the role of what I call 'counterhistorical institutional justifications', which precisely aim to dispel the illusion of a separation between the past and the present in institutional assessment by connecting an institutional target to its (unjust) history and its new reproduction. I conceptualise this peculiar instance of the 'politics of the unjust past', which can be found in activist discourses and practices, by drawing on the example of prison abolitionism in the US. As I explain, counterhistorical institutional justifications are of normative significance not only for their unsettling criticism of the status quo but also because they stimulate our political and social imagination in transformative and unexpected directions.

8.1 Reparations, Historical Accountability and Structural Debt

Since the post–Civil War era, discussions about reparations for slavery (and subsequently also for Jim Crow and racial segregation) have been a permanent feature of African American movements, connecting the fight for national race equality to international racial justice.[3] In contemporary US politics, demands for reparations for slavery and Jim Crow are still on the agenda of African American activism. The National Coalition of Blacks for Reparations in America (N'COBRA) is centred on the claim that the US government (and corporations implicated in past wrongs) should offer reparation for the past injustices it committed.[4] The Movement for Black Lives (MBL) – a coalition of more than fifty organisations across the US, such as the Black Lives Matter Network, the Ella Baker Center for Human Rights, and Mothers Against Police Brutality, which represents the interests of black

---

[2] As I will sum up in § 9.1, reparations should be seen as a component of a multifaceted process of *redress*.

[3] It is sufficient to recall the importance that claims for reparations played in the demands of African American leaders, such as Ida B. Wells, W. E. B. Du Bois, Malcom X and Huey Percy Newton, to name but a few, to see how reparations for domestic and international racial injustice were 'a much more visible theme in the civil rights/Black liberation movement than historical accounts generally acknowledge' (Biondi 2003, 7). For a recent collection of essays and documents on the reparations movement in the US, see Henry (2007). For a history of American racial-reparations movements (and of America's failure to seriously consider their demands), see the contributions in Martin and Yaquinto (2007).

[4] www.ncobraonline.org (accessed 3 July 2018).

persons – includes reparations for '*past* and continuing harms' towards African Americans among their six demands of justice and identifies the US government as one of the main agents accountable for them.[5] To wit, fights for present and future racial justice press *backward-looking* demands for (even distant) past injustices on certain contemporary agents.

Although structural-injustice theorists such as Iris Marion Young and Catherine Lu share many intuitions about the contemporary nature of racial inequalities with African American movements, they have been reluctant to endorse a backward-looking normative analysis to reflect upon responsibility for racial injustices of the distant past. Young completely rejects reparations for slavery as being both conceptually and politically problematic.[6] Echoing long-standing criticisms to such reparation claims, she argues that reparations cannot be morally justified, because they isolate a contemporary agent (i.e. the American state) as accountable for past wrongs (i.e. slavery) whose direct causal connection to present racial inequality and oppression cannot be accurately established.[7] According to Young, present-day racial injustice calls for a forward-looking responsibility to change enduring racial structures, which is shared by all collective agents (e.g. the American state) and individuals (e.g. American citizens) who participate in these structures.[8]

In her recent sophisticated account of justice and reconciliation in world politics, Lu advances a more nuanced model of responsibility for structural injustices implicated in atrocities. Unlike Young, she contends that still-alive individual victim-survivors of wrongs can rightly demand reparations and compensations not only from direct perpetrators but also from other agents participating in unjust structures underpinning such wrongs because of the 'causal implication of structural injustice in contemporary wrongful conduct'.[9] To exemplify, following Lu's account, it could be suggested that, in the case of the Charleston church shooting in South Carolina in June 2015, not only should the perpetrator, the white supremacist Dylann Roof, be punished for the massacre but also the US state should bear reparative responsibilities towards the still-alive victim-survivors (and the immediate families of the murdered victims) because it has arguably failed to address the racial structures at the roots of the shooting. Lu's account does offer a more complex picture of responsibility and accountability for structural injustice, and, in contexts of wrongs whose individual victim-survivors (or their immediate families) are still

[5] https://policy.m4bl.org/reparations/ (accessed 3 July 2018, my emphasis).
[6] Young (2011, chapter 7).   [7] Young (2011, 175).   [8] Young (2011, 184).   [9] Lu (2017, 259).

alive, it ensures that victims receive reparation or compensation by all parties involved (especially when direct perpetrators are unable to fully pay for their wrongful conduct without suffering themselves from distributive or structural injustice). However, when it comes to injustices committed in the distant past (i.e. whose victims and immediate families are not alive) such as slavery in the US, Lu agrees with Young that a backward-looking account of responsibility is misguided.[10] In criticising 'interactional' accounts of international historical justice, such as Daniel Butt's,[11] she argues that, instead of searching for specific agents to hold them accountable for historical wrongs and their effects, we should focus on those contemporary structures originated from past injustices and the forward-looking responsibility that *all* contemporary agents (independently of their possible connection to past injustice) bear to address them.[12]

To be sure, Lu specifies that contemporary agents may also have to acknowledge past wrongs, which may include offering some symbolic 'acknowledgement payments', but argues this amounts to a forward-looking responsibility for reconciliation – that is, it is part of 'the project of constructing a mutually affirmable and affirmed global [and domestic] order'.[13] In other words, according to Lu, reparations as backward-looking demands on specific agents for injustices of the distant past (e.g. slavery), even when these injustices are connected to persisting unjust structures, should not be included in a framework aimed at conceptualising responsibility for structural injustices.[14] What normatively matters is *forward-looking* responsibility for structural injustice and reconciliation.[15]

---

[10] Lu (2017, chapter 5).   [11] Butt (2009).   [12] Lu (2017, 155, 164–65).   [13] Lu (2017, 250).

[14] Lu (2017, 250). In this respect, Lu's position on reparations for historical injustices is similar to that of Spinner-Halev, who rejects reparations in favour of acknowledgement of past wrongs (Spinner-Halev 2012, 85–119).

[15] Note that one could rebut Lu by arguing that proper backward-looking reparations for injustices of a distant past are a precondition for reconciliation (see McGary 2003). How could we even start to establish a mutually affirmable order if agents that committed serious injustices over history did not take full responsibility to repair what they did in the past? Although I share the intuitions behind this possible line of reasoning, in what follows, I pursue a different argument, which does not rely on the idea of reconciliation but on what doing *justice* to the reproduction of an unjust history entails. 'Reconciliation' projects are too easily co-opted by those in power, and thus we should try to theorise reparations for injustices of the distant past independently from calls for reconciliation. Indeed, although in 2008, the US government recognised the importance of 'reconciliation', acknowledged and apologised for the wrongs of slavery and Jim Crow and (especially in the version of the bill passed by the House of Representatives) committed to addressing their present effects, it has avoided taking on a backward-looking responsibility for any 'reparation'. See H. Res. 194, 110th Cong. (2008). By distinguishing reparations from reconciliation, my argument tries to reclaim the irreducibly (and non-negotiable) backward-looking character of obligations of reparations (see McGary 1999, 94) from within a structural perspective.

Movements such as the MBL have a multifaceted agenda, which does encompass forward-looking demands to address present racial structural injustice, such as investment in education, health and safety of black persons, reconstruction of the economy to guarantee equal ownership to black communities, and political empowerment of black persons in all social areas (including effective disenfranchisement).[16] However, they also insist that forward-looking responsibilities do not cancel off the 'compounding moral debt' that certain agents owe to African Americans for their past conduct.[17] How should we interpret this resilience of reparation claims in fights against racial injustice? Do such movements inappropriately hold accountable for past injustices contemporary agents (e.g. the US state) that are 'only' responsible to change persistent structural injustices (and possibly accountable for their present failure to do so)?

I think this interpretation would be mistaken. In the case of historical injustices, dismissing backward-looking reparations demands would leave a significant gap in the moral framework of structural approaches. Indeed, such demands should be read as singling out and holding accountable specific agents not simply for past wrongs (and their effects) but for their historical role in the reproduction of unjust history over time. Reparation demands for injustices such as slavery point out that fully de-temporalising injustice – that is, separating the past and the present in our reflecting upon justice – entails not only forward-looking responsibilities but *also* a backward-looking normative analysis searching for powerful agents that, over history, have significantly enabled the structural reproduction of unjust history. It requires that such agents be held accountable for what can be called their *structural debt* – that is, a debt they have accumulated over time through their actions (and inactions) within unjust structures.[18]

To illustrate what I mean by 'structural debt', consider briefly the history of the systematic infringement of black women's reproductive rights and the role of the US state in it.[19] As black feminist scholars argue, such a history starts with slavery. During slavery, black women

---

[16] https://policy.m4bl.org/reparations/ (accessed 3 July 2018).   [17] Coates (2014).

[18] It is important to clarify that providing a backward-looking justification for reparations is not inconsistent with the claim that backward-looking arguments for why we should care about the unjust past are flawed, which I developed in Chapter 2. The fact that a backward-looking approach is unable to *identify* when and why historical injustices normatively matter does not entail that there are no compelling backward-looking *responsibilities* when it comes to injustices that have kept being reproduced over time.

[19] In what follows, I draw on Dorothy E. Roberts's compelling historical and sociological reconstruction of the 'systematic institutionalized denial of [black women's] reproductive freedom' (2017, 4). See also Nelson (2003); Solinger (2007); Threadcraft (2016).

suffered from sexual violence and exploitation of their reproductive capacities, which were both sanctioned by law. Since enslaved women's offspring was the property of their masters, controlling slaves' reproduction became a source of wealth for slaveholders. Enslaved mothers could be coercively separated from their children or forced not to nurture and to leave them alone while working in the field or caring for their masters' offspring.[20] Slavery marked those recognised as black women as 'unfit mothers' whose reproductive capacities needed to be socially governed and thus 'laid the foundation for centuries of reproductive regulation'.[21]

Such a regulation has been reproduced through legal discrimination during the Jim Crow era in the South and, after the victories of the civil rights movement, through subtler policy making. After the demise of Jim Crow segregation laws, which both had guaranteed the formal exclusion of black women from the gains of the birth control movement in the 1930s and had made them paradoxically less targeted by the pre–World War II eugenic legislation punishing those regarded as 'genetically inferior' and, thus, 'anti-social' (e.g. the 'feebleminded', the poor and migrants),[22] federally sponsored family-planning and welfare programmes started to 'not only encourag[e] Black women to use birth control but coerc[e] them into being sterilized'.[23] In the second half of the 1960s and especially during the 1970s, through policy making that relied on wicked and long-standing ideas about how welfare support encouraged the reproduction of 'inferior' groups and how control of reproduction was effective at addressing social issues, the medical establishment and social workers were enabled to practice widespread sterilisation on black women (and indigenous, Mexican, and Puerto Rican women) without their informed consent or by pressuring them into consenting to the procedure.[24]

With the progressive decrease in sterilisation abuse, other ways to regulate black women's reproduction have been devised by legislators and other policy makers in the US. Dorothy E. Roberts identifies three

---

[20] Roberts (2017, 22–55).   [21] Roberts (2017, 23).

[22] It is important to note that, although pre–World War II eugenics laws were not specifically directed to African Americans, racism theoretically underpinned eugenics (Roberts 2017, 61). A crucial role in linking the eugenics movement with concerns about managing reproduction within African American communities was played by birth control activists, such as Margaret Sanger – the founder of Planned Parenthood – who initially proposed the 'Negro Project'. Implemented in 1939, the project aimed to contain the 'reckless breeding' of African Americans, who were regarded as an illiterate group plagued by economic, health and social problems (Roberts 2017, 72–76).

[23] Roberts (2017, 56).

[24] Roberts (2017, 89–98). See also Hansen and King (2013, 237–58) on the role of welfare legislation and policy making in the sterilisation of African American women during the 1960s and 1970s.

main interconnected strategies, which became prominent in the 1990s. First, Norplant – a levonorgestrel-releasing contraceptive, implanted under the skin and lasting for up to five years, which had harmful side effects (e.g. heavy bleeding and vision impairment) on women's health – started being marketed, distributed to and pushed onto poor women through the joint federal and state programme Medicaid.[25] Second, the welfare system, which previously formally excluded African Americans, became the target of reforms drastically shrinking federal support and framing welfare as 'a means of modifying poor people's behaviour',[26] rather than a tool of distributive justice. For instance, infamously, the Personal Responsibility and Work Opportunity Reconciliation Act of 1996, passed under Bill Clinton's administration, required beneficiaries to work after two years of benefits, placed a five-year lifetime limit on federal funds and granted states increased authority to design their own welfare programmes, such as by adding 'family caps' aimed at deterring women on public assistance from having more babies and excluding large families from support.[27] Third, the criminal-justice system started to implement punitive measures against addicted mothers and pregnant women – especially those smoking crack – by temporarily or permanently removing their babies and prosecuting them for risking to harm the foetuses during pregnancy.[28]

To be sure, unlike slavery laws, such measures did not explicitly target black women but were framed more neutrally as addressing poverty. However, in a context of historical racial structural injustice, they ended up severely restricting the reproductive freedom of black women (and women of colour) not only because black women were (and still are) disproportionately represented in the lowest social classes of the American population. These measures also hinged upon myths and stereotypes of black women as unfit for motherhood (e.g. the 'welfare queen', the 'Jezebel' immoral black woman, the black unwed or negligent mother), which have historically regulated the social control and management of black women's reproductive freedom and still permeated the American imagination.[29] Today, the interplay between policy making and the historical-structural intersection of race, gender and class can be seen, for instance, in how the US child-welfare system operates by punishing parents (and especially mothers), rather than tackling the societal roots of

---

[25] Roberts (2017, 104–38).   [26] Roberts (2017, 202).
[27] Roberts (2017, 202–45). On the racial foundations and development of the American welfare system, see Quadagno (1994).
[28] Roberts (2017, 150–83).   [29] Roberts (2017, 8–21).

poverty. As Roberts shows, for instance, the equation of poverty with child neglect places a disproportionate number of black children into the foster care system, thereby disrupting black families.[30]

Over history, federal and state laws and policy making 'not only injured individual black women, but they [have been] a principal means of justifying [and enabling] the perpetuation of a racist social structure'.[31] In other words, they have constituted a crucial mechanism whereby the history of reproductive injustice against African American women has been reproduced *through* changes in circumstances. In this sense, as Shatelma Threadcraft puts it, the US state should 'answer for decades – centuries – of outright collusion in denying black women's bodily integrity'.[32] It should be held accountable and offer reparation for its 'structural debt'.[33]

Structural debts are accumulated over time by (usually collective) agents that have a significant power to influence structural processes but that instead have sustained unjust structures or failed to intervene to address them. Such a *pattern* of enablement or negligence has contributed to the new reproduction of unjust history over time. Structural debts can be assessed precisely when a de-temporalised framework is endorsed. As seen in Chapter 2, de-temporalising injustice entails conceiving (certain) past and present injustices not simply as connected (e.g. in a cause-effect relation to one another) but as the same injustice reproduced over time through changes and in new ways. When we look at a (past) injustice as a 'moving picture' along a temporal arc (even a very long one),[34] we can evaluate how specific agents have exercised their agency and power during the overarching process of reproduction of that injustice. In this respect, to establish structural debts we do not have to counterfactually ask how the present would look had a specific wrong (e.g. slavery) not been committed and thus trace the causal chain from that past event to the present unjust condition. The relevant normative question is how powerful agents (e.g. the US state) have acted within unjust structures over time – that is, whether such agents have contributed to processes of structural reproduction while they could have instead significantly helped gradually interrupt them.

---

[30] Roberts (2002).   [31] Roberts (2017, 6).   [32] Threadcraft (2016, 157).

[33] Obviously, the US state also played a significant role in many other dimensions of the reproduction of the unjust history of African Americans (e.g. political disenfranchisement, educational and housing segregation and police brutality). I focused on the denial of black women's reproductive rights as a compelling, and traditionally neglected, illustration of what structural debts are and how they are accumulated over time.

[34] On the difference between 'moving pictures' and 'snapshot' views of political and social life, see Pierson (2004).

Unlike 'interactional' accounts,[35] my backward-looking justification for reparations does not focus on single wrongs committed by agents and their effects. Structural debts are about the conduct of powerful agents within unjust structures over time. Unlike other structural-injustice theorists' approaches to responsibility for injustices of the distant past, the notion of structural debt shows how the passage of time does not necessarily weaken backward-looking responsibilities; rather, it can make them even weightier. The longer it passes, the more opportunities an agent with power to influence structural processes has had to address them. If an agent sustains unjust structures or fails at multiple times to intervene in their reproduction, its structural debt increases, rather than decreases. Indeed, structural debts are precisely accumulated by powerful agents *over time.*[36]

To be sure, no single agent, as powerful as it may be, can eradicate unjust structures on its own. Tackling unjust structural processes is a complex task that requires the collaboration of many (collective and individual) agents. Moreover, unjust structural processes are the background context in which all agents act; for instance, the myth and stereotype of the black welfare queen was not created by the drastic reforms of the US welfare system in the 1990s. As seen, these reforms relied and could count on the existence of such structures for support.

That said, considering the institution of slavery, segregation laws, restrictive welfare reforms, reproductive-control policies and criminal-justice legislation and measures as simply by-products of racial ideologies, discourses, norms and stereotypes that were (and still are) promoted and permeated within civil society would be overly simplistic in at least three respects. First, such legislations and policies have *also* importantly contributed to the reproduction of racially unjust structures over time by authorising and legitimising them (e.g. in the case of slavery and racial-segregation legislation) and by sustaining and reinforcing them (e.g. in the case of welfare policy making since the second half of the 1960s). As seen in Chapter 3, there is indeed an interplay between structures and the exercise of agency. Second, although no agent can change structural processes by

---

[35] E.g. Boxill (1972, 2003); Butt (2009).

[36] In this respect, the attempt to ground reparations claims on more recent wrongs against African Americans (e.g. Jim Crow and lawful racist housing practices after World War II) which some reparation scholars have made (e.g. Forde-Mazrui 2004; McCarthy 2004; Valls and Kaplan 2005) can be counterproductive. To assess the whole *structural* debt the US state has accumulated for its role in the reproduction of unjust history, we should start from the outset (i.e. slavery). For an influential argument for grounding reparations on the entire history of racial injustice in the US, see Bittker (1973).

itself, *certain* agents do have the inherent capacity to influence their development over time. The state, with its pervasive coercive and expressive power, is arguably a significant actor within unjust structures. For instance, as seen in Chapter 7, (just and unjust) policy making is a crucial tool to direct persons' actions and interactions towards certain channels, rather than others. Third, the relation between structures and agency is not a deterministic one. Agents can often act otherwise especially if they are powerful.[37] For example, policy making is the result of preferring certain measures over others to regulate an area of political, social and economic life. By adopting punitive measures against addicted mothers and pregnant women, the US state chose not to devise and implement policy making aimed at tackling the intersectional structural roots of poverty and addiction. To wit, in arguing that 'slavery and its aftermath was a social ill, not simply a matter of public policy',[38] Young neglects how the two dimensions were not mutually exclusive; rather, they reinforced one another. Through a patterned and wide-ranging array of legislation and public policies, the US state played (and arguably still plays) an important role in the structural reproduction of the injustice of slavery over time and through change – a role for which it should be held accountable and offer reparation.

To whom should reparations for structural debts be paid? While Young disputes that African Americans can be meaningfully defined as a 'single and continuous group',[39] Lu is sceptical about the 'ancestor-descendant relationship' along family lines upon which backward-looking justifications for reparations of historical injustices often hinge to identify beneficiaries.[40] However, as seen (§ 4.2), there is another promising and compelling way of thinking about descent: that of 'structural descent'. There is a crucial connection between (dead) victims of past injustices and some present agents: the latter are structural descendants of the former as they have inherited their unjust structural position. In a *structural* sense, there is thus a relation of identity between the two categories of persons. Had persons recognised as African Americans today been alive during, say, slavery, they would have suffered from the original form of the injustice (i.e. now newly reproduced) because of their structural membership; they would have occupied the same position as their (structural) ancestors. Therefore, reparations for a structural debt are owed to structural

---

[37] I will come back to the role of powerful agents, and especially of states, within structures in § 9.2.
[38] Young (2011, 177).   [39] Young (2011, 177).
[40] Lu (2017, 162–63). For a defence of claims of reparations for slavery along family lines, see Boxill (1972); Kershnar (1999); Thompson (2002).

descendants of those who have occupied an unjust historical-structural position over time because of the significant contribution some powerful agents have made to sustaining that position.

At this point, one may wonder whether the US state's accountability for its structural debt to African Americans means American citizens should also be blameworthy and accountable for it as they may have to share the costs of reparations through, say, tax paying. Although I cannot discuss issues of how to distribute state's accountability in detail, here I think that, as Robert K. Fullinwider argues, it can be helpful to distinguish between a state's 'corporate accountability' and citizens' 'civic responsibility'.[41] The state – in all its executive, legislative, administrative, juridical and law enforcement branches – can be described as a corporate agent with an internal decision-making structure, which makes it act (or fail to act) intentionally.[42] Indeed, an understanding of states as moral persons that enter into intergenerational agreements, which bind them over time, underpins international law and describes many state practices (e.g. signing treaties).[43] In this respect, the current government and public officials – qua shareholders of a corporate group – are accountable for the past wrongs committed by the state *and* for its patterned conduct within unjust structures and thus should offer reparation for them. Contemporary citizens, however, cannot be easily described as shareholders in a corporate group because, unlike public officials and representatives of the state, their membership is largely involuntary and the costs of exit are too high.[44] Rather than being held accountable for their state's role in the reproduction of unjust structural processes over time, citizens, at least in democratic states, should regard support for reparation programmes as an obligation of citizenship – that is, as an obligation to sustain their state's efforts to achieve (reparative structural) justice.[45] To wit, while reparations for slavery (and the history of racial injustice) should be grounded on a backward-looking justification (i.e. the US state's structural debt),[46]

---

[41] Fullinwider (2004).

[42] See, e.g., Goodin (1995, 35); List and Pettit (2011, 40); Stilz (2011, 195–96).

[43] Stilz (2011, 196); Thompson (2002).   [44] See, e.g., Pasternak (2013); Stilz (2011, 196).

[45] The practice of asking citizens qua citizens to pay reparations for past injustices committed by their state when they were not alive is not completely unprecedented, as shown by the case of Germany's still-running reparation programme for survivors of the Nazi regime.

[46] In addition to the US state, there are other powerful 'corporate' agents that have accumulated a structural debt to African Americans (and thus should be held accountable for reparations); corporations, religious organisations and academic institutions, to name a few, have contributed to the structural reproduction of history. I mainly focus on the US state because of its pervasive – both coercive and expressive – power.

American citizens' support for such reparations should be justified as what being citizens of a democratic state may entail.[47] Disjoining the two types of responsibilities ensures that accountability and blameworthiness fall on the appropriate agents.

There may be a legitimate worry that, even in cases of historical injustices that are newly reproduced, reparations will clash with other compelling demands of present distributive and structural injustice in that prioritising the former will necessarily end up with sacrificing the latter. However, this does not have to be the case. For instance, the content of many demands for reparations advanced by MBL (e.g. full and free access to education, a guaranteed minimum income, public school curricula critically examining the American history of racial injustice, and public memorabilia celebrating struggles for racial equality) resonates with issues of distributive and structural injustice suffered by African Americans.[48] What activists seem to point out is that such measures not only may be justifiable demands of present distributive and structural injustice, as some theorists suggest,[49] but also *should* be justified as reparations for the (structural) debt that certain agents have accumulated over time. More generally, such a worry points out that reparations programmes must be devised through a careful decision-making procedure that considers all legitimate interests at stake; it does not pose a challenge to the justifiability of reparations per se.

One may still be concerned that, by bringing up an unjust history (i.e. still newly reproduced), reparations claims would exacerbate divisions and undermine solidarity efforts.[50] Three observations can be made in reply. First, arguably when, unlike states, *citizens* are asked to support reparations efforts as an obligation of citizenship, rather than as a duty to repair wrongs they should be accountable for, it may be less likely that they – and especially members of historically privileged groups in relation to unjust historical structures (e.g. white Americans in the case of slavery in the US) – would (or should) still feel unfairly blamed.

---

[47] Obviously, the US state and American citizens have also additional responsibilities to tackle present racial structural injustices (see § 9.2). My point is simply that such responsibilities cannot be the substitute for a backward-looking justification for state's reparations for structural debt (and citizens' present obligation to support them). In this respect, my argument is different from accounts for reparations simply grounded on the '*collective responsibility of U.S. citizens as such* for the enduring harms to African Americans that have resulted from legally sanctioned injuries of race under earlier regimes' (McCarthy 2004, 757). See also Balfour (2005, 790).

[48] https://policy.m4bl.org/reparations/ (accessed 3 July 2018).   [49] See, e.g., Shelby (2013).

[50] E.g. Aiyetoro (2003, 473); Darby (2010, 56); Loury (2007, 104); Young (2011, 181).

Second, in the case of a history that keeps being newly reproduced, reparations demands can also have an important educational effect. When reparations are advanced by revealing how certain agents have significantly contributed to the reproduction of history over time (and should be held accountable for it), they can also show how 'the [past] injuries not only perdure, but are inflicted anew'.[51] The new reproduction of an unjust history is difficult to acknowledge by individuals because (1) it involves taken-for-granted institutions and informal structural processes regulating societies (and the transnational order) and individuals' own everyday interactions and (2) it is also enabled by persons' exercise of their agency. Reparations claims open up spaces of discussion and debate within domestic and transnational civil society over how an unjust history has been (and still is) reproduced. Consider, for instance, the array of strategies for mobilisation around the need to repair slavery (and its endurance) that N'COBRA has adopted: from town hall meetings and rallies in cities throughout the US, which have gathered together reparations advocates and sceptics to discuss the necessity of reparations to obtain racial justice, to public education in schools, conferences, radio and television programmes, which raise awareness of the relationship between past injustice and present racial inequality among civil society and citizens.[52]

Third, opposition to reparations demands based on worries about fuelling divisions fails to examine what often lies behind the unwillingness to take such demands seriously. Such an unwillingness may not simply be a strategy whereby persons try to avoid their responsibility for structural injustice.[53] It can also indicate much more problematic dynamics. As Lawrie Balfour contends by drawing on W. E. B. Du Bois's observations, aversion to even reflecting upon the justifiability of reparations claims for slavery has been historically indicative of the 'carelessness' that has defined (the majority of) whites' attitudes towards the conditions of African Americans since the aftermath of slavery.[54] In this respect, the US context is not unique. Indeed, when it comes to past injustices, enduring unconcern for the condition of those groups that suffered from them has too often generated an unwillingness to even recognise (let alone repair) these injustices. Consider, for example, how (West) Germany

---

[51] Hartman (2002), quoted in Balfour (2005, 802).
[52] www.ncobraonline.org (accessed 3 July 2018).
[53] Our failure to recognise structural injustice results from a combination of widespread excuses for avoiding responsibility (Young 2011, chapter 6) and psychological dispositions that characterise human nature (Schiff 2014).
[54] Balfour (2003, 40).

publicly acknowledged the genocide of Sinti and Romani people during the Nazi regime (*Porrajmos*) only in 1982;[55] this late recognition should not come as a surprise if one thinks about how these populations continued to be seriously oppressed in Europe after the end of War Word II through overt forms of discrimination, such as forced sterilisation of Romani women and school segregation of Romani children, some of which still continue today.[56] It is because some groups are still not substantially regarded and treated as equals by the society in which the original form of the injustice has been committed (and by the international community at large) that reparations for such wrongs (or, better, structural debts owed to the groups) are not even taken into consideration. To wit, issues of divisiveness should not be taken at face value, precisely because they may be indicative of the structural reproduction of history.

In sum, 'if the practicalities, not the justice, of reparations are the true sticking point',[57] we should not dismiss reparations demands. In the case of an unjust history that has been reproduced over time, certain agents with the power to influence structural processes have accumulated a structural debt over time in virtue of their significant role in the reproduction of such a history, a debt that they *should* offer reparation for. However, as I will contend in the next sections, this does not mean that mobilising around and devising reparations programmes is straightforward. Nor does my argument imply that addressing the reproduction of an unjust history has only a backward-looking orientation and only amounts to repairing structural debts.

8.2   Towards (and Beyond) a Participatory Approach to Reparations

Demands for reparations very often reveal differences between groups pressing them. For instance, the Caribbean Community, which announced their decision to sue European countries for Caribbean slavery in September 2013, received criticism from the Pan-Afrikan Reparations Coalition of Europe and other organisations and communities of African

[55] On the Romani *Porajmos*, see the contributions in Lewy (2001).
[56] On the ongoing practice of school segregation of Romani children in Europe, see, e.g., Fox and Vidra (2013). To mention a quite recent episode of discrimination of Romani people in Germany, about fifty thousand persons, who were mainly asylum-seekers who originally fled Kosovo during the war, were deported to Kosovo by the German government. These asylum seekers had been living in Germany for ten years by then, and many were children who had been educated in Germany and spoke German as their primary language (Wood 2005).
[57] Coates (2014).

heritage (e.g. the Caribbean Pan-African Network and the Rastafarian Movement) for its too top-down approach to reparations as ill suited to 'achiev[e] the reparations aspirations of the masses of Afrikan descendant and indigenous citizens in the Caribbean'.[58] Instead, according to such organisations, reparations demands should be advanced through a 'participatory' approach, which aspires to include all stakeholders – and, especially, marginalised perspectives on colonial injustice (and its reproduction) – from the very beginning.

Groups fighting for reparations are also *internally* heterogeneous and marked by power imbalances, and they have always been so. Consider how, for instance, gender differences and inequalities have been a crucial (yet often neglected) component of unjust histories (and of their reproduction) by turning back to the case of black reparations in the US.[59]

Since slavery, racial injustice has been gendered in its *forms*. Racial violence and exploitation were perpetrated against women through different means. As previously seen, 'since slave women were classified as "breeders" as opposed to "mothers"',[60] they were also exploited in their reproductive labour and forced to separate from their children or not to nurture them. Later on, because of their gender, black women were subjected to specific types of state-sponsored violence and reproductive control, such as sterilisation. Sexual violence also constituted a systematic strategy to dominate enslaved women, especially those resisting their masters, and represented a tool of racial terror that black women have experienced and have been vulnerable to over history.[61] Overlooking sexual and reproductive exploitation as crucial forms of injustices towards African Americans since slavery would lead to a partial understanding and assessment of the structural debt accumulated by powerful agents over history. Moreover, decisions over what should count as a past wrong (or, better, as a form of injustice that has been reproduced over time) are never neutral.[62] Not only do they often stem from existing power inequalities within groups fighting for reparations, but also they may reveal a general failure to consider certain wrongs (e.g. sexual violence), which have been (and still

---

[58] https://parcoe.wordpress.com/open-letter-to-caricom-on-reparations/ (accessed 3 July 2018).
[59] On the relevance of gender to black reparations in the US, see Balfour (2015); Biondi (2003, 17).
[60] Davis (1983, 7).   [61] E.g. hooks (1982, 18).
[62] Gendered wrongs, such as those connected to the tasks women were expected to perform in the 'private' sphere, have rarely been recognised even in cases of reparations and compensations for human rights violations (Rubio-Marin 2011). For instance, as Ruth Rubio-Marin observes, although (West) German federal reparations laws for victims of the Nazi regime gradually expanded their understanding of the 'damages to freedom' eligible for compensation by including forced labour in factories, they have failed to cover forced housework (Rubio-Marin 2011, 88n55).

are) committed also by (e.g. male) members of such groups, as proper injustices.

Moreover, unjust racial history has been *structured* through gender ideology. Consider, for instance, how, although 'the gendered politics of slavery [and its reproduction over time] denied black [women and] men the freedom to act as ["women"] and "men" within the definition[s] set by white norms, th[ese] notion[s] of [womanhood and] manhood did become a standard used to measure black [female and] male progress'.[63] Through controlling images and myths such as the 'black matriarch' and the 'emasculation of black men', black women have been negatively portrayed as less 'feminine' for not conforming to ideals of the stay-at-home mother,[64] whereas black men have been criticised and disparaged for not always being the main breadwinners in their families. Such a gender ideology was promulgated by governmental discourses (e.g. the infamous Moynihan report of 1965) to frame dynamics stemming from racial injustice (e.g. black men's exclusion from a labour market that, at the same time, marginalised black women) as historical 'pathologies' of black communities.[65] However, gender ideology was also interiorised by some black leaders, which embodied the ideal of male dominance in the family to gain public recognition, and it constituted a continuous source of tension within black families and communities.[66] As a result, rather than being challenged in its partiality, white (middle-class and heteronormative) gender expectations ended up being reinforced.[67]

Finally, reparations for slavery (and its reproduction over time) should factor gender in because their *recipients* belong to different gendered positions, which bears on their access to and benefit from them. It is a general desideratum of reparations programmes that they include as many beneficiaries as possible; however, in cases of reparations directed towards internally gendered differentiated groups, meeting this desideratum might be particularly difficult because some members of the group

---

[63] hooks (1992, 90).   [64] E.g. Collins (2000, 69–96); Davis (1983, 4–5); hooks (1982, 51–86).
[65] E.g. Roberts (2017, 16–17).
[66] To be sure, the fact that some black men may have interiorised a model of patriarchal masculinity and reproduced it in their relations with women does not mean that they fully – materially and symbolically – benefitted from it. The interlocking of gender with race and class guaranteed that their privilege was always partial (hooks 1992). As bell hooks forcefully puts it, 'Black males in the culture of imperialist white-supremacist capitalist patriarchy [have been] feared but they [have] not [been] loved' (hooks 2004, ix).
[67] hooks (1982, 91–100; 1992, 90–94). Obviously, this does not mean that some black men did not resist or problematise the model of masculinity set by white middle-class and heteronormative norms and thus that black male experiences have not been complex and varied (hooks 1992).

might not have an equal say in the groups' decisions or might enjoy even a lesser status than their male counterparts within societies.

As previously argued, reparations for historical injustices rest on a backward-looking justification: they are owed by powerful agents for their structural debt. However, a participatory approach to reparations demands points out that, to be empowering, claimants cannot simply be the passive beneficiaries of an agent's fulfilment of its reparative obligation of justice; they need to be in the vanguard of the entire process.[68] Moreover, as seen, reparations can also have an important educational effect in that they open up spaces of dialogue and discussion on an unjust history and its new reproduction over time. To unleash this educational potential, such spaces should not be monopolised by a single voice but must include heterogeneous perspectives that can cast light on the different dimensions of that history.

Considerations of intersectionality point to the need to include not only plural voices but also different *positions* within those unjust structures that have been reproduced over time through the significant contribution of powerful agents. To wit, mechanisms of participation must also be sensitive to the intersectional dimensions of an unjust history. Although inclusion per se does not guarantee that concerns of intersectionality will be addressed, participatory mechanisms, once properly devised, can be useful also in this respect. For instance, in the case of reparations for slavery in the US, movements demanding reparations should ensure that not only black women but also black feminist organisations and associations are included and have a prominent role in the struggle. Groups such as, to name a few, the National Council of Negro Women, the SisterSong Women of Colour Reproductive Justice Collective, INCITE! and the Women of Color Network have deep insight into the intersectional dynamics of racial historical injustice because they currently fight against the intersectional ways such an unjust history is newly reproduced.[69]

A fully fledged account of a participatory (i.e. inclusive and intersectional) approach to demands for reparations cannot be developed here and arguably should be spelled out precisely by those struggling to obtain them.

---

[68] Amighetti and Nuti (2015, 388).

[69] The National Council of Negro Women is an African American women's organisation founded in 1935 that promotes the interests of black women in the US and internationally; the SisterSong Women of Color Reproductive Justice Collective is a network of eighty grassroots organisations, formed in 1997, that fight for the sexual and reproductive rights of black women (but also Latinos and indigenous ones) at the local, regional and national levels; both INCITE! and the Women of Color Network are US-based activist organisations pushing for an end of violence against women of colour and their communities.

That said, it is important to observe that, for demands for reparations to (1) understand the complex intersectional dimensions of historical injustices (i.e. of an unjust history that has kept being reproduced) and (2) avoid reinforcing power dynamics between and within groups pursuing them, participatory procedures should be in place at every stage of the struggle: during the phase of outreach and mobilisation, in the decision-making process concerning which reparations programmes to establish and involving claimants and representatives of the collective agent paying its structural debt, and at the level of implementation.[70] Developing a truly participatory approach to reparations demands is not straightforward, but it is necessary for reparations to be truly empowering and promote justice.

From within a de-temporalised framework, the task of *redressing* an unjust history requires (backward-looking) reparations for structural debts but also it involves a forward-looking orientation that aims to challenge the very formal and informal set-up in which we daily interact. Indeed, as seen, (certain) unjust histories are newly reproduced into the fabric of our societies (and transnational order). This means that simply achieving equality of outcomes between groups that have been historically mutually constituted is insufficient. In contrast to more old-fashioned attempts to calculate the economic sum America would owe to African Americans for the harms of slavery (and its aftermath),[71] reparations scholars have increasingly contended that reparations should aim to close the gap between African Americans and white Americans that persists in almost every measure of well-being, including wealth, housing, health, education and crime.[72] Equality of outcomes across the two racial groups in the US – that is, equalising where members of the two groups end up in relation to, say, the prison system – is thus perceived as the goal of reparations *and* redress.[73]

Obviously, the significance of equality of outcomes in the context of historical injustice – or of inter- (and intra-)group inequality in general – should not be dismissed. Inequality of outcomes can point to injustices across groups and, specifically, to the lack of substantively equal opportunities members of groups start with.[74] In cases of an unjust history that has

---

[70] For a deliberative democratic approach to achieve reparations that focuses on the cases of international historical injustices (e.g. colonialism and the slave trade), see Amighetti and Nuti (2015).

[71] E.g. Barkan (2000, 288–89); Bittker (1973, 131–32); Browne (1971).

[72] E.g. Boxill (2003); McCarthy (2004); Valls (2007, 118); Valls and Kaplan (2005).

[73] For a definition of equality of outcome, see Phillips (2004, 1).

[74] Phillips (2004); Young (2001b).

been reproduced over time, as Charles Tilly famously argues, opportunities have also been 'hoarded' – that is, members of (historical and) structural groups have gained and monopolised access to valuable resources (e.g. employment), especially when such an access has been facilitated by the social networks in which persons are embedded (e.g. family, friendships and associates).[75]

What I simply want to suggest is that redressing the reproduction of an unjust history should not be limited to equalising outcomes or levelling the playing field. We should ask whether the field we aim to level does not itself have to be dismantled. In greater detail, the challenge with unjust histories that have been newly reproduced is that our very societies – or the informal and formal institutions regulating them – have been organised in a way that contributes to the reproduction of these injustices *through* change.[76] Therefore, redress also means scrutinising the formal and informal institutions that regulate our societies (sometimes even questioning the desirability of their existence) in order to understand the extent to which an unjust history still directs the workings of our institutions and is reproduced through them, and to reveal whether and how such institutions are compromised as a result. We need what can be called *counter-historical institutional justifications* – that is, discourses and narratives that directly question our institutional set-up in connection with unjust histories, rather than taking it for granted or, at best, calling for its reform.

8.3   Counter-historical Institutional Justifications

To unpack what counter-historical institutional justifications amount to and their normative significance, let me start with one example of activism: prison abolitionism in the US. One of the main tropes of prison abolitionists in the US, especially of those activists linking the disestablishment of prisons to racial justice, has been tracing the continuity between slavery and the institution of prison. In the past, organisations that deployed such a connection included the Committee to Abolish Prison Slavery (CAPS), which operated in the late 1970s and early 1980s with the conception that the abolition of imprisonment was necessary to really free African Americans, and the Prison Research Education Action Project (PREAP), which in the 1970s contended that prison reform was insufficient to achieve

---

[75] Tilly (1998, 147–69).
[76] On how the international order has been reorganised to maintain colonial dependency after World War II and, then, decolonisation, see Tully (2008, chapters 5 and 7).

justice and provided some practical suggestions about how the transition from a penal system centred on prisons to a society without prisons could have been realised.[77] Today, in an era characterised by the 'hyper-carceration' of economically marginalised African Americans and other racialised minorities in the US, activists and critical scholars continue to argue that the prison should be regarded as 'the modern day manifestation of the plantation' and denounced as such.[78]

How do prison abolitionists connect the institution of prison with slavery? There are various accounts of such a connection; however, the majority focus on the tie between slavery, the Thirteenth Amendment and the convict-lease system.[79] The Thirteenth Amendment to the US Constitution (ratified by the Senate on 8 April 1864) is deemed crucial as it prescribed the abolition of slavery and involuntary servitude 'except as a punishment for crime whereof the party shall have been duly convicted',[80] and thus inscribed the link between slavery and crime into the US Constitution. According to abolitionists, the amendment authorised the state to exploit convicts' unfree labour by leasing them to private corporations and plantation owners to rebuild the South's infra-structure. Through the establishment and enforcement of 'black codes', which criminalised certain behaviours (e.g. vagrancy, drunkenness and absence from work) only of blacks, the convict-lease system became immediately racialised and, along with Jim Crow legislation, was crucial in reconstructing a racial state.[81] In Angela Davis's words, 'The post-Civil War evolution of the punishment system was in very literal ways the continuation of a slave system, which was not longer legal in the "free" world'.[82]

Prison-abolitionist activists and scholars draw on how the penitentiary system was developed – that is, as an attempt to sustain the racial order under new circumstances – to reflect upon the status of prisons in the present. In analysing the linkage between slavery and the early penitentiary system, they posit the following unsettling question: 'Is racism so deeply entrenched in the institution of the prison that it is not possible to

---

[77] For the two main publications of CAPS and PREAP, see Esposito and Wood (1982) and Morris (1976), respectively.

[78] James (2005, xxiii). See also Best and Hartman (2005); Davis (2003, 2005); Heiner (2016); McLeod (2015); Roberts (2007); Wacquant (2002); Wilderson (2003).

[79] Childs (2015, chapter 2); Davis (2003, chapter 2); Lichtenstein (1996); Mancini (1996).

[80] US Constitution, Amendment XIII.   [81] E.g. Wallenstein (2004).

[82] Davis (2003, 33); see also Lichtenstein (1996, 13). On how the association between crime and blackness, constructed through statistical discourses, is crucial to explain the evolution of the penitentiary system as a system of racial control also in the urban North, see Muhammad (2011).

eliminate one without eliminating the other?'[83] Abolitionists reply affirma-
tively to this question by pointing out that today's prison populations are
profoundly racialised and that the very penitentiary system should be
regarded as a continuation of the institution of slavery. The array of
restrictions ex-felons are subjected to (e.g. political disenfranchisement,
housing and employment discrimination, and ineligibility to public assistance) combined with the 'prison label' – that is, the expressive ways ex-
convicts are relegated to the status of second-class citizens, ensures the
reproduction of a racialised order and the enduring extraction of the social
capital of African American (and other racialised minorities') communities
by disrupting the functioning of families and social networks. In other
words, according to abolitionists, the institution of prison constitutes one
of the main formal mechanisms of the reproduction of the colour line in an
era of supposed colour-blindness. Unlike reformists who aim to decrease
the inmate population and are mainly concerned about the racialised *effects*
of the penitentiary system, abolitionists argue that the very institution of
prison is so structurally connected with slavery and the history of racial
injustice that its eradication is necessary to realise racial justice.[84]
Obviously, they do not contend that abolishing the prison would magically
achieve this goal; abolitionists are well aware that the disestablishment of
the institution of prison must be combined with tackling all the constellation of economic and social structures that are entangled with the penitentiary system.[85] However, what is important to highlight here is that for
abolitionists, without conceiving of and criticising the institution of prison
as a reproduction of slavery, the process of advancing racial justice cannot
even start.

The narratives elaborated by American prison abolitionism suggest that
the unjust past is pervasively interwoven with our present in that the
former keeps being reproduced even in and through our institutional set-
up. They are an example of 'counter-historical institutional justifications' –
that is, political narratives constructed in activist politics and aimed at
explicitly countering the tendency to separate the critical evaluation of the
current formal and informal institutions regulating our societies (and the
transnational order) from their history and their role in reproducing it.

---

[83] Davis (2003, 26).
[84] E.g. Loury (2008). Michelle Alexander's (2012) and Michael Tonry (2011)'s compelling analyses of
the complex web of formal and informal rules whereby the institution of prison maintains a racial
system in the US resonate with abolitionist narratives. However, they are still reformist insofar as
they are not grounded on abolition as a long-term goal.
[85] Davis (2005).

Counter-historical institutional justifications are interconnected to practices of 'counter-memory'. According to Michel Foucault's influential account, counter-memory is the 'insurrection of subjugated knowledges'.[86] Foucault contends that knowledges that have been marginalised and disqualified by the imposed and hegemonic regime of discourse are crucial because they point out how the alleged unity of knowledge is not only an illusion but also the result of a power struggle.[87] For Foucault, resistance is always endogenous, rather than exogenous, to power and counter-memories are critical narratives that can disrupt and challenge the dominant knowledge regime because they are internal to it (i.e. they are what the regime constantly tries to push outside).[88]

In the context of historical injustices, many scholars highlight the importance that retelling the official history can play in reconstructing a social imagination that has excluded certain perspectives and views.[89] As Charles W. Mills contends in the case of racial injustice in the US, the idea of white superiority is sustained through amnesia of the past wrongs committed against African Americans and the contributions African Americans made to American history and society over time. Such a 'management of memory',[90] which denies or marginalises both the brutality of past racial violence and the participation of African Americans in the making of the US, is 'inscribed in textbooks, generated and regenerated in ceremonies and official holidays, concretized in statues, parks, and monuments',[91] thereby imposing itself as the official history of interracial relations. By retrieving those aspects of the past that are silenced in the daily reproduction of domestic and international polities and rewriting the official histories in a way that brings to the forefront its deliberately neglected elements, counter-memory aims to remodel the present social (and international) imagination. W. E. B. Du Bois's *Black Reconstruction* is widely regarded as a paradigmatic example of counter-memory. In his retelling of the story of the Reconstruction era of the South after its defeat in the American Civil War, Du Bois unveils the 'gifts of the black folks' – that is, the contributions African Americans made to their own emancipation from slavery and to the (re-)construction of the US.[92] In so doing, he places slavery and the denial of its effects at the centre of American citizenship.[93]

---

[86] Foucault (2003b, 9–11).   [87] Foucault (2003b, 9).   [88] Foucault (2003b, lecture IV).
[89] E.g. McCarthy (2002).   [90] Mills (2007, 28).   [91] Mills (2007, 29).
[92] Balfour (2011, 26); Blight (1994, 46).   [93] Balfour (2011, chapter 2).

Counter-historical institutional justifications often draw on counter-memories to develop their institutional critique. As Davis observes, 'There are aspects of our history that we need to interrogate and rethink, the recognition of which may help us to adopt more complicated, critical postures toward the present and the future'.[94] In turn, attempts to provide counter-historical institutional justifications may inspire or accelerate the search for counter-memories of an unjust history that can cast new light on the roots and unfolding of the criticised institutions. However, counter-historical institutional justifications are distinctive in being directly aimed at countering the tendency to separate the critical evaluation of current institutions regulating our societies (and the international order) from their connection to an unjust history and their role in its reproduction. To wit, they de-temporalise injustice when it comes to institutional assessment.

All institutions embed a story or, rather, a justification of their purpose that sustains them by creating consensus over their legitimacy and necessity. As Rainer Forst argues, 'When asked why a particular institution exists, one will usually respond with a story that led to [it]'.[95] The institution of prison, for instance, may be supported by narratives centred on the need to deter crime, to punish or rehabilitate those breaking the social contract, or to incapacitate dangerous individuals, and constructed to show that prisons constitute the best and only way to meet these needs. However, institutional justifications may sometimes be ideological – that is, they may hide some institutions' problematic workings, which would question their very desirability. In so doing, they may also conceal alternative ways to think about and regulate social issues. Challenging institutional justifications is particularly difficult. We rarely interrogate them not only because we tend to take our structural background for granted but also because institutional justifications are often a crucial aspect of our collective identity – that is, of how we conceive of ourselves as a community (e.g. a community that is tough on crime and strives to keep itself safe).[96]

By providing an alternative history of institutions and of their rationale, counter-historical institutional justifications criticise dominant institutional narratives by exposing their ideological function and may reveal the role such institutions have played in the reproduction of an unjust

---

[94] Davis (2003, 36).   [95] Forst (2017, 56).

[96] On the relation between institutions and identity and especially on how identities become institutionalised, see Hayward (2013). For a recent analysis of the role of 'public consciousness' in mass incarceration in the US, see Enns (2016).

history. For instance, prison abolitionism in the US prompts us to raise unsettling questions about what the institution of prison is really for. It tries to lift the justificatory veil by contrasting dominant rationales (e.g. deterrence, retribution, rehabilitation and incapacitation) with an alternative narrative that constructs the institution of the prison as 'underpinning a system of racial capitalism' and as 'an evolution of the regime of control and exploitation that began with slavery'.[97] Prison abolitionists also attempt to denounce the ideological character of the main justifications for the institution of prison in the US by asking whether, especially under conditions of injustice, some of the social goods the institution of prison is meant to provide (e.g. safety) are best delivered by regimes of punishment and surveillance.

In so doing, counter-historical institutional justifications aim to correct the 'failure of moral, legal and political *imagination*'[98] that is caused by the acritical acceptance of dominant institutional justifications. In other words, they combine a criticism of the status quo with an alternative understanding of how social problems should be framed and addressed. For instance, prison abolitionists in the US have proposed different and multifaceted strategies of progressive decarceration which aim to tackle the structural issues prisons have been systematically relied on as a solution for.[99] Such measures include, but are not limited to, disinvesting from carceral infrastructures and investing in social welfare and public education, supporting organisations that try to address structural (intersecting) inequalities that are often at the roots of resort to crime, decriminalising minor offences such as personal possession of drugs and sex work, and empowering local communities to build internal mechanisms of accountability and restorative justice that do not rely on federal and state criminal-justice apparatuses while still providing safe shelter for vulnerable persons.[100] In this sense, prison abolitionists are not opposed to reforms but insist reforms must be driven by a completely different vision of how society should be regulated, rather than simply being the end point.[101] According to prison abolitionists, incremental change thus should be at the service of 'the founding of a new society'[102] – a society in which resort to prisons will become 'obsolete'.[103]

---

[97] Akbar (2018, 410, 449).   [98] McLeod (2015, 1156, my italics).   [99] Gilmore (2007, 5).
[100] For a recent abolitionist blueprint for action, see McLeod (2015).
[101] For an interesting account of the relation between prison-abolitionist activism and reforms, see Berger, Kaba and Stein (2017).
[102] Moten and Harney (2004, 114).   [103] Davis (2003).

In sum, counter-historical institutional justifications, of which US prison abolitionism is an example, are normatively crucial because they compel us to change the horizon of our political thinking and reorient our sight towards what is unfamiliar and seems impossible within the boundaries of our existing order. They help detect how our institutional set-up may be compromised by its unjust history and may constitute a crucial mechanism of its reproduction while also opening up new frontiers for our political and social imagination. In other words, they unleash the potential of what de-temporalising (in)justice can accomplish.

CHAPTER 9

Conclusion: Responsibility and the Process of Redress

When and why does an unjust history matter for considerations of justice? In this book, I argued for de-temporalising injustice – that is, refusing to separate, in certain cases, the past from the present. I started with developing a *structural account of history*, which conceives of history itself as comprising enduring long-term structures, as the most congenial starting point to reflect on the normative significance of historical injustice and the limits of existing approaches to past wrongs (Chapter 2). I then offered an account of historical injustice – *historical-structural injustice* – that is sensitive to how history can operate under new circumstances and explains why egalitarians who strive for justice in the present cannot dismiss unjust history (Chapter 3). The implication of this account is that some ongoing injustices should be theoretically and normatively conceptualised as the reproduction of unjust history under new circumstances and through changes. Unjust histories are newly reproduced into the fabric of societies (and the transnational order) and constitute the structural conditions of persons' interactions. At the same time, persons' interactions are also one way such structures are sustained over time. I put an emphasis on the 'banal radicality' of the reproduction of unjust history to show the subtle and often difficult-to-tackle mechanisms whereby an unjust history can be reproduced in the present and how these mechanisms provide some of the conditions of possibility for radical injustices to occur and repeat. De-temporalising injustice broadens and enriches our understanding of those groups that now suffer from an unjust history – or rather, from its new reproduction (Chapter 4). In particular, it challenges the assumption that descent should be mainly regarded along family lines. Contemporary persons occupying historical-structural positions are in a relation of 'structural descent' with those who have been previously categorised in the same way, and it is on this basis that they should be entitled to, for instance, reparations for historical injustices. By looking at the interplay between history and injustice, I put forward a spectrum of structural groups that also enables us to refine our views on structural injustice and start disentangling the various forms such injustices can take. Not all structural injustices are analogous in every respect, and if we aim to overcome them, acknowledging their differences becomes tantamount to recognising their common characteristics.

The central part of the book focused on the group of 'women', which has been under-theorised in the literature over past wrongs, to expand and apply my account of historical-structural injustice. I argued that women are a historical-structural group in that the very position of women is rooted in a history of injustice that is still structurally reproduced. Conceiving of women in these terms has been fruitful in at least three respects. First, it provided an account of what makes women a collective, which improves on Iris Marion Young's influential notion of seriality by (1) reducing its still-essentialist aspects and (2) giving a historically driven interpretation of intersectionality (Chapter 5). Second, it offered an approach to contemporary issues of gender injustice within egalitarian contexts, which explains how even some dimensions of gender inequality characterising the 'private' sphere, such as intimate-partner violence and the gendered division of domestic labour, are significantly connected to a structurally reproduced unjust history. Moreover, it suggested that certain differences in women's and men's life patterns, such as those resulting from a horizontally segregated job market, would remain normatively problematic even if economic or time resources were more equally distributed among genders because of their role in reproducing an unjust history (Chapter 6). Third, it showed that policy making holding to the promise of getting to the roots of the unjust condition of women within societies that are no longer formally discriminatory can be successfully devised only when the complex interplay between history and structure is taken into full consideration (Chapter 7).

De-temporalising injustice also cast light on 'the politics of the unjust past' (Chapter 8). In particular, I put forward a backward-looking yet structural justification for claims of reparations for historical injustices of even a distant past, and I identified a compelling form of activist discourse – that is, 'counter-historical institutional justifications' – which plays a crucial role in redressing the reproduction of an unjust history.

In this conclusion, my aim is twofold. First, I intend to pull together the threads of my argument about the process of redress and clarify some of its aspects. Redressing injustices of a structural nature requires the collaboration of many individual and collective actors, which are responsible for their eradication. My second goal is to offer some normative considerations on how we should think about responsibility within unjust structures and, in particular, how responsibility should be sensitive to the different types of agents involved.

9.1 The Process of Redress

Redressing injustices that are both historical and structural is extremely urgent and yet particularly challenging because of the very nature and complex mechanisms of their reproduction. It means embarking on a long and unsettling process aimed at, first, dismantling the institutional, material, cultural, discursive and symbolic channels whereby the unjust history is reproduced in the present and, second, constructing new forms of organisation of our societies, the transnational order and our personal relations. In the book, I identified three required (yet not exhaustive) forms of interventions that should be undertaken in the process of redress: reparations, transformative policy making and counter-historical institutional interventions.

A de-temporalised framework highlights (rather than obviates) the necessity of *reparations* for structurally reproduced historical injustices (of even a distant past). The process of redress should thus entail a backward-looking normative analysis holding contemporary powerful agents morally responsible for their significant contribution to the reproduction of an unjust history over time and thus accountable to repair their 'structural debt'. Reparations demands should be pursued through a participatory approach, which sees claimants at the forefront of the mobilisation and decision-making process. As the activist politics of reparations shows,[1] reparations demands usually are both 'redistributive' (e.g. free and public educational programmes, a guaranteed minimum liveable income and affirmative actions) and about 'recognition' (e.g. changes in school curricula, national holidays and public practices of commemoration) and thus they already tend to be quite encompassing in scope (as they should be).

That said, reparations should be complemented by other (more forward-looking) interventions. This is not only because sometimes movements fighting for historical and structural inequalities do not seem to put reparations on their agenda or reparations may not be as successful as initially hoped at repairing unjust historical structures,[2] but also because

---

[1] See, for instance, the Movement for Black Lives's demands for reparations: https://policy.m4bl.org/reparations/ (accessed 3 July 2018).

[2] Feminist movements, for instance, do not ask for reparations for the history of injustice against women but mainly focus on what I called 'transformative measures' and 'counter-historical

redressing the new reproduction of an unjust history calls for an ongoing commitment to preventing its possible 'reactivation' and remodelling our background conditions (also through institutional innovation).

Transformative policy making should aim to devise and implement measures that avoid the structural reactivation of an unjust history by intervening especially (but not only) on the more insidious banal mechanisms whereby that history is reproduced in day-to-day interactions. To wit, policy making must be sensitive to the historical-structural conditions in which it intervenes. As seen, this is because it takes place against a background that is not historically neutral. At the same time, in cases of historical and structural injustices, policy making often significantly contributes to enabling the structural reproduction of an unjust history under new circumstances. For instance, any policy decision regarding child protection in the US is undertaken within a system of reproductive rights and child services that, as discussed in Chapter 8, has been historically structured in relation to the historical injustices against African American women and that still seems to represent a crucial means whereby such a history can be reproduced today. However, as argued in Chapter 7, when properly framed, policy making can be creative in that it has the potential to channel persons' actions into new directions.

To de-temporalise justice, historically sensitive policy making needs to operate along with and in light of *counter-historical institutional justifications*. Counter-historical institutional justifications, which are developed in activist politics, critically examine whether and how our societies (and the transnational order) have been constructed to make an unjust history reproduce through changes. They are such a core and necessary component of redress because, by advancing an alternative narrative about rationales and workings of those institutions that we take for granted, they urge us to scrutinise whether precisely such institutions facilitate the endurance of (unjust) history or are themselves ways such a history is reproduced through changes. In doing so, counter-historical institutional justifications constitute the bedrock of the very process of redress.

---

institutional justifications' (e.g. the critique of the institution of marriage and the case for its disestablishment). Does this mean women could or should not be entitled to reparations? To many, the very idea of 'women' reparations would seem bizarre. On one hand, I think it is important to respect the ways movements frame their requests. On the other hand, the fact that these claims for reparations are not pursued does not mean that, if they were, they would have no moral force and plausibility. In this respect, my account of 'structural debt' could show that there is indeed a case for 'women' reparations.

A fundamental feature of the process of redress is that this process requires a thorough understanding of how *specific* historical injustices have been constantly and newly reproduced over time. This means that remedies that are created to tackle a newly reproduced unjust history may not be effective for other cases of historical and structural injustices. For instance, I argued for horizontal affirmative action as a transformative measure to address gendered occupational segregation (§ 7.2). This is a highly integrative measure which aims to include women in traditionally male-dominated jobs and men in occupations that are regarded as stereotypically female. In this case, integration works because the reproduction of the unjust history of women is rooted in ideas about what women (and men) should be that occupational segregation precisely reinforces. However, when a history of injustice has been characterised by forced and brutal assimilation, such as that of indigenous peoples in the US, Canada and Australia, integrative policies may turn out to reproduce that history instead of dismantling it. Moreover, integrative measures, such as horizontal affirmative action, may not be the obvious and best response to all forms of segregation reproducing an unjust history, such as racial neighbourhood segregation in the US. A full examination of how the history of unjust racial relations has developed in the US may show that, in this case, desegregation through integration (of African American persons in mainly residential areas inhabited by whites) is detrimental to the cause of historical justice. For instance, it may be likely to sever those social ties and networks that persons have established over time with determinate neighbours that have been crucial to their sense of belonging and in resisting oppression. In other words, by asking African Americans to leave their neighbours, integration is bound to continue to dismiss what many (although not all) persons who are categorised as African American value the most.[3]

The process of redress thus should be tailored not only to the specificities of the historical injustices at stake but also to the ways the interplay between history and structures has impacted the dynamics of the groups that suffer from it. Now, in my account of structural groups, I contended that whether a person identifies with a (historical or not) structural group is not important in determining membership from the point of view of structural injustice (of a historical nature or not); in this respect, all that matters is external recognition from someone who has the authority to place that person in a structural group within that determinate context (§ 4.1). My conception

---

[3] See Shelby (2014).

denies that the bonds of solidarity and affinity that those belonging to the same structural group may (or may not) develop and their (potential) feeling of having a shared identity should play a central role in (1) defining criteria of membership in a structural group and (2) determining whether these groups suffer from injustices that are both historical and structural. That said, my account also acknowledges that other dimensions of membership in structural groups, such as how persons experience their belonging to such collectives, the value they place on their membership, and the networks they establish with those similarly positioned, become highly relevant when we consider the actions that should be taken to address the condition of injustice these structural groups suffer from. Recognising that for many African Americans residing in black neighbourhoods, membership in a historical-structural racial group not only means being classified as such by others but also creates profound ties and strong networks, entails factoring such ties and networks in when solutions to the historical injustice of segregation are theorised. Conceiving of structural groups in terms of a spectrum (§ 4.5) precisely eschews the neglect of important differences among structural groups – differences that are often the result of the peculiar ways histories of injustices have been perpetuated and are still newly reproduced.

Once we take history seriously, thus, the aim of the political theorist should not be to come up with a detailed blueprint for repairing all the historical injustices that are structurally reproduced. Indeed, such a goal is not only undoubtedly ambitious but also likely to backfire on the very prospect of achieving historical justice because it overlooks the specificity of histories and their new reproduction. What instead we should do, and what I have tried to accomplish in this book, is put forward a framework to understand the normative significance of history, its complex reproduction through change, and the different components that should constitute the process of redressing it.

A crucial and interrelated second characteristic of the process of redress is that it should take into consideration how a historical injustice and its reproduction have been impacting in different ways those who suffer from them. Importantly, this means that thinking about the ways unjust long-term structures have *historically intersected* becomes of paramount importance if we want to bring about historical justice. For instance, I argued that reparations programmes that neglect intersectionality run the risk of providing a partial account of history (and of its new reproduction) and thus proposing forms of reparations that reinforce power imbalances that are (at least partially) connected with the historical injustices in question. Moreover, a concern for intersectionality has been central in determining which measures that aim at tackling the structural reproduction of unjust history are actually 'transformative'. In other words, historical and structural injustices can be overcome only through *a process of intersectional redress*. Although much work still needs to be done to explore the implications of such a process of redress, here I merely point out that the very conceptualisation of redress as an intersectional process has been made possible by theorising women as a group that suffers from the new reproduction of history. Indeed, bringing women to the forefront of the debate over historical injustices has led to a profound reformulation of which groups should receive historical justice, of notions of descent, of why redress is a demand of justice, and of how it should be achieved. To wit, 'gender' proved to be not a secondary element in questions of history and injustice but a primary category of normative analysis that can and should orientate our reflections on these issues.

In this book, my main aim has been developing a framework to understand when and why history matters for considerations of justice, which highlights the complexity of the relation between persistence and change and reconceptualises unjust history as newly reproduced. There are still many pressing questions that such a reproduction raises. For instance, how should we assign responsibility to redress it? This question points to the more general problem of conceptualising responsibility for structural injustices. Here I can only venture to make some normative considerations which identify the need for a more fine-grained understanding of responsibility for structural injustice than that provided by existing notions of a shared responsibility based on an allegedly equal contribution.

9.2   Present Responsibility within Unjust Structures

As seen in Chapter 3, unjust structures constitute the background conditions against which wrongs occur. Many collective and individual agents contribute to these structures and their reproduction by exercising their agency. According to Iris Marion Young, agents should be held morally responsible and blameworthy only for wrongs directly caused either by their voluntary actions whose consequences they sufficiently know (e.g. someone stealing a wallet) or by their culpable negligence (e.g. a police officer leaving her loaded gun around her children). In cases of structural injustices (e.g. homelessness), Young argues that this quasi-legal notion of moral responsibility is ill suited and insufficient. It simply isolates a few agents who interact in a blameworthy way (e.g. a landlord who denies tenancy to a single mother because of his sexist views), whereas unjust structures positioning individuals in a condition of vulnerability results from the combination of many agents simply acting within them.[4] For Young, just by participating and thus contributing to unjust structures, agents share a 'political' responsibility to eradicate them, a responsibility for which they are not blameworthy but that they can be criticised for not taking on.[5] Because Young is aware that, in our deeply interconnected world, we participate in an enormous number of processes leading to structural injustices but do not have the time, energy and means to address all of them, she suggests some 'parameters of reasoning' (e.g. power, privilege, interest and collective ability) that agents can use to think about 'what it makes the most sense for them … to do in the effort to remedy injustice'.[6] Such parameters can help us discharge our responsibility for structural injustice, but we still share responsibility for all structural injustices we participate in.

In her recent account of justice and reconciliation in world politics, Catherine Lu does not challenge the idea that agents share responsibility for structural injustice because they contribute to those processes causing it. However, she contends that agents share responsibility for structural injustice but are not without blame; because unjust structures have causal 'implication … in contemporary wrongful conducts', those who participate in these structures but fail to fulfil their responsibility to address them are morally responsible for such a failure and for the consequences of structural injustices (although they are not blameworthy for the wrongful conduct of others within such structures).[7] In this sense, structural injustice is overdeterminate but that does not mean that agents contributing to it are blameless. Although Lu advances this argument in order to attribute present reparative obligations to states and transnational institutions in cases of 'political catastrophes', the implication of her account is that any contributing agent is blameworthy if they do not discharge their responsibility for structural injustice. If one endorses Lu's account, it seems that even ordinary individuals should be held morally responsible for structural injustices (and their consequences) because, as discussed in Chapter 3, they also contribute to structural injustice (i.e. they reproduce it through the exercise of their agency).

While Young is (rightly) worried about placing blame on ordinary individuals for their participation in processes leading to structural injustice but ends up arguing that *nobody* is blameworthy for their contribution to structural injustices, Lu (rightly) thinks that contribution to structural

---

[4] Young (2011, 97–104).   [5] Young (2011, 109–11).   [6] Young (2011, 124).   [7] Lu (2017, 259).

injustice can be blameworthy, but her account turns out to place blame on *everyone* who fails to address the unjust structures they contribute to. The problem with (and the implausibility of) both Young's and Lu's understandings of responsibility for structural injustice comes down to grounding (either political or moral) responsibility on the allegedly equal contribution all agents participating in structures make to their sustainment. They both overlook differences among types of agents within structures and, in particular, that the different power agents display make their specific contributions normatively salient when it comes to attribution of moral responsibility and blame.[8]

To be sure, as already mentioned, no agent, as powerful as they may be, can on their own transform unjust structures. However, some agents *inherently* have a significant capacity to influence structural processes in virtue of their features (e.g. states) or the role they occupy in a society or internationally (e.g. the US president), and they possess this capacity independently of whether they choose to use it.[9] For instance, states not only have extensive power in the sense that their power is ramified in many (e.g. executive, legislative, administrative, juridical and law enforcement) branches but also because their power is both coercive and expressive (i.e. the state 'speaks' and communicates values when it acts).[10] Consider intimate-partner violence and the gendered structures (which intersect with racial and class structures) constituting the background conditions against which it takes place. Although the state cannot eradicate such structures by itself, its actions can play a crucial role in addressing them by, for example, publicly funding not only shelters and legal and counselling aid for survivors but also through preventive initiatives led by feminist organisations (e.g. the bystander

---

[8] Recall that, for Young, 'potential or actual power or influence over processes that produce the outcomes' is one parameter that *can* guide agents' actions in discharging their 'political' responsibility and not a characteristic that makes an agent morally responsible for structural injustices (Young 2011, 144–45). On the neglect of 'power' in Young's account of responsibility, see also Goodhart (2017, 182–83).

[9] Scholars of power usually define the power an agent has attached to its specific agency as 'dispositional power' (see, famously, Lukes 2005). Such a view is contrasted with a more 'systematic' understanding of power, which characterises power as networks of practices and social boundaries (i.e. structures) (see, e.g. Hayward 2000). Although I cannot enter into this fascinating debate about the nature of power, I want to clarify that arguing that some agents have a greater capacity to influence structural processes does not commit myself to an exclusively agent-centric view of power. We can still recognise the power of structures while also acknowledging that some agents within structures inherently have power to significantly influence (yet not to determine) change in structural processes.

[10] On coercion and expression as two crucial components of state power, see Brettschneider (2012).

programmes) and by denouncing the structural nature of intimate-partner violence through public campaigns.[11]

In other words, what both Young's and Lu's understandings of responsibility for structural injustices neglect is that, precisely because of their inherent capacity to influence structural processes, the contributions of certain agents (such as states) to such structures have effects that are profound and tangible. Therefore, when such agents act (or fail to act) in a way that reinforces (rather than trying to address) structural injustice, they should be held morally responsible for it. This moral intuition is captured by movements' and activist organisations' accusations of the role played by agents such as states in structural injustices. Consider, for instance, the fierce and restless attacks that Sisters Uncut, a British feminist direct-action group founded in November 2014, has directed against the UK state for how austerity policies (e.g. cuts to domestic violence services, welfare support, and preventive initiatives, and denial of access to public services and benefits to migrants) have impacted intimate-partner violence and the structural processes underlying it. Sisters Uncut is well aware that individual perpetrators should be held accountable for the abuse they commit, and thus it does not blame the UK government for having directly caused episodes of intimate-partner violence. At the same time, it insists that intimate-partner violence 'and sexual violence do not exist in a vacuum'.[12] Such wrongs happen within structural processes that, as discussed in Chapters 2 and 3, have 'explanatory autonomy' when it comes to the conditions of possibility and repetition of these wrongs. The 'cycle of violence' can be broken only if such structural processes are transformed. When Sisters Uncut directs its message to 'those in power',[13] it holds them morally responsible and blameworthy because their actions (and failure to act) within structural processes have significantly contributed to reinforcing them and placing women (especially those in abusive relationships) in a more vulnerable position. In other words, even if arguably the governmental measures did not deliberately intend to have that impact, their consequences in a context of unjust social and transnational structures were predictable. Moreover, powerful agents such as the UK state have a responsibility to act within structures in a non-negligent way because of

---

[11] Serena Parekh has also highlighted the important role of states in eradicating gender violence (2011, 683–84). Although her analysis is illuminating in many respects, she still conceives of states as 'politically' responsible and thus open to criticism but not to blame for their failure to address gender structures.

[12] www.sistersuncut.org/feministo/ (accessed 3 July 2018).

[13] www.sistersuncut.org/feministo/ (accessed 3 July 2018).

their inherent capacity to reinforce structural processes or influence their change.[14]

To be sure, structural change is not usually initiated by agents that have an inherent capacity to influence it but by social and transnational movements pressing for it. However, this does not mean these agents should not be held morally responsible and blameworthy by such movements for their role in structural injustices;[15] indeed, as seen in Chapter 8, such agents also accumulate a 'structural debt' over time when they have significantly enabled the structural reproduction of an unjust history. Moreover, since agents such as states tend to either have an interest in sustaining unjust structures or align with the interests of those who are in a position of advantage within structures,[16] it is unlikely that they would take any substantive action to address structural injustice if their responsibility were levelled to that of everyone else.

One implication of this discussion about moral responsibility for structural injustice and an agent's inherent capacity to influence change is that contribution alone is insufficient to ascribe the former to those who do not possess the latter. Ordinary individuals should not be blamed for failing to address structural injustices, although they contribute to their reproduction. As seen in Chapter 3, there is a crucial interplay between individuals' exercise of agency and structural processes. Structural processes constrain and enable individual agency, and, at the same time, we contribute to the reproduction of structures just by exercising agency. More precisely, structures are also reproduced through the *repetition of many* ordinary individuals' actions within them – that is, through *patterns* of ways we exercise our agency. This is why, for instance, as discussed in Chapter 7, policy making disrupting the banal mechanisms of the reproduction of unjust history and channelling persons' actions towards new directions is so important. However, the contribution of a *specific* ordinary individual does not have a profound and tangible impact, because she does not have the inherent capacity to influence structural change. Ordinary individuals

---

[14] The blameworthy 'carelessness' characterising the UK government's austerity policies is particularly emphasised by Sisters Uncut in, for instance, suggesting in their manifesto that the government 'think[s] that [it] can get away with [such policies] because [they] have targeted people who [it] perceive[s] as powerless'; www.sistersuncut.org/feministo/ (accessed 3 July 2018).

[15] It is important to acknowledge, especially when we consider the inequalities in power at the international level, that even agents having that inherent capacity may act within constraints. Obviously, if such constraints are very serious (e.g. coercion and duress), moral appraisal (i.e. blame) should be suspended (see, e.g. Scanlon 1998, 279).

[16] Young (2011, 148).

thus should not be held morally responsible and blameworthy for their failure to address structural injustice.

Does this mean ordinary individuals share equal *political* responsibility to organise and resist structural injustice and can be all criticised for not doing so? According to Young, both those who are privileged vis-à-vis unjust (e.g. racial) structures (e.g. white Americans) and those who are comparatively disadvantaged (e.g. African Americans) share political responsibility for structural injustice and thus can be criticised by others for their failure to address it because they both contribute to unjust structures through their actions or inactions. For Young, their different positions within such structures just give them different reasons for wanting to prioritise the eradication of, say, racial structural injustice in their efforts at discharging political responsibility. Although Young's way of conceptualising ordinary individuals' responsibility within structures does not amount to 'victim blaming', as political responsibility is blameless,[17] I think it is still problematic when attributed to those who are in a disadvantaged position within specific structural processes. In particular, it still equalises too much their responsibility with that of those who are comparatively privileged vis-à-vis the same structures.[18] If we take structural injustice (and, especially, injustice that is the new reproduction of an unjust history) seriously, we should pay particular attention to relations and mutually constituted positions within structures and offer an account of political responsibility that is deeply sensitive to them. Moreover, we need to ask *who* can criticise *whom* for their failure to discharge political responsibility for a structural injustice by, for instance, calling them out and pushing them to do more.

One avenue, which I cannot fully explore here, is to avoid conceiving of ordinary individuals' political responsibility as a responsibility that everyone shares in virtue of their contribution to structural injustice. In other words, we should distinguish between (1) the sociological analysis of how structures are sustained and reproduced over time (i.e. through individuals' exercise of their agency) and (2) considerations of responsibility and criticism. Position within unjust structures, rather than (1), should be the main basis for (2).

---

[17] Lu's account of responsibility is even more problematic when it comes to those who suffer from structural injustice (2017, 171). Since, as discussed above, for Lu, any agent participating in structural injustice who fails to address it is blameworthy, her account does not blame 'the oppressed' for the wrongs committed against them but does end up making them *morally* responsible for their contributions and thus blameworthy for their inaction.

[18] My criticism differs, in this respect, from that developed by Carol Gould, who, focusing on the case of 'sweatshops', criticises Young for holding 'victims' of structural injustice politically responsible while, according to her, they are 'coerced' into participating in unjust structures (2009, 203).

Those who are privileged vis-à-vis certain structures should be politically responsible for their eradication, and because of their privilege should be criticised for failing to discharge their responsibility. As Peggy McIntosh famously argues, privilege is an 'invisible knapsack' which systematically and unjustifiably confers advantages and assets to some over others because of their membership in a structural group.[19] Privilege is intrinsically relational because it always corresponds to a disadvantage that others have or a set of assets that others do not possess. Importantly, privilege is given to ordinary individuals *only* by their being identified as members of specific structural groups by someone who has the authority to do so in a determinate context (§ 4.1) and not necessarily because of the individuals' actions. For instance, just by being recognised as a man, an academic is more likely than a colleague who is identified as a woman to be quickly promoted, presumed to be willing to sacrifice family over career, asked his opinion during meetings, have fewer pastoral duties, and not be sexually harassed by students or other colleagues. Privilege encompasses a wide range of institutionalised entitlements and advantages, material resources, opportunities and statuses persons have in their daily life. Consider 'heterosexual privilege'.[20] By being and being recognised as a heterosexual, for instance, an Italian citizen can civilly marry and get access to all the entitlements conferred by marital status (e.g. migration rights, inheritance, visitation rights in hospital, alimony in case of divorce), and kiss her partner publicly without fear of being physically or verbally attacked; moreover, she has her type of family represented in children's literature and she does not have to come out and announce her sexuality to friends, family and colleagues by, say, correcting assumptions about her partner's gender.

Those privileged vis-à-vis certain structures, because of their privilege, should be politically responsible to contribute to eradicating such structures and thus creating a society (or transnational order) in which their unjustified advantages are eliminated or become everyone's entitlements. Since the injustice is structural in nature, they should do so not simply by changing their attitudes but by engaging with others (e.g. calling out similarly positioned persons) and, especially, participating in or organising collective actions.[21] When privileged ordinary individuals fail to take on their political responsibility, they should be rightly criticised as they keep having unjustified advantages and assets while doing nothing to change their position. Now, those privileged in relation to, say, gender structures

---

[19] McIntosh (1989).   [20] Simoni and Walters (2001).   [21] Young (2011, 111).

(i.e. those identified as men) are also subjected to and thus may be also constrained by such structures (e.g. by gendered expectations about how men should behave) and suffer as a result. However, recognising that there are mutually constituting positions within social structures entails acknowledging one's own privilege within them, even if sufferance from gendered expectations can be real. This, as bell hooks argues, entails that 'while [men] do not need to blame themselves [for the new reproduction of the unjust history of women], they must assume responsibility for eliminating it'.[22]

What about those who are at a disadvantage within unjust structures? It is crucial to recognise the pivotal role that those suffering from injustice play in struggles for justice and equality. Over history, it has been through the *collective* power of the oppressed that change has been brought about. There are ways to respect and theorise the oppressed as agents of justice that resonate with how activists themselves conceptualise their political commitment and explain why they have become activists which do not rely on their contribution to the structural injustice they suffer from.

Realising that one has to take on responsibility and join others in fighting against their unjust conditions is often a necessity. As compellingly observed by Martin Luther King Jr., 'Freedom is never voluntarily given by the oppressor; it must be demanded by the oppressed'.[23] In addition to painfully understanding that struggle is necessary for progress and often for sheer survival, for many activists, standing up *with others* for one's rights and against one's own injustice is empowering. As Billy McMillan, a leading activist in ACT UP's Chicago chapter established during the AIDS crisis in the late 1980s, recalls, 'I felt empowered that there were other gays and lesbians who, like myself . . . believed that we had to take matters into our hands to help our community'.[24] The nexus between empowerment and activism underpinned the practice of consciousness raising in feminist movements during the 1960s and 1970s. By sharing one's own experiences with similarly structurally positioned others, participants realised that what they felt as personal faults, an isolated experience and a fate they had no power over (e.g. having had an illegal abortion, surviving rape, being domestically abused and fighting daily with their male partner over housework) were

---

[22] bell hooks (1984, 72). Similarly, recognising, say, men's privilege does not imply that those who have it equally benefit from it. As hooks observes, 'Patriarchy does not negate the existence of class and race privilege or exploitation' (1984, 68). Intersectionality means that the extent to which one person is overall privileged depends on their intersectional position and that one person may be privileged vis-à-vis certain structures but not others.

[23] King ([1963] 1991, 292).   [24] D. B. Gould (2009, 187).

actually the result of structural injustice (and of the reproduction of an unjust history), and, in so realising, they could take back control over their lives. In Susan Brownmiller's words,

> My solitary efforts to forge my own destiny were fragments of women's shared, hidden history, links to past and future generations, pieces of the puzzle called sexual oppression. The simple technique of consciousness-raising had brought my submerged truths to the surface, where I learned that I wasn't alone.[25]

Fighting against one's own injustice as part of a collective becomes a way to love oneself and believe in one's own value and abilities. Activists, however, very often describe taking on responsibility as significantly driven by other-regarding reasons. It is seen as an expression, or even a duty, of solidarity towards those similarly positioned within unjust structures in the present and across generations – something owed to future members of structural groups (i.e. 'structural descendants') but also to those previous generations that made sacrifices and stood up for their rights before (i.e. 'structural ancestors'). As Deja Nicole Greenlaw, a trans activist and advocate, passionately argues in addressing other trans* individuals:

> We will pave the way for [future trans* persons] just as others have paved the way for us at Stonewall in New York City and the Compton Riots in San Francisco. Do it for these brave Trans men and women who suffered and even lost their lives. Do it so that they won't have suffered and died in vain. Do it for all those Transpeople who have died and we remember them every year in our yearly November 20th Transgender Day of Remembrance. Do it for our Trans brothers and sisters who aren't even born yet, so that they will not have to endure what we had to in our lives.[26]

It is on the basis of such responsibilities of solidarity among similarly positioned persons that activists criticise, often vehemently, those who instead remain silent. For instance, during the 1980s and 1990s, when AIDS became a real epidemic in the US and the governmental and medical establishment kept reacting with indifference to it, ACT UP activists – in their demonstrations, direct actions, speeches and writings – persisted in giving 'wake-up calls' to those more affected by AIDS (in particular to homosexuals) so as to push them to mobilise and join the fight.

Such a criticism has moral force and, in this sense, is legitimate because it is voiced by persons who have what can be called 'structural standing' vis-à-vis a specific injustice – that is, members of structural groups suffering from that

---

[25] Brownmiller (1990, 7).   [26] Greenlaw (2009).

injustice who are fighting for achieving freedom and equality for *all* those similarly positioned in society. They can criticise those who, like them, suffer from the same (historical or not) structural injustice but do nothing to overcome it not only because their resistance will also benefit structural members who do not participate in the struggle but also because the improvement of *their own* condition hinges on others' joining the fight. As, in 1983, Larry Kramer, one of the founders of ACT UP New York, wrote in the *New York Native* to other gay men: 'Our continued existence depends on how angry you can get'.[27] Moreover, this form of criticism can be constructive and empowering as, in expressing it, activists also set an example for those who may feel powerless by showing the force of collective action.

However, criticism is problematic and rightly perceived as unfair when it is voiced by privileged persons (e.g. white Americans) towards those who are disadvantaged (e.g. African Americans) in relation to the (e.g. racial) structures that confer them a privilege. The problem is that privileged individuals lack the 'structural standing' to compel the structurally disadvantaged to do more to address the structural injustice they suffer from, especially when the relations between privileged and disadvantaged structural groups have been historically characterised by violence, exploitation, negligence, unconcern and indifference. Such a lack of 'structural standing' explains, for instance, the frustration that members of disadvantaged structural groups experience when those with privilege ask them to 'educate' them about their injustice. To be sure, the epistemic access to the unjust workings of social (and transnational) structures that those suffering from structural injustice may uniquely develop can serve as a reason for them to mobilise and empower themselves. However, when the 'privileged' use it to demand that members of disadvantaged structural groups do more (by, for instance, explaining to them how racial structures function), the former does not only further burden the latter but also 'maintain[s] their position and evade[s] their responsibility' to collectively address the unjust structures in which they occupy a privileged space.[28] Discharging that responsibility starts with embarking on a long learning journey to understand structural injustice and one's own privileges in relation to it. Awareness of such privileges is, then, shown by directing criticism about failure to tackle unjust structures more fairly – that is, at others similarly privileged.

These final observations do not want to deny that those disadvantaged within certain (e.g. gendered) structures (e.g. women) contribute to structural

---

[27] Kramer (1989, 39).   [28] Lorde (2007, 115).

injustices by exercising their agency. I have simply tried to suggest that there are other ways to normatively conceptualise their fundamental role in bringing about (historical and) structural justice that are sensitive to the relations between groups that are differently positioned within such unjust structures and often, as in the case of women and men, have been mutually constituted through injustices over history.

De-temporalising injustice is crucial to conceptually and normatively theorise certain present injustices, which are not simply the passive legacy or effects of historical injustices but the new reproduction of an unjust history. De-temporalising injustice and thus understanding when, why and how an unjust history matters for consideration of justice entails examining both historical persistence and change, and, especially, their interplay. It urges us not to dismiss the 'banal' ways unjust history is reproduced and their relation to the radical forms of such a reproduction. De-temporalising injustice means recognising the historical accountability of certain powerful agents, and their obligations to repair their structural debts, while also conceiving of redress as a long and challenging process involving many different agents. This process gives us the responsibility to investigate whether and how unjust history is newly reproduced in the very 'apparatus' of societies (and the transnational order) – that is, in the complex web of different and interconnected 'discourses, institutions, architectural forms, regulatory decisions, laws, administrative measures, scientific statements, philosophical, moral and philanthropic propositions',[29] practices and stereotypes that regulate our existence and that we take for granted.

The process of redress may seem overly disheartening but can also be invigorating because it offers us the opportunity to imagine new ways of organising our political and social life together. This process may look too strenuous or even vain, but, in the words famously attributed to Nelson Mandela, 'it always seems impossible until it's done'.

---

[29] Foucault (1980, 194).

References

Abdel-Nour, Farid. 2003. 'National Responsibility'. *Political Theory* 31 (5): 693–719.

Ahrens, Courtney E., Marc D. Rich and Jodie B. Ullman. 2011. 'Rehearsing for Real Life: The Impact of the InterACT Sexual Assault Prevention Program on Self-Reported Likelihood of Engaging in Bystander Interventions'. *Violence Against Women* 17 (6): 760–76.

Aiyetoro, Adjoa A. 2003. 'Formulating Reparations Litigation through the Eyes of the Movement'. *NYU Annual Survey of American Law* 58 (4): 457–74.

Akbar, Amna. 2018. 'Toward a Radical Imagination of Law'. *NYU Law Review* 93 (3): 405–79.

Alcoff, Linda Martin. 2006. *Visible Identities: Race, Gender, and the Self.* New York: Oxford University Press.

Alexander, Michelle. 2012. *The New Jim Crow.* New York: The New Press.

Amighetti, Sara and Alasia Nuti. 2015. 'Towards a Shared Redress: Achieving Historical Justice through Democratic Deliberation'. *Journal of Political Philosophy* 23 (4): 385–405.

Amnesty International. 2007. *Maze of Injustice: The Failure to Protect Indigenous Women from Sexual Violence in the USA.* New York: Amnesty International USA. www.amnestyusa.org/pdfs/mazeofinjustice.pdf.

2010. 'Case Closed: Rape and Human Rights in the Nordic Countries. Summary Report'. London: Amnesty International-International Secretariat. www.amnesty.org/en/documents/ACT77/001/2010/en/.

Anderson, Benedict. 1991. *Imagined Communities: Reflections on the Origin and Spread of Nationalism.* Revised and extended edn. London: Verso.

Anderson, Elizabeth. 2010. *The Imperative of Integration.* Princeton, NJ: Princeton University Press.

Appiah, K. Anthony. 1994. 'Identity, Authenticity, Survival: Multicultural Societies and Social Reproduction'. In *Multiculturalism: Examining the Politics of Recognition,* edited by Charles Taylor, 149–64. Princeton, NJ: Princeton University Press.

Arendt, Hannah. 1970. *Men in Dark Times.* New York: Houghton Mifflin Harcourt.

Assies, Willem. 2003. 'David versus Goliath in Cochabamba: Water Rights, Neoliberalism, and the Revival of Social Protest in Bolivia'. *Latin American Perspectives* 30 (3): 14–36.

Austin, John L. [1962] 1975. *How to Do Things with Words*. Edited by James O. Urmson and Marina Sbisá. 2nd edn. Cambridge, MA: Harvard University Press.

Badassi, Giovanna and Federica Gentile. 2016. 'Rapporto Mamme 2016 – Le Equilibriste'. Rome: Save the Children. https://s3.savethechildren.it/public/files/uploads/pubblicazioni/rapporto-mamme-2016-le-equilibriste.pdf.

Balfour, Lawrie. 2003. 'Unreconstructed Democracy: W.E.B. Du Bois and the Case for Reparations'. *American Political Science Review* 97 (1): 33–44.

2005. 'Reparations after Identity Politics'. *Political Theory* 33 (6): 786–811.

2011. *Democracy's Reconstruction: Thinking Politically with W.E.B. Du Bois*. New York: Oxford University Press.

2015. 'Ida B. Wells and "Color Line Justice": Rethinking Reparations in Feminist Terms'. *Perspectives on Politics* 13 (3): 680–96.

Balibar, Etienne. 1990. 'Paradoxes of Universality'. In *The Anatomy of Racism*, edited by David Theo Goldberg, 283–94. Minneapolis: University of Minnesota Press.

Banyard, Victoria L., Elizabethe G. Plante and Mary M. Moynihan. 2004. 'Bystander Education: Bringing a Broader Community Perspective to Sexual Violence Prevention'. *Journal of Community Psychology* 32 (1): 61–79.

Barclay, Linda. 2013. 'Liberal Daddy Quotas: Why Men Should Take Care of the Children, and How Liberals Can Get Them to Do It'. *Hypatia* 28 (1): 163–78.

Barkan, Elazar. 2000. *The Guilt of Nations: Restitution and Negotiating Historical Injustices*. New York: W. W. Norton.

Batkins, Sam. 2013. 'Red Tape Challenges to America's Veterans'. *American Action Forum*, 2 July. http://americanactionforum.org/insights/red-tape-challenges-to-americas-veterans.

Bekkengern, Lisbeth. 2006. 'Men's Parental Leave: A Manifestation of Gender Equality or Child-Orientation?'. In *Gender Segregation: Divisions of Work in Post-industrial Welfare States*, edited by Lena Gonas and Jan C. Karlsson, 149–62. Aldershot: Ashgate.

Benjamin, Walter. [1942] 2003. 'On the Concept of History'. In *Selected Writings: Volume 4, 1938–1940*, edited by Michael W. Jeggings and Howard Eiland, 388–400. Cambridge, MA: Belknap of Harvard University Press.

Benson, Jennifer. 2014. 'Freedom as Going Off Script'. *Hypatia* 29 (2): 355–70.

Berger, Dan, Mariame Kaba and David Stein. 2017. 'What Abolitionists Do'. 24 August. http://jacobinmag.com/2017/08/prison-abolition-reform-mass-incarceration.

Berkowitz, Alan D. 2002. 'Fostering Men's Responsibility for Preventing Sexual Assault'. In *Preventing Violence in Relationships: Interventions across the Life Span*, edited by Paul A. Schewe, 163–96. Washington, DC: American Psychological Association.

Berlin, Ira. 2000. *Many Thousands Gone: The First Two Centuries of Slavery in North America*. Cambridge, MA: Harvard University Press.

Berlin, Isaiah. [1979] 2013. 'Nationalism: Past Neglect and Present Power'. In *Against the Current: Essays in the History of Ideas*, edited by Henry Hardy, 420–48. Princeton, NJ: Princeton University Press.

Bertrand, Marianne, Emir Kamenica and Jessica Pan. 2015. 'Gender Identity and Relative Income within Households'. *The Quarterly Journal of Economics* 130 (2): 571–614.

Best, Stephen and Saidiya Hartman. 2005. 'Fugitive Justice'. *Representations* 92 (1): 1–15.

Bettcher, Talia Mae. 2014. 'Trapped in the Wrong Theory: Rethinking Trans Oppression and Resistance'. *Signs: Journal of Women in Culture and Society* 39 (2): 383–406.

Bia, Silvia. 2016. 'Aborto, l'Esilio Dei Medici Non Obiettori in Italia: Soli in Sala Operatoria, Costretti Ad Auto-Assistersi e Senza Carriera'. *Il Fatto Quotidiano*, 11 April. www.ilfattoquotidiano.it/2016/04/11/aborto-lesilio-dei-medici-non-obi ettori-italia-soli-sala-operatoria-costretti-ad-auto-assistersi-e-senza-carriera/2626 543/.

Bianchi, Suzanne, Nancy Folbre and Douglas Wolf. 2012. 'Unpaid Care Work'. In *For Love or for Money: Care Provision in the United States*, edited by Nancy Folbre, 40–64. New York: Russell Sage Foundation.

Bickford, Susan. 1997. 'Anti-Anti-Identity Politics: Feminism, Democracy and the Complexities of Citizenship'. *Hypatia* 12 (4): 111–31.

Billig, Michael. 1995. *Banal Nationalism*. London: Sage.

Biondi, Martha. 2003. 'The Rise of the Reparations Movement'. *Radical History Review* 2003 (87): 5–18.

Bird, S. Elizabeth. 1999. 'Gendered Construction of the American Indian in Popular Media'. *Journal of Communication* 49 (3): 61–83.

Birmingham, Peg. 2003. 'Holes of Oblivion: The Banality of Radical Evil'. *Hypatia* 18 (1): 80–103.

Bittker, Boris. 1973. *The Case for Black Reparations*. New York: Vintage Books.

Bittman, Michael, Paula England, Liana Sayer, Nancy Folbre and George Matheson. 2003. 'When Does Gender Trump Money? Bargaining and Time in Household Work'. *American Journal of Sociology* 109 (1): 186–214.

Blackburn, Robert M., Jude Browne, Bradley Brooks and Jennifer Jarman. 2002. 'Explainig Gender Segregation'. *The British Journal of Sociology* 53 (4): 513–36.

Blackburn, Robert M. and Jennifer Jarman. 2006. 'Gendered Occupations Exploring the Relationship between Gender Segregation and Inequality'. *International Sociology* 21 (2): 289–315.

Blake, Jamilia J., Bettie Ray Butler, Chance W. Lewis and Alicia Darensbourg. 2011. 'Unmasking the Inequitable Discipline Experiences of Urban Black Girls: Implications for Urban Educational Stakeholders'. *The Urban Review* 43 (1): 90–106.

Blau, Peter. 1977. *Inequality and Heterogeneity: A Primitive Theory of Social Structure*. New York: Free Press.

Blight, David W. 1994. 'W. E. B. Du Bois and the Struggle for American Historical Memory'. In *History and Memory in African-American Culture*, edited by Geneviève Fabre and Robert O'Meally, 45–71. New York: Oxford University Press.

Bloksgaard, Lotte. 2011. 'Masculinities, Femininities and Work: The Horizontal Gender Segregation in the Danish Labour Market'. *Nordic Journal of Working Life Studies* 1 (2): 5–21.

Booth, W. James. 2011. '"From This Far Place": On Justice and Absence'. *American Political Science Review* 105 (4): 750–64.

Bourdieu, Pierre. 1984. *Distinction: A Social Critique of the Judgement of Taste*. Translated by Richard Nice. Cambridge, MA: Harvard University Press.

Boxill, Bernard R. 1972. 'The Morality of Reparation'. *Social Theory and Practice* 2 (1): 113–22.

2003. 'A Lockean Argument for Black Reparations'. *The Journal of Ethics* 7 (1): 63–91.

Brenner, Lisa A., Lisa M. Betthauser, Beeta Y. Homaifar, Edgar J. Villarreal, Jeri Harwood, Pamela J. Staves and Joseph A. Huggins. 2011. 'Posttraumatic Stress Disorder, Traumatic Brain Injury, and Suicide Attempt History among Veterans Receiving Mental Health Services'. *Suicide and Life-Threatening Behavior* 41 (4): 416–423.

Brettschneider, Corey. 2012. *When the State Speaks, What Should It Say? How Democracies Can Protect Expression and Promote Equality*. Princeton, NJ: Princeton University Press.

Brighouse, Harry and Erik O. Wright. 2008. 'Strong Gender Egalitarianism'. *Politics and Society* 36 (3): 360–72.

Bronski, Michael. 2011. *A Queer History of the United States*. Boston, MA: Beacon Press.

Browne, Jude. 2005. *Gender Inequality and Social Change: Segregation in the Modern Labour Market*. Bristol: Policy Press.

2013. 'The Default Model: Gender Equality, Fatherhood, and Structural Constraint'. *Politics and Gender* 9 (2): 152–73.

2014. 'The Critical Mass Marker Approach: Female Quotas and Social Justice'. *Political Studies* 62 (4): 862–77.

Browne, Robert S. 1971. 'The Economic Basis for Reparations to Black America'. *The Review of Black Political Economy* 2 (2): 67–80.

Brownmiller, Susan. 1990. *In Our Time: Memoir of a Revolution*. New York: Dial Press.

Brownstein, Michael. 2015. 'Implicit Bias'. In *The Stanford Encyclopedia of Philosophy*, edited by Edward N. Zalta. http://plato.stanford.edu/archives/spr2015/entries/implicit-bias/.

Brubaker, Rogers. 2002. 'Ethnicity without Groups'. *European Journal of Sociology* 43 (2): 163–89.

Bubeck, Diemut E. 1995. *Care, Gender, and Justice*. Oxford: Clarendon Press.

1999. 'A Feminist Approach to Citizenship'. In *Gender and the Use of Time*, edited by Olwen Hufton and Yota Kravariton, 401–28. Dordrecht: Kluwer Academic.

Bushway, Shawn D. 2004. 'Labor Market Effects of Permitting Employer Access to Criminal History Records'. *Journal of Contemporary Criminal Justice* 20 (3): 276–91.

Butler, Judith. 1990. *Gender Trouble: Feminism and the Subversion of Identity*. New York: Routledge.

Butt, Daniel. 2009. *Rectifying International Injustice: Principles of Compensation and Restitution between Nations*. Oxford: Oxford University Press.

Calhoun, Cheshire. 2002. *Feminism, the Family, and the Politics of the Closet: Lesbian and Gay Displacement*. New York: Oxford University Press.

Cameron, Claire. 2001. 'Promise or Problem? A Review of the Literature on Men Working in Early Childhood Services'. *Gender, Work and Organization* 8 (4): 430–53.

Canovan, Margaret. 1996. *Nationhood and Political Theory*. Cheltenham: Edward Elgar.

Carastathis, Anna. 2014. 'The Concept of Intersectionality in Feminist Theory'. *Philosophy Compass* 9 (5): 304–14.

Carbado, Devon W. 2013. 'Colorblind Intersectionality'. *Signs: Journal of Women in Culture and Society* 38 (4): 811–45.

Card, Claudia. 1996. 'Against Marriage and Motherhood'. *Hypatia* 11 (3): 1–23.

Casey, Erin, Juliana Carson and Sierra Two Bulls. 2016. 'Gender Transformative Approaches to Engaging Men in Gender-Based Violence Prevention: A Review and Conceptual Model'. *Trauma, Violence, and Abuse* 19 (2): 231–46.

Chakrabarty, Dipesh. 2007. *Provincializing Europe: Postcolonial Thought and Historical Difference*. Princeton, NJ: Princeton University Press.

Charles, Maria. 2003. 'Deciphering Sex Segregation Vertical and Horizontal Inequalities in Ten National Labor Markets'. *Acta Sociologica* 46 (4): 267–87.

Childs, Dennis. 2015. *Slaves of the State: Black Incarceration from the Chain Gang to the Penitentiary*. Minneapolis: University of Minnesota Press.

Cho, Sumi, Kimberlé W. Crenshaw and Leslie McCall. 2013. 'Toward a Field of Intersectionality Studies: Theory, Applications, and Praxis'. *Signs: Journal of Women in Culture and Society* 38 (4): 785–810.

Coates, Ta-Nehisi. 2014. 'The Case for Reparations'. *The Atlantic*, June. www.theatlantic.com/magazine/archive/2014/06/the-case-for-reparations/361631/.

Code, Lorraine. 1993. 'Taking Subjectivity into Account'. In *Feminist Epistemologies*, edited by Linda Alcoff and Elizabeth Potter, 15–48. New York: Routledge.

Cohen, Andrew I. 2009. 'Compensation for Historic Injustices: Completing the Boxill and Sher Argument'. *Philosophy and Public Affairs* 37 (1): 81–102.

Cohen, Gerald A. 2000. '"Where the Action Is: On the Site of Distributive Justice"'. In *If You're an Egalitarian How Come You're So Rich?*, by Gerald A. Cohen, 134–47. Cambridge, MA: Harvard University Press.

Coker, Ann L., Patricia G. Cook-Craig, Corrine M. Williams, Bonnie S. Fisher, Emily R. Clear, Lisandra Garcia and Lea M. Hegge. 2011. 'Evaluation of Green Dot: An Active Bystander Intervention to Reduce Sexual Violence on College Campuses'. *Violence Against Women* 17 (6): 777–96.

Collins, Patricia H. 2000. *Black Feminist Thought: Knowledge, Consciousness, and the Politics of Empowerment*. New York: Routledge.

Conti, Fulvio. 2013. 'La Secolarizzazione Inconsapevole. Laicità e Dimensione Pubblica Nell'Italia Contemporanea'. *Memoria e Ricerca* 43: 45–65.

Copp, David. 2002. 'Social Unity and the Identity of Persons'. *The Journal of Philosophy* 10 (4): 365–91.

Correll, Joshua, Bernadette Park, Charles M. Judd and Bernd Wittenbrink. 2007a. 'The Influence of Stereotypes on Decisions to Shoot'. *European Journal of Social Psychology* 37 (6): 1102–17.

Correll, Joshua, Bernadette Park, Charles M. Judd, Bernd Wittenbrink, Melody S. Sadler and Tracie Keesee. 2007b. 'Across the Thin Blue Line: Police Officers and Racial Bias in the Decision to Shoot'. *Journal of Personality and Social Psychology* 92 (6): 1006–23.

Crenshaw, Kimberlé W. 1991. 'Mapping the Margins: Intersectionality, Identity Politics, and Violence Against Women of Color'. *Stanford Law Review* 43 (6): 1241–1299.

  2012. 'From Private Violence to Mass Incarceration: Thinking Intersectionally about Women, Race, and Social Control'. *UCLA Law Review* 59 (6): 1419–72.

Crenshaw, Kimberlé W., Priscilla Ocen and Jyoti Nanda. 2015. 'Black Girls Matter: Pushed Out, Overpoliced and Underprotected'. New York: African American Policy Forum and Center for Intersectionality and Social Policy Studies. www.law.columbia.edu/sites/default/files/legacy/files/public_affairs/2015/february_2015/black_girls_matter_report_2.4.15.pdf.

Cudd, Ann E. 2006. *Analyzing Oppression*. New York: Oxford University Press.

Dalton, Susan and Denise D. Bielby. 2000. '"That's Our Kind of Constellation": Lesbian Mothers Negotiate Institutionalized Understandings of Gender within the Family'. *Gender and Society* 14 (1): 36–61.

Darby, Derrick. 2010. 'Reparations and Racial Inequality'. *Philosophy Compass* 5 (1): 55–66.

Davies, Lizzy. 2013. 'Italian Integration Minister Issues Defiant Response to Banana Stunt'. *The Guardian*, 24 July. www.theguardian.com/world/2013/jul/28/italian-cecile-kyenge-banana-stunt.

Davis, Angela Y. 1983. *Women, Race and Class*. New York: Vintage Books.

  2003. *Are Prisons Obsolete?* New York: Seven Stories Press.

  2005. *Abolition Democracy: Beyond Empire, Prisons, and Torture*. New York: Seven Stories Press.

Deer, Sarah. 2004. 'Federal Indian Law and Violent Crime: Native Women and Children at the Mercy of the State'. *Social Justice* 31 (4): 17–30.

Dobash, Rebecca Emerson and Russell Dobash. 1998. 'Cross-Border Encounters: Challenges and Opportunities'. In *Rethinking Violence Against Women*, edited by Rebecca Emerson Dobash and Russell Dobash, 1–23. Thousand Oaks, CA: Sage.

Edwards, Alice. 2010. *Violence Against Women under International Human Rights Law*. New York: Cambridge University Press.

Eisikovits, Nir. 2014. 'Transitional Justice'. In *The Stanford Encyclopedia of Philosophy*, edited by Edward N. Zalta. http://plato.stanford.edu/archives/win2014/entries/justice-transitional/.

Elman, R. Amy. 2001. 'Unprotected by the Swedish Welfare State Revisited: Assessing a Decade of Reforms for Battered Women'. *Women's Studies International Forum* 24 (1): 39–52.

Eltis, David. 2000. *The Rise of African Slavery in the Americas*. Cambridge: Cambridge University Press.

Enander, Viveka. 2010. '"A Fool to Keep Staying": Battered Women Labeling Themselves Stupid as an Expression of Gendered Shame'. *Violence Against Women* 16 (1): 5–31.

Enns, Peter K. 2016. *Incarceration Nation*. New York: Cambridge University Press.

Eriksson, Maria and Keith Pringle. 2005. 'Introduction: Nordic Issues and Dilemmas'. In *Tackling Men's Violence in Families: Nordic Issues and Dilemmas*, edited by Maria Eriksson et al., 1–12. Bristol: Policy Press.

Ertürk, Yakin. 2006. 'Implementation of General Assembly Resolution 60/251 of 15 March 2006 Entitled "Human Rights Council". Report of the Special Rapporteur on Violence Against Women, Its Causes and Consequences. Mission to Sweden'. New York: United Nations.

Espin-Andersen, Gosta. 2009. *Incomplete Revolution: Adapting to Women's New Roles*. Cambridge: Polity Press.

Esposito, Barbara and Lee Wood. 1982. *Prison Slavery*. Maryland: Abolish Prison Slavery.

European Agency for Fundamental Rights. 2014. 'Violence Against Women: An EU-Wide Survey: Main Results'. Vienna: FRA. http://fra.europa.eu/en/publication/2014/violence-against-women-euwide-survey.

Evertsson, Marie and Magnus Nermo. 2004. 'Dependence within Families and the Division of Labor: Comparing Sweden and the United States'. *Journal of Marriage and Family* 66 (5): 1272–86.

Fabre, Cecile. 2008. *Whose Body Is It Anyway? Justice and the Integrity of the Person*. Oxford: Oxford University Press.

Falcinelli, Daniela and Sveva Magaraggia. 2013. '"Double Yes" for Whom? Gender Innovation in Italian Families'. *Journal of Contemporary European Studies* 21 (2): 290–303.

Falcon, Sylvanna. 2001. 'Rape as a Weapon of War: Advancing Human Rights for Women at the US–Mexico Border'. *Social Justice* 28 (2): 31–50.

Fishkin, James S. 1984. *Justice, Equal Opportunity and the Family*. New Haven, CT: Yale University Press.

Fiske, Susan and Tiane L. Lee. 2008. 'Stereotypes and Prejudice Create Workplace Discrimination'. In *Diversity at Work*, edited by Arthur P. Brief, 13–52. Cambridge: Cambridge University Press.

Folbre, Nancy. 1994. *Who Pays for the Kids? Gender and the Structures of Constraint*. New York: Routledge.

Folbre, Nancy, Suzanne Bianchi and Douglas Wolf. 2012. 'Unpaid Care Work'. In *For Love or Money: Care Provision in the United States*, edited by Nancy Folbre, 40–64. New York: Russell Sage Foundation.

Folbre, Nancy and Erik O. Wright. 2012. 'Defining Care'. In *For Love and Money: Care Provision in the United States*, edited by Nancy Folbre, 1–21. New York: Russell Sage Foundation.

Forde-Mazrui, Kim. 2004. 'Taking Conservatives Seriously: A Moral Justification for Affirmative Action and Reparations'. *California Law Review* 92 (3): 683–753.

Forst, Rainer. 2017. 'On the Concept of a Justification Narrative'. In *Normativity and Power: Analyzing Social Orders of Justification*, 55–68. Oxford: Oxford University Press.

Foucault, Michel. 1980. *Power/Knowledge: Selected Interviews and Other Writings, 1972–1977*. Edited by Colin Gordon. New York: Pantheon Books.

  2003a. *Abnormal: Lectures at the Collège de France, 1974–1975*. Translated by Burchell Grahman. London: Verso.

  2003b. *Society Must Be Defended: Lectures at the Collège de France, 1975–76*. Translated by David Macey. New York: Picador.

Fox, John and Zsuzsanna Vidra. 2013. 'Applying Tolerance Indicators: Roma School Segregation'. Fiesole: European Institute. https://cps.ceu.hu/sites/default/files/publications/cps-policy-brief-accept-roma-school-segregation-indicators-2013.pdf.

Fraser, Nancy. 1997a. 'From Redistribution to Recognition? Dilemmas of Justice in a "Postsocialist" Age'. In *Justice Interruptus: Critical Reflections on the 'Postsocialist' Condition*, 11–40. London: Routledge.

  1997b. 'After the Family Wage: A Postindustrial through Experiment'. In *Justice Interruptus: Critical Reflections on the 'Postsocialist' Condition*, by Nancy Fraser, 41–68. New York: Routledge.

Freeman, Michael. 2008. 'Historical Injustice and Liberal Political Theory'. In *The Age of Apology: Facing Up to the Past*, edited by Mark Gibney, Rhoda E. Howard-Hassmann, Jean-Marc Coicaud and Niklaus Steiner, 45–60. Philadelphia: University of Pennsylvania Press.

Frye, Marilyn. 1996a. 'The Necessity of Differences: Constructing a Positive Category of Women'. *Signs: Journal of Women in Culture and Society* 21 (4): 991–1010.

  1996b. 'The Possibility of Feminist Theory'. In *Women, Knowledge, and Reality: Explorations in Feminist Philosophy*, edited by Ann Garry and Marilyn Pearsall, 34–47. New York: Routledge.

Fullinwider, Robert K. 2004. 'The Case for Reparations'. In *Reparations for Slavery: A Reader*, edited by Ronald Paul Salzberger and Mary C. Turck, 141–50. Lanham, MD: Rowman and Littlefield.

Gallo, Filomena. 2016. 'Legge 194, Un Pericoloso Ritorno Al Passato'. *Il Manifesto*, 12 April. https://ilmanifesto.it/legge-194-un-pericoloso-ritorno-al-passato/.

Gans, Chaim. 2003. *The Limits of Nationalism*. New York: Cambridge University Press.

Garcia-Moreno, Claudia, Naeemah Abrahams, Karen Devries, Christina Pallitto, Max Petzold, Heidi Stöckl and Charlotte Watts. 2013. 'Global and Regional Estimates of Violence Against Women: Prevalence and Health Effects of Intimate Partner Violence and Non-Partner Sexual Violence'. World Health Organization. http://apps.who.int/iris/bitstream/10665/85239/1/9789241564 625_eng.pdf.

Gatens, Moira. 1996. *Imaginary Bodies: Ethics, Power, and Corporeality*. London: Routledge.

Gauthier, DeAnn K. and William B. Bankston. 2004. '"Who Kills Whom" Revisited: A Sociological Study of Variation in the Sex Ratio of Spouse Killings'. *Homicide Studies* 8 (2): 96–122.

Gheaus, Anca. 2008. 'Basic Income, Gender Justice and the Costs of Gender-Symmetrical Lifestyles'. *Basic Income Studies* 3 (3): 1–8.

2012. 'Gender Justice'. *Journal of Ethics and Social Philosophy* 6 (1): 1–24.

Gheaus, Anca and Ingrid Robeyns. 2011. 'Equality-Promoting Parental Leave'. *Journal of Social Philosophy* 42 (2): 173–91.

Giddens, Anthony. 1979. *Central Problems in Social Theory: Action, Structure, and Contradiction in Social Analysis*. Berkeley: University of California Press.

Gilbert, Margaret. 1989. *On Social Facts*. New York: Routledge.

Gilmore, Ruth Wilson. 2007. *Golden Gulag: Prisons, Surplus, Crisis, and Opposition in Globalizing California*. Berkeley: University of California Press.

Goldman, Alan H. 1976. 'Affirmative Action'. *Philosophy and Public Affairs* 5 (2): 178–95.

Gooden, Susan T. 1999. 'The Hidden Third Party: Welfare Recipients' Experiences with Employers'. *Journal of Public Management and Social Policy* 5 (1): 69–83.

Goodhart, Michael. 2017. 'Interpreting Responsibility Politically'. *Journal of Political Philosophy* 25 (2): 173–95.

Goodin, Robert E. 1995. *Utilitarianism as a Public Philosophy*. Cambridge: Cambridge University Press.

2013. 'Disgorging the Fruits of Historical Wrongdoing'. *American Political Science Review* 107 (3): 478–91.

Goodwin, Morag. 2004. 'The Romani Claim to Non-territorial Nation Status: Recognition from an International Legal Perspective'. *Roma Rights Journal* 1 (1): 54–64.

Gornick, Janet C. and Marcia Meyers. 2005. *Families That Work: Policies for Reconciling Parenthood and Employment*. New York: Russell Sage Foundation.

Gottzén, Lucas. 2013. 'Encountering Violent Men: Strange and Familiar'. In *Men, Masculinities and Methodologies*, edited by Barbara Pini and Bob Pease, 197–208. London: Palgrave Macmillan.

Gould, Carol C. 2009. 'Varieties of Global Responsibilities: Social Connection, Human Rights, and Transnational Solidarity'. In *Dancing with Iris: The Philosophy of Iris Marion Young*, edited by Ann Ferguson, 199–212. New York: Oxford University Press.

Gould, Deborah B. 2009. *Moving Politics*. Chicago, IL: University of Chicago Press.

Green, Rayna. 1975. 'The Pocahontas Perplex: The Image of Indian Women in American Culture'. *The Massachusetts Review* 16 (4): 698–714.

Greenlaw, Deja Nicole. 2009. 'Transactivism: Like "Milk's" Message Come Out, Be True to Who You Are!' *Rainbow Times*, September. www.therainbowtimesmass.com/septo9.pdf.

Gunnarsson, Lena. 2011. 'A Defence of the Category "Women"'. *Feminist Theory* 12 (1): 23–37.

Hakim, Catherine. 2010. '(How) Can Social Policy and Fiscal Policy Recognise Unpaid Family Work?' *Renewal* 18 (1–2): 23–24.

Halberstam, Judith. 1998. *Female Masculinity*. Durham, NC: Duke University Press.

Hall, David. 2004. 'The Spirit of Reparation'. *BC Third World Law Journal* 24: 1.

Hancock, Ian F. 2008. 'Responses to the Porrajmos: The Romani Holocaust'. In *Is the Holocaust Unique? Perspectives on Comparative Genocide*, edited by Alan S. Rosenbaum, 75–102. Boulder, CO: Westview Press.

Hansen, Randall and Desmond King. 2013. *Sterilized by the State: Eugenics, Race, and the Population Scare in Twentieth-Century North America*. New York: Cambridge University Press.

Haraway, Donna. 1988. 'Situated Knowledges: The Science Question in Feminism and the Privilege of a Partial Perspective'. *Feminist Studies* 14 (3): 575–99.

Harris, Leslie M. 2004. *In the Shadow of Slavery: African Americans in New York City, 1626–1863*. Chicago, IL: University of Chicago Press.

Hartman, Saidiya V. 2002. 'The Time of Slavery'. *The South Atlantic Quarterly* 101 (4): 757–77.

Haslanger, Sally. 2000. 'Gender and Race: (What) Are They? (What) Do We Want Them to Be?' *Noûs* 34 (1): 31–55.

2012. *Resisting Reality: Social Construction and Social Critique*. New York: Oxford University Press.

2015. 'Distinguished Lecture: Social Structure, Narrative and Explanation'. *Canadian Journal of Philosophy* 45 (1): 1–15.

Hattery, Angela. 2007. *Intimate Partner Violence*. Lanham, MD: Rowman and Littlefield.

Hausmann, Ricardo et al. 2017. 'Gender Gap Report 2017'. Geneva: World Economic Forum. www3.weforum.org/docs/WEF_GGGR_2017.pdf.

Hautanen, Teija. 2005. 'Bypassing the Relationship between Fatherhood and Violence in Finnish Policy and Research'. In *Tackling Men's Violence in Families: Nordic Issues and Dilemmas*, edited by Maria Eriksson, Marianne Hester, Suvi Keskinen and Keith Pringle, 67–82. Bristol: Policy Press.

Hayward, Clarissa R. 2000. *De-facing Power*. New York: Cambridge University Press.

2013. *How Americans Make Race: Stories, Institutions, and Spaces*. New York: Cambridge University Press.

Hearn, Jean and Linda McKie. 2010. 'Gendered and Social Hierarchies in Problem Representation and Policy Processes: 'Domestic Violence' in Finland and Scotland'. *Violence Against Women* 16 (2): 136–58.

Hearn, Jeff. 1998. *The Violences of Men: How Men Talk about and How Agencies Respond to Men's Violence to Women*. London: Sage.

Heiner, Brady. 2016. 'The Procedural Entrapment of Mass Incarceration'. *Philosophy and Social Criticism* 42 (6): 594–631.

Hendrix, Burke A. 2005. 'Memory in Native American Land Claims'. *Political Theory* 33 (6): 763–85.

Henry, Charles P. 2007. *Long Overdue: The Politics of Racial Reparations from Forty Acres to Atonement and Beyond*. New York: New York University Press.

Herstein, Ori J. 2009. 'Historic Injustice, Group Membership and Harm to Individuals: Defending Claims for Historic Justice from the Non-identity Problem'. *Harvard Journal of Racial and Ethnic Justice* 25: 229–75.

Hodson, Gordon, John F. Dovidio and Samuel L. Gaertner. 2002. 'Processes in Racial Discrimination: Differential Weighting of Conflicting Information'. *Personality and Social Psychology Bulletin* 28 (4): 460–71.

Holden, Stephen. 2011. '"Even the Rain", Icíar Bollaín's Political Film – Review'. *New York Times*, 17 February. www.nytimes.com/2011/02/18/movies/18even.html.

Holzer, Harry J., Steven Raphael and Michael Stoll. 2006. 'Perceived Criminality, Criminal Background Checks, and the Racial Hiring Practices of Employers'. *Journal of Law and Economics* 49 (2): 451–80.

hooks, bell. 1982. *Ain't I a Woman: Black Women and Feminism*. London: Pluto Press.

1984. *Feminist Theory: From Margin to Center*. Boston: South End Press.

1992. 'Reconstructing Black Masculinity'. In *Black Looks: Race and Representation*, 87–113. Boston: South End Press.

2004. *We Real Cool: Black Men and Masculinity*. New York: Routledge.

Hoschschild, Arlie. 2012. *The Second Shift: Working Families and the Revolution at Home*. Revised edn. London: Penguin Books.

Hoskins, Zachary. 2014. 'Ex-Offender Restrictions: Ex-Offender Restrictions'. *Journal of Applied Philosophy* 31 (1): 33–48.

Hussey, Andrew. 2014. *The French Intifada: The Long War between France and Its Arabs*. London: Granta Books.

Ibañez, Gladys E., Barbara VanOss Marín, Stephen A. Flores, Gregorio A. Millett and Rafael M. Díaz. 2009. 'General and Gay-Related Racism Experienced by Latino Gay Men'. *Cultural Diversity and Ethnic Minority Psychology* 15 (3): 215–22.

Iceland Ministry of Welfare. 2012. 'Male Violence Against Women in Intimate Relationships in Iceland. Report of the Minister of Welfare'. Reykjavík: Minister of Welfare. http://eng.velferdarraduneyti.is/media/rit-og-sky rslur2012/Ofbeldi_gegn_konum_enska_feb_2012.pdf.

Ivison, Duncan. 2000. 'Political Community and Historical Injustice'. *Australasian Journal of Philosophy* 78 (3): 360–73.

   2002. *Postcolonial Liberalism*. Cambridge: Cambridge University Press.

   2008. 'Historical Injustice'. In *The Oxford Handbook of Political Theory*, edited by John S. Dryzek, Bonnie Honig and Anne Phillips, 507–25. Oxford: Oxford University Press.

Jackson, Kathy M. 1996. 'Redesigning Pocahontas: Disney, the 'White Man's Indian', and the Marketing of Dreams'. *Journal of Popular Film and Television* 24 (2): 90–98.

Jafnréttisstofa. 2012. 'Gender Equality in Iceland. Information on Gender Equality Issues in Iceland'. Akureyri: The Centre for Gender Equality Iceland. https:// rafhladan.is/bitstream/handle/10802/9259/Gender-Equality-in-Iceland.pdf? sequence=1.

James, Joy. 2005. 'Introduction: Democracy and Captivity'. In *The New Abolitionists: (Neo)Slave Narratives and Contemporary Prison Writings*, edited by Joy James, xxi–xlii. New York: State University of New York Press.

Jewkes, Rachel, Michael Flood and James Lang. 2015. 'From Work with Men and Boys to Changes of Social Norms and Reduction of Inequities in Gender Relations: A Conceptual Shift in Prevention of Violence Against Women and Girls'. *The Lancet* 385 (9977): 1580–89.

Johnson, Michael P. 2008. *A Typology of Domestic Violence: Intimate Terrorism, Violent Resistance, and Situational Couple Violence*. Boston: Northeastern University Press.

Johnson, Walter. 1999. *Soul by Soul: Life inside the Antebellum Slave Market*. Cambridge, MA: Harvard University Press.

Judd, Terri and Tom Foot. 2013. 'Benefits Crackdown 'Humiliates' Disabled Army War Veterans'. Independent, 17 May. www.independent.co.uk/new s/uk/home-news/benefits-crackdown-humiliates-disabled-army-war-veter ans-8633610.html.

Kalajdzic, Jasminka. 1996. 'Rape, Representation and Rights: Permeating International Law with the Voices of Women'. *Queen's Law Journal* 21: 457–97.

Kandiyoti, Deniz 1991. 'Identity and Its Discontents: Women and the Nation'. *Millennium – Journal of International Studies* 20 (3): 429–43.

Kang, Jerry. 2005. 'Trojan Horses of Race'. *Harvard Law Review* 118 (5): 1489–593.

Kant, Immanuel. [1784] 2004. 'An Answer to the Question: "What Is Enlightenment?"' In *Kant: Political Writings*, translated by H. Barry Nisbet, 2nd edn., 54–63. Cambridge: Cambridge University Press.

Karraker, Katherine H., Dena A. Vogel and Margaret A. Lake. 1995. 'Parents' Gender-Stereotyped Perceptions of Newborns: The Eye of the Beholder Revisited'. *Sex Roles* 33 (9–10): 687–701.

Katz, Jackson, H. Alan Heisterkamp and Wm. Michael Fleming. 2011. 'The Social Justice Roots of the Mentors in Violence Prevention Model and Its Application in a High School Setting'. *Violence Against Women* 17 (6): 684–702.

Kemp, Janet and Robert Bossarte. 2012. 'Suicide Data Report 2012'. Washington, DC: Department of Veterans Affairs. www.va.gov/opa/docs/Suicide-Data-Report-2012-final.pdf.

Kershnar, Stephen. 1999. 'Are the Descendants of Slaves Owed Compensation for Slavery?' *Journal of Applied Philosophy* 16 (1): 95–101.

Keskinen, Suvi. 2005. 'Commitments and Contradictions: Linking Violence, Parenthood and Professionalism'. In *Tackling Men's Violence in Families: Nordic Issues and Dilemmas*, edited by Maria Eriksson, Marianne Hester, Suvi Keskinen and Keith Pringle, 31–48. Bristol: Policy Press.

King, Martin Luther, Jr. [1963] 1986. 'Letter from Birmingham City Jail'. In *A Testament of Hope: The Essential Writings and Speeches of Martin Luther King, Jr.*, edited by James M. Washington, 289–302. New York: HarperCollins.

[1967] 2010. *Where Do We Go from Here: Chaos or Community?* Boston: Beacon Press.

Koselleck, Reinhart. 2002. *The Practice of Conceptual History: Timing History, Spacing Concepts*. Translated by Todd Samuel Presner. Stanford, CA: Stanford University Press.

2005. *Futures Past: On the Semantics of Historical Time*. Translated by Keith Tribe. New York: Columbia University Press.

2006. 'Conceptual History, Memory and Identity: An Interview with Reinhart Koselleck'. Interview by Javiér Fernández Sebastián and Juan Francisco Fuentes. *Contributions to the History of Concepts* 2: 99–127.

Krafft-Ebing, Richard Freiher von. [1886] 2011. *Psychopathia Sexualis*. Translated by Franklin S. Klaf. New York: Arcade.

Kramer, Larry. 1989. *Reports from the Holocaust: Making of an AIDS Activist*. London: Penguin.

Kurz, Demie. 1996. 'Separation, Divorce, and Woman Abuse'. *Violence Against Women* 2 (1): 63–81.

Kymlicka, Will. 1995. *Multicultural Citizenship: A Liberal Theory of Minority Rights*. New York: Oxford University Press.

2001. *Politics in the Vernacular: Nationalism, Multiculturalism, and Citizenship*. New York: Oxford University Press.

Langhinrichsen-Rohling, Jennifer, John D. Foubert, Hope M. Brasfield, Brent Hill and Shannon Shelley-Tremblay. 2011. 'The Men's Program:

Does It Impact College Men's Self-Reported Bystander Efficacy and Willingness to Intervene?' *Violence Against Women* 17 (6): 743–59.

Lawrence, Jane. 2000. 'The Indian Health Service and the Sterilization of Native American Women'. *The American Indian Quarterly* 24 (3): 400–419.

Lewy, Guenter, ed. 2001. *The Nazi Persecution of the Gypsies*. New York: Oxford University Press.

Lichtenstein, Alex. 1996. *Twice the Work of Free Labor: Political Economy of Convict Labor in the New South*. London: Verso.

List, Christian and Philip Pettit. 2011. *Group Agency: The Possibility, Design, and Status of Corporate Agents*. Oxford: Oxford University Press.

Lorde, Audre. 2007. 'Age, Race, Class, and Sex: Women Redefining Difference'. In *Sister Outsider: Essays and Speeches*, 114–23. Freedom, CA: Crossing Press.

Loury, Glenn C. 2002. *The Anatomy of Racial Inequality*. Cambridge, MA: Harvard University Press.

  2007. 'Transgenerational Justice: Compensatory versus Interpretative Approaches'. In *Reparations: Interdisciplinary Inquiries*, edited by Jon Miller and Rahul Kumar, 87–113. New York: Oxford University Press.

  2008. *Race, Incarceration, and American Values*. Cambridge, MA: MIT Press.

Lu, Catherine. 2017. *Justice and Reconciliation in World Politics*. Cambridge: Cambridge University Press.

Lukes, Steven. 2005. *Power: A Radical View*. 2nd edn. Basingstoke: Palgrave Macmillan.

Lundgren, Eva, Gun Heimer, Jenny Westerstrand and Anne-Marie Kalliokoski. 2002. *Captured Queen: Men's Violence Against Women in 'Equal' Sweden : A Prevalence Study*. Translated by Julia Mikaelsson and Geoffrey French. Stockholm: Fritzes Offtliga Publikationer.

Lutz, Helma. 2011. *The New Maids: Transnational Women and the Care Economy*. Translated by Deborah Shannon. London: Zed Books.

MacDonald, Graham and Philip Pettit. 1980. *Semantics and Social Science*. London: Routledge.

Malone, Kareen and Rose Cleary. 2002. '(De)Sexing the Family: Theorizing the Social Science of Lesbian Families'. *Feminist Theory* 3 (3): 271–93.

Mancini, Matthew J. 1996. *One Dies, Get Another: Convict Leasing in the American South, 1866–1928*. Columbia: University of South Carolina Press.

Manos, James A. 2015. 'From Commodity Fetishism to Prison Fetishism: Slavery, Convict-Leasing, and the Ideological Productions of Incarceration'. In *Death and Other Penalties: Philosophy in a Time of Mass Incarceration*, edited by Geoffrey Adelsberg, Lisa Guenther and Scott Zeman, 43–59. New York: Fordham University Press.

Maraini, Dacia. 1963. *L'Età del Malessere*. Torino: Einaudi.

Margalit, Avishai and Joseph Raz. 1990. 'National Self-Determination'. *The Journal of Philosophy* 87 (9): 439–461.

Martin, Michael T. and Marilyn Yaquinto, eds. 2007. *Redress for Historical Injustices in the United States: On Reparations for Slavery, Jim Crow, and Their Legacies*. Durham, NC: Duke University Press.

Mason, Andrew. 2000. *Community, Solidarity, and Belonging: Levels of Community and Their Normative Significance*. Cambridge: Cambridge University Press.

May, Larry. 1987. *The Morality of Groups: Collective Responsibility, Group-Based Harm, and Corporate Rights*. Notre Dame, IN: University of Notre Dame Press.

McCarthy, Thomas. 2002. 'Vergangenheitsbewältigung in the USA: On the Politics of the Memory of Slavery'. *Political Theory* 30 (5): 623–48.

2004. 'Coming to Terms with Our Past, Part II: On the Morality and Politics of Reparations for Slavery'. *Political Theory* 32 (6): 750–72.

McGary, Howard. 1999. *Race and Social Justice*. Malden, MA: John Wiley.

2003. 'Achieving Democratic Equality: Forgiveness, Reconciliation, and Reparations'. *The Journal of Ethics* 7 (1): 93–113.

McGillivray, Anne and Brenda Comaskey. 1999. *Black Eyes All of the Time: Intimate Violence, Aboriginal Women, and the Justice System*. Toronto: University of Toronto Press.

McIntosh, Peggy. 1989. 'White Privilege: Unpacking the Invisible Knapsack'. *Peace and Freedom*, July/August: 10–12.

McLeod, Allegra. 2015. 'Prison Abolition and Grounded Justice'. *UCLA Law Review* 62: 1156–239.

McMahon, Sarah and Victoria L. Banyard. 2012. 'When Can I Help? A Conceptual Framework for the Prevention of Sexual Violence through Bystander Intervention'. *Trauma, Violence, and Abuse* 13 (1): 3–14.

McMahon, Sarah and Alexandria Dick. 2011. '"Being in a Room with Like-Minded Men": An Exploratory Study of Men's Participation in a Bystander Intervention Program to Prevent Intimate Partner Violence'. *The Journal of Men's Studies* 19 (1): 3–18.

McMahon, Sarah, Judy L. Postmus and Ruth Anne Koenick. 2011. 'Conceptualizing the Engaging Bystander Approach to Sexual Violence Prevention on College Campuses'. *Journal of College Student Development* 52 (1): 115–30.

McVeigh, Michael and Tracy McVeigh. 2009. 'Eluana Englaro's Father Tells of His Long Legal Battle to Allow Her to Pass Away Peacefully'. *Guardian*, 8 February. www.theguardian.com/world/2009/feb/08/eluana-englaro-assisted-suicide.

Memmi, Albert. [1965] 2003. *The Colonizer and the Colonized*. Translated by Howard Greenfeld. London: Earthscan.

Meyer, Lukas. 2014. 'Intergenerational Justice'. In *The Stanford Encyclopedia of Philosophy*, edited by Edward N. Zalta. http://plato.stanford.edu/archives/win2014/entries/justice-intergenerational/.

Mikkola, Mari. 2010. 'Gender Concepts and Intuitions'. *Canadian Journal of Philosophy* 39 (4): 559–83.

2016. *The Wrong of Injustice: Dehumanization and Its Role in Feminist Philosophy*. New York: Oxford University Press.

Miller, David. 1995. *On Nationality*. Oxford: Oxford University Press.

2000. *Citizenship and National Identity*. Cambridge: Polity Press.

2007. *National Responsibility and Global Justice*. Oxford: Oxford University Press.

2008. 'A Response'. *Critical Review of International Social and Political Philosophy* 11 (4): 553–67.

Mills, Charles W. 2007. 'White Ignorance'. In *Race and Epistemologies of Ignorance*, edited by Shannon Sullivan and Nancy Tuana, 13–38. Albany: State University of New York Press.

Minow, Martha. 1998. *Between Vengeance and Forgiveness: Facing History after Genocide and Mass Violence*. Boston: Beacon Press.

Mitchell, Karen S. and Jennifer L. Freitag. 2011. 'Forum Theatre for Bystanders: A New Model for Gender Violence Prevention'. *Violence Against Women* 17 (8): 990–1013.

Mogul, Joey L., Andrea J. Ritchie and Kay Whitlock. 2011. *Queer (In)Justice*. Boston: Beacon Press.

Mohanty, Chandra T. 1991. 'Under Western Eyes'. In *Third World Women and the Politics of Feminism*, edited by Chandra T. Mohanty, Ann Russo and Lourdes Torres, 1–80. Bloomington: Indiana University Press.

Moore, Margaret. 2001. *The Ethics of Nationalism*. New York: Oxford University Press.

Moore, Mignon. 2011. *Invisible Families: Gay Identities, Relationships, and Motherhood among Black Women*. Berkeley: University of California Press.

Morris, Mark, ed. 1976. *Instead of Prisons: A Handbook for Abolitionists*. Syracuse, NY: Prison Research Education Project.

Moses, Wilson J. 1988. *The Golden Age of Black Nationalism, 1820–1925*. New York: Oxford University Press.

Moten, Fred and Stefano Harney. 2004. 'The University and the Undercommons: Seven Theses'. *Social Text* 22 (2): 100–15.

Muhammad, Khalil. 2011. *The Condemnation of Blackness: Race, Crime, and the Making of Modern Urban America*. Cambridge, MA: Harvard University Press.

Murphy, Mary C. and Valerie J. Taylor. 2011. 'The Role of Situational Cues in Signaling and Maintaining Stereotype Threat'. In *Stereotype Threat: Theory, Process, and Application*, edited by Michael Inzlicht and Toni Schmader, 17–33. New York: Oxford University Press.

Murray, Charles. 2000. 'Affirmative Racism'. In *Morality in Practice*, edited by James P. Sterba, 6th ed., 248–60. Belmont, CA: Wadsworth.

Nakba. 2003. 'Haifa Declaration'. Haifa: Mada al-Camel. http://mada-research .org/wp-content/uploads/2007/09/watheeqat-haifa-english.pdf.

Nandy, Ashis. 1995. 'History's Forgotten Doubles'. *History and Theory* 34 (2): 44–66.

Native Women's Association of Canada. 2011. 'Fact Sheet: Violence Against Aboriginal Women'. Ottawa, ON: Native Women's Association of Canada.

Nelson, Jennifer. 2003. *Women of Color and the Reproductive Rights Movement*. New York: NYU Press.

Nordborg, Gudrun. 2005. 'Children's Peace? The Possibility of Protecting Children by Means of Criminal Law and Family Law'. In *Tackling Men's Violence in Families: Nordic Issues and Dilemmas*, edited by Maria Eriksson, Marianne Hester, Suvi Keskinen and Keith Pringle, 101–18. Bristol: Policy Press.

Norton, Michael I., Joseph A. Vandello and John M. Darley. 2004. 'Casuistry and Social Category Bias'. *Journal of Personality and Social Psychology* 87 (6): 817–31.

Nozick, Robert. 1974. *Anarchy, State and Utopia*. New York: Basic Books.

Nuti, Alasia. 2018. 'Temporary Labor Migration within the EU as Structural Injustice'. *Ethics & International Affairs* 32 (2): 1–23.

n.d. 'On Structural Descent'. Unpublished manuscript.

Office for National Statistics. 2013. 'Women in the Labour Market'. Newport: Office for National Statistics. www.ons.gov.uk/ons/dcp171776_328352.pdf.

Okin, Susan M. 1979. *Women in Western Political Thought*. Princeton, NJ: Princeton University Press.

1989. *Justice, Gender, and the Family*. New York: Basic Books.

Oliver, William. 2000. 'Preventing Domestic Violence in the African American Community: The Rationale for Popular Culture Interventions'. *Violence Against Women* 6 (5): 533–49.

Olsen, Frances E. 1985. 'The Myth of State Intervention in the Family'. *University of Michigan Journal of Law Reform* 18: 835–64.

Pacelli, Lia, Silvia Pasqua and Claudia Villosio. 2013. 'Labor Market Penalties for Mothers in Italy'. *Journal of Labor Research* 34 (4): 408–32.

Pager, Devah. 2007. *Marked: Race, Crime, and Finding Work in an Era of Mass Incarceration*. Chicago: University of Chicago Press.

Parekh, Serena. 2011. 'Getting to the Root of Gender Inequality: Structural Injustice and Political Responsibility'. *Hypatia* 26 (4): 672–89.

Parfit, Derek. 1984. *Reasons and Persons*. Oxford: Oxford University Press.

Pasolini, Caterina. 2014. 'Roma, "Io, Abbandonata in Bagno Ad Abortire"'. *LaRepubblica*, 3 November. http://roma.repubblica.it/cronaca/2014/03/11/news/io_abbandonata_in_bagno_ad_abortire-80714684/.

Pasternak, Avia. 2013. 'Limiting States' Corporate Responsibility'. *Journal of Political Philosophy* 21 (4): 361–81.

Pateman, Carole. 1989. 'Feminist Critiques of the Public/Private Dichotomy'. In *The Disorder of Women: Democracy, Feminism and Political Theory*, by Carole Pateman, 118–40. Stanford, CA: Stanford University Press.

Payne, Keith B. 2001. 'Prejudice and Perception: The Role of Automatic and Controlled Processes in Misperceiving a Weapon'. *Journal of Personality and Social Psychology* 81 (2): 181–92.

Perez, Nahshon. 2012. *Freedom from Past Injustices: A Critical Evaluation of Claims for Intergenerational Reparations*. Edinburgh: Edinburgh University Press.

Perreault, Thomas. 2006. 'From the Guerra Del Agua to the Guerra Del Gas: Resource Governance, Neoliberalism and Popular Protest in Bolivia'. *Antipode* 38 (1): 150–72.

Phillips, Anne. 1999. *Which Equalities Matter?* Cambridge: Polity Press.

  2004. 'Defending Equality of Outcome'. *Journal of Political Philosophy* 12 (1): 1–19.

Pierson, Paul. 2004. *Politics in Time: History, Institutions and Social Analysis.* Princeton, NJ: Princeton University Press.

Poeschl, Gabrielle. 2008. 'Social Norms and the Feeling of Justice about Unequal Family Practices'. *Social Justice Research* 21 (1): 69–85.

Potter, Sharyn J. and Victoria L. Banyard. 2011. 'Guest Editors' Introduction'. *Violence Against Women* 17 (6): 679–83.

Quadagno, Jill. 1994. *The Color of Welfare: How Racism Undermined the War on Poverty.* New York: Oxford University Press.

Rao, Rahul. 2010. *Third World Protest: Between Home and the World.* Oxford: Oxford University Press.

Rawls, John. 1999. *A Theory of Justice.* Revised edn. Cambridge, MA: Harvard University Press.

  2005. *Political Liberalism.* Expanded edn. New York: Columbia University Press.

Renan, Ernest. [1882] 1990. 'What Is a Nation?' In *Nation and Narration*, edited by Homi K. Bhabha, 8–22. London: Routledge.

Reskin, Barbara F. 2000. 'The Proximate Causes of Employment Discrimination'. *Contemporary Sociology* 29 (2): 319–28.

Rhode, Deborah L. 1999. *Speaking of Sex: The Denial of Gender Inequality.* Cambridge, MA: Harvard University Press.

Ridge, Michael. 2003. 'Giving the Dead Their Due'. *Ethics* 114 (1): 38–59.

Ridgeway, Cecilia L. 2011. *Framed by Gender: How Gender Inequality Persists in the Modern World.* New York: Oxford University Press.

Roberts, Dorothy E. 2002. *Shattered Bonds: The Color of Child Welfare.* New York: Basic Civitas Books.

  2007. 'Constructing a Criminal Justice System Free of Racial Bias: An Abolitionist Framework'. *Columbia Human Rights Law Review* 39 (1): 261–85.

  2017. *Killing the Black Body: Race, Reproduction, and the Meaning of Liberty.* 2nd edn. New York: Vintage Books.

Robeyns, Ingrid. 2000. 'Hush Money or Emancipation Fee?' In *Basic Income on the Agenda: Policy Objectives and Political Chances*, edited by Robert van der Veen and Loek Groot, 121–36. Amsterdam: Amsterdam University Press.

  2001. 'Will a Basic Income Do Justice to Women?' *Analysis und Kritik* 23 (1): 88–105.

Robinson, Dean E. 2001. *Black Nationalism in American Politics and Thought.* Cambridge: Cambridge University Press.

Roseneil, Sasha and Shelley Budgeon. 2004. 'Cultures of Intimacy and Care beyond 'the Family': Personal Life and Social Change in the Early 21st Century'. *Current Sociology* 52 (2): 135–59.

Ross, Fiona C. 2003. *Bearing Witness Women and the Truth and Reconciliation Commission in South Africa.* London: Pluto Press.

Rubio-Marin, Ruth. 2011. 'The Gender of Reparations in Transitional Societies'. In *The Gender of Reparations: Unsettling Sexual Hierarchies While Redressing Human Rights Violations*, edited by Ruth Rubio-Marin, 63–120. Cambridge: Cambridge University Press.

Ruspini, Elisabetta. 2013. *Diversity in Family Life: Gender, Relationships and Social Change*. Bristol: Policy Press.

Sabbadini, Linda Laura. 2018. 'Le 900 Mila Madri Single Dimenticate Dalla Politica'. *LaStampa. It*, 20 April. www.lastampa.it/2018/04/20/cultura/le-mil a-madri-single-dimenticate-dalla-politica-SBYbpRXVCQkqLSuW4F7YRP/p agina.html.

Said, Edward W. 1994. *Culture and Imperialism*. London: Vintage Books.

Sander, Richard H. 2004. 'A Systemic Analysis of Affirmative Action in American Law Schools'. *Stanford Law Review* 57: 367–483.

Sander, Richard H. and Stuart Taylor Jr. 2012. *Mismatch: How Affirmative Action Hurts Students It's Intended to Help, and Why Universities Won't Admit It*. New York: Basic Books.

Sardar, Ziauddin. 1996. 'Walt Disney and the Double Victimisation of Pocahontas'. *Third Text* 10 (37): 17–26.

Sarti, Raffaella and Francesca Scrinzi. 2010. 'Introduction to the Special Issue: Men in a Woman's Job, Male Domestic Workers, International Migration and the Globalization of Care'. *Men and Masculinities* 13 (1): 4–15.

Sartre, Jean-Paul. 1976. *Critique of Dialectical Reason*. Translated by Alan Sheridan-Smith. New York: New Left Books.

Scanlon, Thomas. 1998. *What We Owe to Each Other*. Cambridge, MA: Harvard University Press.

Schiff, Jade. 2014. *Burdens of Political Responsibility: Narrative and The Cultivation of Responsiveness*. New York: Cambridge University Press.

Schilt, Kristen. 2010. *Just One of the Guys? Transgender Men and the Persistence of Gender Inequality*. Chicago: University of Chicago Press.

Schneider, David J. 2003. *The Psychology of Stereotyping*. New York: Guilford Press.

Schor, Naomi. 1994. 'This Essentialism Which Is Not One: Coming to Grips with Irigaray'. In *The Essential Difference*, edited by Elizabeth Weed and Naomi Schor, 40–62. Bloomington: Indiana University Press.

Schwarzenbach, Sibyl A. 2009. *On Civic Friendship: Including Women in the State*. New York: Columbia University Press.

Scott, Jacqueline L. and Anke C. Plagnol. 2012. 'Work-Family Conflict and Well-Being in Northern Europe'. In *Gendered Lives: Gender Inequalities in Production and Reproduction*, edited by Shirley Dex, Jacqueline L. Scott and Anke Plagnol, 174–205. Cheltenham: Edward Elgar.

Scott, Joan W. 1986. 'Gender: A Useful Category of Historical Analysis'. *The American Historical Review* 91 (5): 1053–75.

Secretary-General UN Women. 2006. 'Ending Violence Against Women: From Words to Action'. New York: United Nations. www.unwomen.org/~/media/ Headquarters/Media/Publications/UN/en/EnglishStudy.pdf.

Seth, Sanjay. 2004. 'Reason or Reasoning? Clio or Siva?' *Social Text* 22 (1): 85–101.

Shelby, Tommie. 2007. 'Justice, Deviance, and the Dark Ghetto'. *Philosophy and Public Affairs* 35 (2): 126–60.

2011. 'Reparations, Leadership, and Democracy: A Comment on Balfour and Gooding-Williams'. *Du Bois Review* 8 (2): 395–99.

2013. 'Racial Realities and Corrective Justice: A Reply to Charles Mills'. *Critical Philosophy of Race* 1 (2): 145–62.

2014. 'Integration, Inequality, and Imperatives of Justice: A Review Essay'. *Philosophy and Public Affairs* 42 (3): 253–85.

Sher, George. 1979. 'Reverse Discrimination, the Future, and the Past'. *Ethics* 90 (1): 81–87.

2005. 'Transgenerational Compensation'. *Philosophy and Public Affairs* 33 (2): 181–200.

Shklar, Judith N. 1990. *The Faces of Injustice*. New Haven, CT: Yale University Press.

1991. *American Citizenship: The Quest for Inclusion*. Cambridge, MA: Harvard University Press.

Simon, Robert. 1974. 'Preferential Hiring: A Reply to Judith Jarvis Thomson'. *Philosophy and Public Affairs* 3 (3): 312–20.

Simoni, Jane M. and Karina L. Walters. 2001. 'Heterosexual Identity and Heterosexism'. *Journal of Homosexuality* 41 (1): 157–72.

Skaria, Ajay. 1999. 'Some Aporias of History: Time, Truth and Play in Dangs, Gujarat'. *Economic and Political Weekly* 34 (15): 897–904.

Smith, Andrea. 2005. *Conquest: Sexual Violence and American Indian Genocide*. Boston: South End Press.

Solinger, Rickie. 2007. *Pregnancy and Power: A Short History of Reproductive Politics in America*. New York: NYU Press.

Sørensen, Annemette and Heike Trappe. 1995. 'The Persistence of Gender Inequality in Earnings in the German Democratic Republic'. *American Sociological Review* 60 (3): 398–406.

Sørensen, Bo Wagner. 2001. '"Men in Transition": The Representation of Men's Violence Against Women in Greenland'. *Violence Against Women* 7 (7): 826–47.

Spelman, Elizabeth V. 1988. *Inessential Woman: Problems of Exclusion in Feminist Thought*. London: Women's Press.

Spinner-Halev, Jeff. 2012a. 'Historical Injustice'. In *The Oxford Handbook of Political Philosophy*, edited by David Estlund, 319–35. Oxford: Oxford University Press.

2012b. *Enduring Injustice*. New York: Cambridge University Press.

Stark, Evan. 2007. *Coercive Control: The Entrapment of Women in Personal Life*. New York: Oxford University Press.

2009. 'Rethinking Coercive Control'. *Violence Against Women* 15 (12): 1509–25.

Steele, Claude M. 2010. *Whistling Vivaldi: How Stereotypes Affect Us and What We Can Do*. New York: W. W. Norton.

Sterba, James P. 2003. 'Defending Affirmative Action, Defending Preferences'. In *Affirmative Action and Racial Preferences: A Debate*, by Carl Cohen and James P. Sterba, 191–278. Oxford: Oxford University Press.

Stilz, Anna. 2011. 'Collective Responsibility and the State'. *Journal of Political Philosophy* 19 (2): 190–208.

Stoljar, Natalie. 1995. 'Essence, Identity, and the Concept of Woman'. *Philosophical Topics* 23 (2): 261–93.

Stone, Alison. 2004. 'Essentialism and Anti-Essentialism in Feminist Philosophy'. *Journal of Moral Philosophy* 1 (2): 135–53.

Stone, Jon. 2016. 'Andrea Leadsom Says Men Should Not Be Hired to Do Childcare as They May Be Paedophiles'. *Independent*, 15 July. www.independent.co.uk/news/uk/politics/andrea-leadsom-men-paedo philes-childcare-workers-hired-sensible-a7139351.html.

Sweden Population Statistics Unit. 2012. 'Women and Men in Sweden: Facts and Figures 2012'. Stockholm: Statistics Sweden, Population Statistics Unit. www.scb.se/statistik/_publikationer/LE0201_2012A01_BR_X10B R1201ENG.pdf.

Tamir, Yael. 1993. *Liberal Nationalism*. Princeton, NJ: Princeton University Press.

Tan, Kok-Chor. 2007. 'Colonialism, Reparations, and Global Justice'. In *Reparations: Interdisciplinary Inquiries*, edited by Jon Miller and Rahul Kumar, 280–306. New York: Oxford University Press.

    2008. 'National Responsibility, Reparations and Distributive Justice'. *Critical Review of International Social and Political Philosophy* 11 (4): 449–64.

Taylor, Rae and Jana L. Jasinski. 2011. 'Femicide and the Feminist Perspective'. *Homicide Studies* 15 (4): 341–62.

Taylor, Robert S. 2009. 'Rawlsian Affirmative Action'. *Ethics* 119 (3): 476–506.

Thompson, Janna. 2001. 'Historical Injustice and Reparation: Justifying Claims of Descendants'. *Ethics* 112 (1): 114–35.

    2002. *Taking Responsibility for the Past: Reparation and Historical Injustice.* Cambridge: Polity.

Thomson, Judith Jarvis. 1973. 'Preferential Hiring'. *Philosophy and Public Affairs* 2 (4): 364–84.

Threadcraft, Shatema. 2016. *Intimate Justice: The Black Female Body and the Body Politic*. New York: Oxford University Press.

Tilly, Charles. 1998. *Durable Inequality*. Berkeley: University of California Press.

Tomasi di Lampedusa, Giuseppe. [1958] 2007. *The Leopard*. Translated by Archibald Colquhoun. London: Vintage Books.

Tonry, Michael. 2011. *Punishing Race: A Continuing American Dilemma*. New York: Oxford University Press.

Torpy, Sally J. 2000. 'Native American Women and Coerced Sterilization: On the Trail of Tears in the 1970s'. *American Indian Culture and Research Journal* 24 (2): 1–22.

Truth Commission Special Report. 1996. 'Human Rights Violations Hearings'. http://sabctrc.saha.org.za/documents/hrvtrans/worcester/56170.htm?t=%2Bkhu twane+%2Byvonne&tab=hearings.

Tully, James. 2008. *Public Philosophy in a New Key: Volume 2, Imperialism and Civic Freedom*. Cambridge: Cambridge University Press.

Ullman, Sarah. 2002. 'Rape Avoidance: Self-Protection Strategies for Women'. In *Preventing Violence in Relationships: Interventions across the Life Span*, edited by Paul A. Schewe, 137–62. Washington, DC: American Psychological Association.

UN Women. 2013. 'Violence Against Women Prevalence Data: Surveys by Country (as by December 2012)'. New York: United Nations. www.endvawnow.org/uploads/browser/files/vawprevalence_matrix_june2013.pdf.

US Census Bureau. 2016. 'Veterans Status Poverty in the Last 12 Months'. Washington, DC: US Census Bureau. https://factfinder.census.gov/bkmk/table/1.0/en/ACS/16_1YR/B21007/0400000US10.

USICH. 2010. 'Homelessness among Veterans. Supplemental Document to the Federal Strategic Plan to Prevent and End Homelessness: June 2010'. Washington, DC: US Interagency Council on Homelessness (USICH). www.usich.gov/resources/uploads/asset_library/BkgrdPap_Veterans.pdf.

Valls, Andrew. 2007. 'Reconsidering the Case for Black Reparations'. In *Reparations: Interdisciplinary Inquiries*, edited by Jon Miller and Rahul Kumar, 114–29. New York: Oxford University Press.

Valls, Andrew and Jonathan Kaplan. 2005. 'Justice and Racial Residential Segregation: Housing Discrimination as a Basis for Black Reparations'. *Public Affairs Quarterly* 21 (3): 255–73.

Vernon, Richard. 2003. 'Against Restitution'. *Political Studies* 51 (3): 542–57.

Virgili, Fabrice. 2002. *Shorn Women: Gender and Punishment in Liberation France*. Translated by John Flower. Oxford: Berg.

Wacquant, Loïc. 2002. 'From Slavery to Mass Incarceration'. *New Left Review* 13: 41–60.

Waite, Linda J. and Mark Nielsen. 2001. 'The Rise of the Dual-Earner Family, 1963–1997'. In *Working Families: The Transformation of the American Home*, edited by Rosanna Hertz and Nancy L. Marshall, 23–41. Berkeley: University of California Press.

Waldron, Jeremy. 1992. 'Superseding Historic Injustice'. *Ethics* 102 (1): 4–28.

    2002. 'Redressing Historic Injustice'. *The University of Toronto Law Journal* 52 (1): 135–60.

Wallace, Anthony F. C. 1993. *The Long, Bitter Trail: Andrew Jackson and the Indians*. New York: Hill and Wang.

Wallenstein, Peter. 2004. *Blue Laws and Black Codes: Conflict, Courts, and Change in Twentieth-Century Virginia*. Charlottesville: University of Virginia Press.

Walzer, Michael. 1983. *Spheres of Justice: A Defence of Pluralism and Equality*. New York: Basic Books.

Weaver, Hilary N. 2009. 'The Colonial Context of Violence: Reflections on Violence in the Lives of Native American Women'. *Journal of Interpersonal Violence* 24 (9): 1552–63.

Weitzman, Susan. 2000. *'Not to People Like Us': Hidden Abuse in Upscale Marriages.* New York: Basic Books.

Wenar, Leif. 2006. 'Reparations for the Future'. *Journal of Social Philosophy* 37 (3): 396–405.

Wiklund, Maria, Eva-Britt Malmgren-Olsson, Carita Bengs and Ann Öhman. 2010. '"He Messed Me Up": Swedish Adolescent Girls' Experiences of Gender-Related Partner Violence and Its Consequences over Time'. *Violence Against Women* 16 (2): 207–32.

Wilderson, Frank B. 2003. 'The Prison Slave as Hegemony's (Silent) Scandal'. *Social Justice* 30 (2): 18–27.

Williams, David R. and Chiquita Collins. 2004. 'Reparations: A Viable Strategy to Address the Enigma of African American Health'. *American Behavioral Scientist* 47 (7): 977–1000.

Williams, Melissa S. 1998. *Voice, Trust, and Memory: Marginalized Groups and the Failings of Liberal Representation.* Princeton, NJ: Princeton University Press.

Wolf-Devine, Celia. 2005. 'Preferential Policies Have Become Toxic'. In *Contemporary Debates in Applied Ethics*, edited by Andrew I. Cohen and Christopher Heath Wellman, 59–74. Oxford: Blackwell.

Wolff, Jonathan and Avner De-Shalit. 2007. *Disadvantage.* New York: Oxford University Press.

Wood, Nicholas. 2005. 'Germany Sending Gypsy Refugees Back to Kosovo'. *The New York Times*, 19 May. www.nytimes.com/2005/05/19/international/europe/19kosovo.html.

Woodly, Deva. 2015. 'Seeing Collectivity: Structural Relation through the Lens of Youngian Seriality'. *Contemporary Political Theory* 14 (3): 213–33.

Woolf, Virginia. [1938] 2006. *Three Guineas.* London: Houghton Mifflin Harcourt.

Yack, Bernard. 2012. *Nationalism and the Moral Psychology of Community.* Chicago: University of Chicago Press.

Young, Iris M. 1990. *Justice and the Politics of Difference*. Princeton, NJ: Princeton University Press.

   1997a. 'Gender as Seriality'. In *Intersecting Voices: Dilemmas of Gender, Political Philosophy, and Policy*, 12–37. Princeton, NJ: Princeton University Press.

   1997b. 'A Multicultural Continuum: A Critique of Will Kymlicka's Ethnic-Nation Dichotomy'. *Constellations* 4 (1): 48–53.

   1998. 'Polity and Group Difference: A Critique of the Ideal of Universal Citizenship'. In *Feminism and Politics*, edited by Anne Phillips, 401–29. Oxford: Oxford University Press.

   2000. *Inclusion and Democracy.* New York: Oxford University Press.

   2001. 'Equality of Whom? Social Groups and Judgments of Injustice'. *Journal of Political Philosophy* 9 (1): 1–18.

   2002. 'Lived Body vs Gender: Reflections on Social Structure and Subjectivity'. *Ratio* 15 (4): 410–28.

   2004. 'Responsibility and Global Labor Justice'. *Journal of Political Philosophy* 12 (4): 365–88.

2006. 'Taking the Basic Structure Seriously'. *Perspectives of Politics* 4 (1): 91–97.

2011. *Responsibility for Justice*. New York: Oxford University Press.

Yuval-Davis, Nira. 1997. *Gender and Nation*. London: Sage.

Zheng, Robin. 2018. 'Bias, Structure, and Injustice: A Reply to Haslanger'. *Feminist Philosophy Quarterly* 4 (1): Article 4.

Index

'Western' societies, 97

ableism, 33
abnormality, 61, 97
abortion
  illegal, 1
  legal access to, 88, 100
abortionists, backstreet, 1
acceleration, 20
accountability, 48, 155, 157–160, 163
ACT UP, 192
activist politics, 32, 191
adaptive preferences, 90
admissions criteria, university, 39
affirmative action
  already-advantaged benefited by, 150
  descent problem with, 149
  horizontal vs. vertical, 148
  integrative model of, 147
  men and women targeted by, 148
  revaluing occupations via, 148
  supplementing, 148
  types of, 146, 147
  underachievement problem with, 150
African Americans. *See also* slavery, race
  as ascriptive group, 56
  criminalisation of, 42
  deactivating stereotypes about, 50
  desegregation, 182
  in employment decisions, 39
  enslaved women who were, 124
  equality with white Americans, 170
  historical consciousness of, 79
  HSG characteristics of, 78
  nations compared to, 77
  on spectrum of structural groups, 77–79
  othermothering among, 122, 144
  prison system's effect on, 173
  redressing HSI against, 79
  relative position of, 55
  reparations movement among, 154

  separatism among, 78
  societal context of, 38, 78
  stereotypes interiorised by, 168
  stereotypes reinforcing segregation, 37
  stereotypes' context, 38
  stereotypes' direct and indirect
    effects, 39
  stereotypical criminality of, 39, 42, 50
  stereotypical hypersexuality of, 137
  in university admissions criteria, 39
  US government's accountability to,
    155
  women, 102, 158, 167–169
agency, human, 27, *See also* collective agents
  patterns of exercise of, 188
  structures' interplay with, 48, 188
AIDS epidemic, 192
American Indian movement, 35
American indigenous peoples
  expulsion of, 37
  narratives about, 37
American South, 36
Americas, discovery of, 35
ancestry, 56
Anderson, Elizabeth, 147
anti-Semitism, 72
Apartheid, 91
Arendt, Hannah, 72
assets as inheritance, 63
asymmetric power, 55, 63
attributes, individual, 39
Austin, John L., 56
authorities, on abnormality, 61
authority conditions, 56
automobiles, effects of, 33

Balfour, Lawrie, 165
Bamboozled, 56
banal mechanisms, 41, 109
  of GDDL, 124
banal radicality, 43, 113, 120

219

banlieues, 35
Banyard, Victoria, 133
basic structure, 32
Bekkengern, Lisbeth, 141
Benjamin, Walter, 45
Bettcher, Talia Mae, 100
biases, implicit, 39–41
Birmingham, Peg, 44
black codes, 36, 172
black market for abortion, 1
Blackburn, Robert M., 118
blackness. *See* African Americans
Blair, Tony, 51
body politic, exclusion from, 60
Bolivia, 30
Booth, W. James, 15
Brooks, Bradley, 118
Browne, Jude, 118
Brownmiller, Susan, 93, 192
Butler, Judith, 94
Butt, Daniel, 14
bystander approach
    breadth of 'bystanders' in, 137
    community account of, 134
    definition of 'bystanders', 133
    HSI version of, 136–137
    intersectionality in, 137
    to IPV vs. other abuse, 135
    self-reflection in, 136
    theatre groups in, 137

care work
    mandatory, 142–144
    sandwich care, 140
    unpaid, 55, 141
caste system, 34
categorisation of persons
    divisions as cause and effect of, 55
    gender-based, 55
    occupation-based, 55
    race-based, 56
    roles and expectations via, 55
Catholic Church, influence of, 88
Catholic identity, 91
chain of women, 94
change
    banal mechanisms' role in, 42
    persistence in relation to, 45
    in racial injustice, 45
    salience of, 4
    in structural understanding of history, 27
Charleston (South Carolina) church
    shooting, 155
Cherokee nation, 37

childcare, 139–142, 145
citizens, responsibility of, 163, 164
citizenship
    benefits of, 71
    classes of, 60, 70, 78
    ideal of abstract, 86
city planning, 33
cluster concepts, 101
clusters of disadvantage, 103
Cochabamba Water War, 30
collective actions, 190–192
collective agents
    nations as, 69
    nonstructural groups, 58
    power of, 186–188
    structural debts of, 160–162, 163
collective identity, 6
collective narrative, 7
colonial history, 5
    of Africa and Asia, 35, 37, 75
    of the Americas, 30, 35, 61
colonial powers, 17, 30
    English, 37
Columbus Day, 35
Columbus, Christopher, 30, 35
Committee to Abolish Prison Slavery (CAPS), 171
community-responsibility bystander approaches,
    133–135
    gender-neutrality emphasis of, 135
    norms unchallenged by, 135
    stereotypes reinforced by, 134
conscientious objectors
    health care providers as, 1, 88, 89
    to mandatory caregiving service, 143
consciousness-raising, 93, 191
constraints, unjust, 101
contexts
    stereotyping in different, 38
    structural groups in local, 78, 98, 113
convict-lease system, 172
convicts, 79, 80, 172
corporate accountability, 163
counterhistorical institutional justifications, 12,
    171–177, 181
    countermemory's connection to, 174
    definition of, 174
    prison-abolitionism example, 171–173
countermemory, 174
criminalisation of race, 42
criminality, stereotypical trait of, 37
criminal-justice system, 159
cultural capital, 34
cultural markers, 70
cultural schemas, 36

Davis, Angela, 36, 172, 175
dead victims, 15, 16, 51, 62
default options, 139
democratic representation of women,
    86
Denmark, 118
descendants. *See also* structural descendants
    new account of, 7
    of original victims, 5
desegregation, 182
de-temporalising injustice, 194
    implications of, 11
    meaning of, 8, 51
    need for, 13
    structural debts in light of, 160
    via counterhistorical institutional
        justifications, 175
disability, 32
discrimination
    formal, 36, 80
    against prisoners, 80
    racial, 36, 39
disenfranchisement, 60
distant past, 2
    in backward-looking approaches, 15,
        16
    entitlements surviving from, 3
    normative salience of, 4
distribution of advantages and privileges, 55,
    71, 96
divisions, reparations exacerbating, 164
domestic services and caring. *See* care work
domestic violence. *See* violence against
    women (VAW)
domestic-violence organisations, 54
double shift, 122
Du Bois, W. E. B., 174

education on injustice, 51, 165, 169
egalitarian institutions, formal, 50
egalitarian societies. *See* liberal democracies
egalitarianism. *See also* equality of opportunity
    scepticism of historical justice in, 18
elderly, respect for, 91
employment decisions, 39
encompassing identities, nations as
    argument for, 71
    interpretive problem with, 72
    normative problem with, 72
enduring-injustice account, 6, 41
Englaro, Eluana, 89
environmental structures, 33
equality of opportunity
    apparent compatibility with, 50
    focus on, 5, 10, 170

equality of outcomes, 170
essentialism, in Young's account, 90–93
eugenics movement, 158
Europe, stereotyping in, 38
Even the Rain (También la lluvia), 30
events
    definition of, 23
    irreducible nature of, 23
    repetition of, 24
    unique, 24
evil, 44
external categorisation
    of nations, 68, 70
    personal identity vs., 57
    of women, 98

Fabre, Cécile, 142
false consciousness, 90
family arrangements. *See also* gendered division
        of domestic labour (GDDL)
    non-nuclear, 139, 144
    transformations in, 121
family resemblances, 101
fatherhood, 141, 145
feminist collectives, 85, 93, 169, 187
feminist revolution, stalled, 121
feminist scholarship
    defining women in, 82
    essentialism, 90
    groups debate in, 6
Finland, 131
Forst, Rainer, 175
Foucault, Michel, 174
France, colonial history of, 35
Fraser, Nancy, 138
Frederick the Great, 24
freedom, demanding one's, 191
Fullinwider, Robert K., 163

Gatens, Moira, 94
gay and lesbian persons, 71, 190, 191
gender categorisation, care work
    assigned via, 55
gender differences and inequalities, 167–169
gender dynamics in existing
    literature, 5
gender equality, 135, 141
gender identity, 33
gender ideology, 168
gender neutrality, 135
gender structures, 100
    normative weight of, 106
    pre-identification of, 87
    public respectability, 88
    in Young's account, 85

gendered division of domestic labour (GDDL),
    121–126
    affirmative measures against, 138
    banal mechanisms of, 124
    double shift, 122
    family arrangements characterised by, 122
    HSI reinforced by, 125
    migrants' role in, 126
    motives concerning, 89
    opinions vs. practice, 121
    payment for housework, 123
    persistence of, 121
    as sign of history's presence, 126
    symbolic meaning of, 124
    time surveys on, 123
    transformative measures against, 138
genealogy. *See* women* as a genealogy
genetic disease, 1
Germany, 163, 165, 166, 167
Green Dot programme, 135
Greenlaw, Deja Nicole, 192
group representation, 86
groups
    clubs and organisations as, 54
    internally differentiated, 167–169
    structural vs. nonstructural, 53, 67
    women, 6, 10
groups, members of, 183
    as rightful claimants, 5–7
    external recognition as, 53, 68, 70, 98
    non-identity problem and, 5
    self-identification as, 53, 56, 68
groups, nonstructural
    as collective agents, 58
    historical embeddedness of, 59
    internal organisation of, 58
    mobilisation for justice, 58
    recognition sought by, 71
groups, structural
    African Americans, 77–79
    ascriptive aspect of, 56–58
    identifying types of, 66
    prisoners, 79, 80
    in relation to one another, 55
    relational aspects of, 54
    standing in, 192
    structures related to, 54
    taxonomy of, 9, 59
gynecologists as conscientious objectors, 1

habitus, 34
Hancock, Ian, 7
Haslanger, Sally, 89
Hayward, Clarissa Rile, 45
health care, 1, 88

heterosexual coupledom, 139
hierarchy, caste-based, 34
highways, 33
historical groups with structural dynamics
    (HGSDs), 68–76, *See also* nations
    definition of, 68
    HSI's illumination of, 81
    remedying injustice against, 81
historical injustice, backward-looking account of,
    14–16
    backward-looking responsibility vs., 157
    dead-victims basis for, 15
    HSI vs., 46
    impracticability objection to, 15
    rectification-based, 14
    temporalisation in, 21
historical injustice, existing accounts of, 3
    enriched understanding of, 10
    non-identity problem in, 5
    undisputed relevance of
    weaknesses of, 3, 46
historical injustice, forward-looking account of,
    14, 16
    egalitarian sceptic of, 18
    HSI vs., 48
    legacy basis of, 17, 18, 22, 48
    merits to, 17
    pragmatic justification for, 16
    redundancy objection to, 17, 49
    temporalising justice in, 22
    trust basis of, 16, 18, 22
historical injustices
    'past', 51
    identifying structural, 47
    past, 51
    reproduction of, 46
    romanticisation of, 37
    script constructed by, 48
    significant relation to stereotypes, 38
    stereotypes' relevance to, 37
    structural aspect of, 45, 48
historical justice. *See also* redress of injustice
    interactional accounts of, 156
    non-identity problem as challenge to, 5
    present justice vs., 16, 164
    quixotic enterprise of, 16
    rectification principle of, 14
    sceptics of, 3, 21
historical memory, 4, 174
historical structural group, women* as, 96–103
    ascriptive membership of, 98
    definition of, 98
    essentialism avoided in, 101
    interplay of past and present in, 103
    as one conception, 100

potentiality aspect of, 98
specificity of, 103
structures indeterminate in, 100
historical structural groups (HSGs)
African Americans compared to, 78
definition of, 60
existence and disappearance of, 63
HSI illuminating, 81
identifying, 66
inheritance of position in, 62
origins of, 61
remedying injustice against, 67
historical structural injustice (HSI), 8
'past', 51
bystander approach in light of, 136
definition of, 44
as gearbox, 126
HGSDs illuminated via idea of, 81
HSGs illuminated via idea of, 81
HSGs' existence tied to, 63
identifying, 47
origins of, 60
persistence and change in, 45
scripts' role in, 48, 109
terminology of, 45
variation across societies, 47
VAW through lens of, 113, 136–137
women as victims of, 97
historiography, 20
history
consciousness of, 79
particularities of, 75
structural conception of, 23–29
structure in relation to, 45
study of, 21
temporalisation of, 20
undertheorisation of, 13, 19
homeless people, 65
homosexuality, 62
hooks, bell, 168, 191
housework. *See* gendered division of domestic
labour (GDDL)

Iceland, 111
identity
Catholic woman's, 91
external categorisation vs., 57
group membership as, 6
nation as encompassing, 71–73
personal, 57
self-identification, 53, 56
ideology, 175
Igbo, 75
impracticability objection, 15
India, 34

Indian Removal Act, 37
indigenous peoples
antimodern conception among, 18
expulsion of, 37
mistrust among, 17
symbols of oppression of, 35
VAW among, 116
wrongdoings toward, 41
individuals, blaming, 185
inequalities
enduring, 10
household. *See* gendered division of domestic
labour (GDDL)
legacy of intergroup, 18
inheritance from victims of injustice, 63
injustice. *See also* specific types of injustice
diagnosing, 66
dynamic conception of, 44
global, 32
intergenerational, 114
of interpretations of femininity, 95
radical, 41
recognising, 165
systematic, 60, 75, 78, 97
temporalising, 21, 147
institutions
limited set of, 32
public and private, 98
integration
gender. *See* collective action
of outsiders, 35
intergenerational bonds, 76, 79
internalisation, 34, 168
international relations, 14, 75
interpretations of femininity, 94
intersectionality, 59, 92, 103
colour-blind, 105
in IPV prevention, 137
Khutwane example of, 91
in policy making, 151, 183
and privilege's gradations, 191
race/gender, 102, 115, 137, 167–169
violence's forms in view of, 115
intimate partner violence (IPV)
banal HSI deployed by, 109
as capillary control, 108
form in liberal democracies, 108
HSI-informed view of, 136–137
norms underlying, 134
physical and other aspects of, 108
prevalence of, 107
reproduction of HSI via, 108
states' role in addressing, 186
IPV policy measures. *See also* IPV prevention
protective, 129

IPV policy measures (cont.)
  relational, 132
  restorative, 130
  types of, 129
IPV prevention, 130–136, *See also* bystander
  approach
  men's programmes, 131, 132
  self-defence classes, 130
Irish potato famine, 51
Israel, 74
Italy
  abortion in, 1, 88, 100
  Law 194, 2, 88
  nation of, 70
Ivison, Duncan, 17

Jackson, Andrew, 37
Jarman, Jennifer, 118
Jewishness, 72
Jim Crow era, 17, 158
just-world fallacy, 40

Kalajdzic, Jasminka, 115
Khutwane, Yvonne, 91
King, Martin Luther, Jr., 191
knowledge regime, 174
Koselleck, Reinhart, 19–21
  modernity analysis of, 21
  role in author's argument, 20
  structures and events, 23–25
Kramer, Larry, 193
Kurdistan Democratic Party, 74
Kyenge, Cécile, 70

labour force
  exclusion from, 61, 97
  women's entry into, 117
Law 194, 2, 88
law enforcement, 42, 102
legacy, historical, 17, 18, 22, 28, 48
legal interventions, racial dimension of, 45
liberal democracies. *See also* Nordic countries
  enduring injustice in, 60
  gender injustices in, 5
  persistence of GDDL in, 121, 126
  systematic past injustice in, 60
  women* as HSG in, 105
liberal nationalism, 15, 68–71
libertarian outlook on historical injustice, 14
Lu, Catherine, 5, 185–187
  racial injustice, 155
  women as group, 82

managerial attributes, 39
mandatory arrest policies, 102

mandatory caregiving service, 142–144
  entailments of, 143
  insufficiency of, 144
  outcomes sought by, 143
  shortcomings avoided by, 144
  sufficientarian rationale for, 142
Mandela, Nelson, 194
marriage, right of, 71
masculinity, 132
MC Serch, 56
McIntosh, Peggy, 190
McMahon, Sarah, 133
McMillan, Billy, 191
  meanings of femininity, 94
membership. *See* groups
Memmi, Albert, 37
men
  control of lives of, 110
  responsibility of, 190
  as series, 87, 96
Mentors in Violence Prevention (MPV), 131
mentorship, 131
Mexican women, 92
migrants, female, 126
migration, 35
military service, 143
Miller, David, 15
Mills, Charles W., 174
miscarriage, 1
mistrust, 16, 18
modernity, 20
moment of conversion, 68
Movement for Black Lives (MBL), 154, 164
movies, 30

National Coalition of Blacks for Reparations in
  America (N'COBRA), 154, 165
national record, setting straight the, 15
nationalism, liberal vs. communitarian, 69
nations
  acceptance as members of, 70
  as encompassing identities, 71–73
  ascriptive membership in, 68, 70
  collective agency of, 69
  cultural markers of, 70
  elective membership in, 68
  historical character of, 75
  in liberal-nationalist thought, 68–71
  intergenerational bonds within, 76
  moment of conversion, 68
  obligations of members of, 69
  privileges via membership in, 71
  recognition as, 75
  relational means of maintaining, 73
  renouncing membership in, 70

reproduction of, 72
self-determination of, 74
solidarity within, 75
structural nature of, 71
territorial aspect of, 74
in wartime, 72
Nigeria, 75
nonhistorical structural groups (NHSGs)
definition of, 64
identifying, 66
nonhistorical aspect of, 65
structural aspect of, 64
non-identity problem, 5, 62
Nordic countries
abusive men's perception in, 113
formal response to VAW in, 110
narrative of progress in, 111–113
occupational segregation in, 118
pigeonholing of VAW in, 111
self-defence in, 130
VAW's prevalence in, 110, 111
victims of VAW in, 112
normalisation, 32, 36
norms, informal, 88
Norplant, 159
North Africa, colonisation of, 35
Nozick, Robert, 14
nuclear family, 139

occupational categorisations, 55, 61
occupational segregation
illusion of progress, 117
in Nordic countries, 118
pink-collar ghetto, 119, 149
problematic horizontal, 119
vertical vs horizontal, 118, 148, 149
occupations, servile/menial, 97
Okin, Susan Moller, 121
Oliphant v. Suquamish Indian Tribe, 116
opportunities, hoarded, 170
othermothering, 122, 144

parameters of reasoning, 185
Parekh, Serena, 108
parental leave, equal
banal mechanisms underestimated by, 141
care reduced to childcare via, 140
fatherhood mistaken for equality in, 141
justifying, 145
normalising of heterosexual coupledom via, 139
participation in reparations process, 166
past. *See also* distant past
as detached from present, 20, 51
as script, 48

paternal leave, 139
patriarchal motifs, 132
persistence, 27
banal mechanisms' role in, 42
change in relation to, 45
in racial injustice, 45
personal identity. *See* identity
personal motives, 115
Personal Responsibility and Work Opportunity
Reconciliation Act, 159
perspective(s), social, 85, 90–93, 101
Pierson, Pier, 13
pink-collar occupations, 119, 149, 150
Pocahontas, 37
police
abuse of power by, 42, 48, 91
authority of, 56
raids by, 56
policies. *See also* IPV prevention
agents' use of, 160
austerity, 187
context-dependent, 151, 182
counterproductive or ineffective, 102, 129
decarceration, 176
intersectional, 151
mandatory-arrest, 102, 129
migration, 126
normative framework for proposing, 11
power to make, 186
relational, 150
transformative measures of, 138, 151, 180
on work-family balance, 145
political parties, 74
political theory, historical arguments in, 5
positions of individuals, 34, 169, 189
potentiality vs. actuality, 98, 107
poverty, 159
power, 186–188
praxis, 32, 191
present injustice, historical injustice vs., 16
present-past, 47, 49
princess, 'Indian', 37
Prison Research Education Action Project
(PREAP), 171
prison system
abolition of, 171–173, 175
narratives supporting, 175
progressive decarceration, 176
prisoners and ex-prisoners, 79, 80, 172
private sphere
interference in, 124
public sphere's interplay with, 98, 124, 136
women in, 124
privilege
in academia, 190

privilege (cont.)
    distribution of, 55, 96
    heterosexual, 190
    lack of, 190–193
    male, 132, 190
    responsibility's sensitivity to, 189–191
    as result of injustice, 63
    structural standing among those with,
        193
progressive view of history
    abusive men's perception in, 113
    in liberal democracies, 111–113
    misleading picture offered by, 112
    origins of, 61
    victims of IPV in, 112
Protocol on the Rights of Women in Africa
    (PRWA), 107
public and private, interplay of, 98, 124, 136
public respectability, 88

race. *See also* African Americans
    criminalisation of, 42, 172
    discrimination on basis of, 36, 39
    profiling on basis of, 42
    stereotypes about, 37, 39
racial injustice, 154–164
    desegregation approach, 182
    gendered aspect of, 167–169
    nonstate agents accountable
        for, 163
    prison system bound up with,
        171–173
    US government's accountability/
        responsibility, 154–157
racial/ethnical categorisations, 55, 70
racialized spaces, 45
racism, overt, 40
rape, 102
reality enforcement, 100
reconciliation, 156
rectification principle, 14
redress of injustice, 180–184
    context-sensitive, 79, 182
    forward-looking element of,
        170, 180
    GDDL's role in, 124
    group membership considered in,
        183
    historical-structural interplay in, 182
    identifying candidates for, 3
    intersectional aspect of, 183
    parameters of reasoning about, 185
    as a process, 12, 194
redundancy objection, 17, 18, 49
religion, in public life, 88

religious identity, 91
reparations, 180
    and groups' internal differences, 167–169
    in backward-looking approaches, 14
    for slavery. *See* slavery, reparations for
    in forward-looking approaches, 17, 170
    groups' differing demands for, 166
    in HSI perspective, 79, 80
    participatory approach to, 166
    recipients of, 168
    reconciliation vs., 156
repetition of events, 24
representation, 86
reproduction of gender injustice in egalitarian
        societies
    banal, 141, 145
    generalizations about, 105
    indicative account of, 105
reproduction of injustice
    banal mechanisms for, 41, 141
    banal radicality of, 43, 119
    changes' salience in, 4, 27, 45
    gender inequality vis-a-vis, 106
    mechanisms of, 38
    radical mechanisms for, 41
    structural, 27, 45, 51
reproductive injustice
    black women's suffering of, 157–160
    continuity and change in, 2
responsibility
    of oppressed people, 189, 191–192
    of ordinary individuals, 188–189
    of powerful agents, 186–188
    parameters of reasoning about, 184
    political, 189–191
    shared and heterogeneous, 12, 186, 189
return-of-the-past narrative
    abortion example of, 2
    weaknesses of, 2
Ridge, Michael, 15, 16
riots, 35
Roberts, Dorothy E., 158
roles and expectations, gendered, 55
    GDDL's effect on, 125
    IPV enabled through, 108
    likelihood of conditioning by, 90
    structural determination of, 98
    of womanhood, 130
Romani peoples, 7, 75, 165, 166
romanticisation, 37
Rome, 1
routine experiences, 86, 90–93, 101
Rubio-Marin, Ruth, 167
rules-based structures, 33, 35
Rwandan genocide, 3

sacrifice during wartime, 72
Sanger, Margaret, 158
SAT scores, 39
school, disciplinary action at, 102
Scott, Joan, 7
scripts
  GDDL maintained via, 126
  going off, 50
  historical construction of, 48
  IPV sustained via, 109
  occupational segregation reinforcing, 119
self-defence classes
  benefits of, 130
  deleterious effects of, 130
  in Nordic countries, 130
self-determination
  conditions undermining women's, 2
  national, 74
  in reproductive decisions, 2
self-identification, 53, 56
self-reflection, 136
separatism, black political, 78
seriality, 10
series. *See also* women* as series
  definition of, 84
settler societies, 17, 30, 35, 37
Seven Years' War, 24
sexual assault, 91, 102
sexual harassment, 91, 92, 136
Shelby, Tommie, 19
Shklar, Judith, 60
Sinti, 7, 165
Sisters Uncut, 187
slavery
  African American women during, 124, 158
  aftermath of, 36
  backward-looking accounts of, 155–157
  Caribbean, 166
  event and structures of, 25, 26
  forward-looking accounts of, 156
  and groups' different demands, 166
  prisons linked to, 171–173
  US state's accountability and responsibility, 155
slavery, reparations for, 17, 154, 156–157, 161–165
  clash with other demands, 164
  divisions exacerbated by, 164
  movement for, 154
  recipients of, 162
  rejection of, 155
  reparations for recent wrongs vs., 161
societal context, variation in, 38, 47, 98
solidarity, 192

black, 78
  national, 75
South Africa, 91
spectrum of structural groups, 9, 77–81
  benefits of idea of, 77, 79
  prisoners on, 79
spectrum of stuctural groups
  African Americans on, 77–79
speech acts, 56
Spinner-Halev, Jeff, 6, 41
Stark, Evan, 109
stereotypes
  activation of, 40
  of American Indians, 37
  attention to, 36
  banality of, 41
  direct use of, 39
  historical connection of, 38
  indirect use of, 39
  injustice justified via, 37
  interiorised, 168
  internal processes of, 40
  narrative significance of, 37
  normalisation via, 36
  of African Americans. *See under* African Americans
  resistance to evidence, 50
  violence facilitated by, 38, 43, 44
  of women, 97
sterilisation, 158
Stoljar, Natalie, 101
Stone, Alison, 94
stories sustaining institutions, 175
structural accounts of women*, 83
structural conception of history
  change in, 27
  de-temporalising injustice via, 25
  determinism in, 28
  explication of, 23–25
  persistence in, 27
  structural reproduction in, 27, 46
structural debts, 11
  distribution of, 163
  powerful agents' liability for, 160–162, 163
structural descendants
  African Americans as, 162
  identity of, 62, 162
  inheritance of, 63
  women as, 149
structural groups. *See* groups, structural
structural injustice
  agency's interplay with, 161–162

structural injustice (cont.)
  civil society's responsibility for, 161
  definition of, 8
  enriched understanding of, 10
  as historical in some cases, 46
  historical vs. nonhistorical, 66
  pluralistic account of, 10
  powerful agents' role in, 186–188
  remedying types of, 67
  transnational cases of, 32
  VAW as, 114
structural reproduction, 27
structural standing, 192
structural stories, 67
structures
  agency's interplay with, 48
  environmental, 33
  history relative to, 45
  intersection of, 101
  positional aspect of, 34, 55
  practico-inert aspect of, 33
  reproduction of, 34, 73
  rules-based, 33, 35, 44
  as sites of justice, 49
  stereotypes as part of, 36
  unjust origins of, 35
structures, long-term
  as background conditions, 23, 48
  definition of, 23
  noncausal nature of, 24
  persistence of, 23
subjectivity, feminine, 94
Sweden, 112, 118
symbolism, 35
systemic racism, 41

taxonomy of groups
  structural groups, 9, 59
taxonomy, of groups
  nonstructural groups, 58
  structural vs. nonstructural groups, 53
Taylor, Robert S., 146
temporalising injustice, 21, 147
territory, national, 74
Thirteenth Amendment, 172
Threadcraft, Shatelma, 160
Tilly, Charles, 170
toilets, public, 33
Trail of Tears, 37
transgender persons, 33, 95
  reality enforcement against, 100
  solidarity among, 192
transitional justice, 3
trust, relations of, 16, 18

United Kingdom, 117, 187
United States
  African American experience in, 36,
    39, 155, 172
  government's responsibility/accountability,
    154–157, 163
  university admissions, 39
Unrepresented Nations and Peoples
    Organisation (UNPO), 76
urban landscape, 33, 35

veterans
  harsh conditions among, 64
  history's bearing on, 66
  structurally unjust condition of, 64
  unintended effects on, 64
victims. *See also* dead victims
  living, 51
  self-understanding of, 18
violence, 37, 44
violence against women (VAW), 106–117
  African American women, 102
  culture-based, 113
  definition of, 107
  economic dimension of, 107
  HSI view of, 113
  life-cycle duration of, 114
  norms underlying, 134
  objection to gender-based accounts of,
    115
  racism as factor in, 115
  simplistic understanding of, 107
violence, stereotypes' sustaining role in, 37
voluntariness, of group membership, 53
vote, right to, 60, 97

Waldron, Jeremy, 4
wartime, national identity in, 72
welfare programs, 158
Wenar, Leif, 16
womanhood, in Nordic countries, 130
women
  African-American, 102, 158–161, 167–169
  differences among, 6, 90–93
  as a group, 6
  as ladies of the house, 109
  not systematically subordinated, 90
  protection of families by, 130
  reparations for wrongs against, 167
  as reproducers of nations, 72
  self-determination of, 2
  shame among, 112
  stereotypes about, 97, 168
women* as a cluster concept, 101

women* as genealogy, 94–96
women* as series, 83–94
  'non-oppressed' women, 89
  differential positioning in, 85
  essentialism of, 90–93
  merits of, 87
  perspective shared in, 86
  pre-identification of structures in, 87–89
  structures orienting, 85
women*, defining, 82
women*, structural accounts of, 83
work, meaningful, 61

World Health Organisation, 106
World Wildlife Fund, 54

Young, Iris Marion
  democratic-representation theory, 86
  parameters of reasoning, 185, 186
  purposes of, 84
  racial injustice, 155, 162
  structural injustice, 8, 32, 64, 66, 155, 185, 189
  women* as a series. *See* women* as a series

Zheng, Robin, 41

For EU product safety concerns, contact us at Calle de José Abascal, 56–1°,
28003 Madrid, Spain or eugpsr@cambridge.org.

www.ingramcontent.com/pod-product-compliance
Ingram Content Group UK Ltd.
Pitfield, Milton Keynes, MK11 3LW, UK
UKHW020329140625
459647UK00018B/2079

*9 7 8 1 1 0 8 4 1 2 6 6 7 *